Confederate Florida

D1553795

Confederate

The Ro

Florida

...d to Olustee

William H. Nulty

**The University of
Alabama Press**

Tuscaloosa

Copyright © 1990
The University of Alabama Press
Tuscaloosa, Alabama 35487-0380
All rights reserved
Manufactured in the United States of America

The paper on which this book is printed meets the minimum requirements
of American National Standard for Information Science-Permanence of Paper
for Printed Library Materials, ANSI A39.48-1984.

First Paperbound Edition 1994

3   4   5   6   7   •   02   01

Library of Congress Cataloging-in-Publication Data

Nulty, William H.
Confederate Florida: the road to Olustee / William H. Nulty
p. cm.
Bibliography: p.
Includes index.
ISBN 0-8173-0748-6
1. Olustee (Fla.), Battle of, 1864. 2. Florida—History—Civil
War, 1861-1864—Campaigns. 3. United States—History—Civil War,
1861-1865—Campaigns. I. Title.
E476.43.N85   1990   89-33849
973.7′3—dc20

Contents

Illustrations

The Battle of Olustee *Frontispiece*
Scenes from the 1864 Federal Expedition 77
Olustee Battlefield Monument 204

Maps

Preface

Florida was the third state to secede from the Union, taking that action on January 10, 1861. Psychologically, economically, socially, and politically, Florida was closely attuned with the other Southern states, and the state's leadership believed it was in her best interest to take this step. An undetermined segment of the population was against secession, but their voices and their votes were overshadowed by the vocal majority. Florida's initial enthusiasm for the Southern cause was demonstrated by her haste to secede and her efforts to support that cause loyally with men and material. The amount of moral support, enthusiasm, and loyalty that Florida contributed, however, was not needed as much as were more tangible assets such as manpower, arms, and manufactured goods; unfortunately, these were in short supply in Florida.

Early in the Civil War, Florida found herself abandoned militarily by the Confederacy. There was nothing of any major strategic importance to the Confederacy within Florida, and her liabilities, particularly her long, vulnerable coastline and limited transportation network, far outweighed her assets. Her manpower resources were comparatively limited in relation to other Southern states, and after an early period of recruiting competition between state and Confederacy, most of what was even remotely available ended up in the Confederate army and had departed the state by the end of 1862. When this happened, Florida was left to defend herself as best she could, using her own resources. These resources included a mostly irregular military force that was small in size, poorly armed, unevenly trained, and widely dispersed over the state.

By early 1862, Federal forces occupied Fernandina, St. Augustine, Key West, and Fort Pickens and controlled Pensacola, Apalachicola, and the entrances to the St. Johns and Chattahoochee rivers. A tightening Federal naval blockade strangled the state's economic life, and a continuing series of small-scale raids by Federal forces caused destruction and created havoc and terror in coastal communities. Many Floridians withdrew into the interior of the state, where the remaining hard-core Confederate supporters were congregated. By the end of 1863, Florida's enthusiasm for secession had long since withered; militarily, economically, psychologically, and politically, she was vulnerable to Federal exploitation.

At the end of 1863, the Federal forces in the Department of the South, which comprised the South Atlantic coastal states, were stalemated. An abortive attack on Charleston had resulted in a standoff, and large numbers of Federal land and naval forces were tied up in seige operations against Charleston and Savannah that showed little progress or promise. These forces were available for employment elsewhere within the Department of the South. The commander of that department, Maj. Gen. Quincy A. Gillmore, requested permission of his superiors to use those forces for an expedition into Florida. To support his request, he listed objectives of recruiting blacks for his Negro regiments, cutting off commissary supplies that were going from Florida to other parts of the Confederacy, disrupting the railroad system within Florida, and preventing Confederate attempts to remove rails from that system for use elsewhere. Later, General Gillmore added the objectives of opening a Florida port to trade and the restoration of Florida to the Union. The requests for the expedition were approved, and on February 7, 1864, Federal forces landed at Jacksonville, Florida, with high hopes and a very strong probability of success in achieving their objectives.

The Federal expedition into Florida was a limited operation in terms of time, resources committed, geography, and objectives. It was not part of any larger strategic plan and was not coordinated with other activities going on at the same time. Lasting about a month, it received little notice at the time and today is rarely mentioned in any general history of the Civil War or recognized outside of the state of Florida. It was, however, the largest Civil War engagement in Florida and contained a Union defeat at the six-hour-long battle of Olustee that, by proportion of casualties to men engaged, was the third bloodiest defeat of the entire war for the Union.[1] At the same time, it came very close to severing Florida from the Confederacy, it forced the Confederacy to divert seventeen thousand men from a thinly manned defense of Charleston and Savannah, it delayed the critical reinforcement of the Southern Army of the Tennessee at a time when that army was fighting desperately to prevent the Union invasion of northwestern Georgia, it gave further proof of the ability of black soldiers to fight, and for a time it put a severe crimp in the subsistence supply lines that fed two Southern armies. In respect to the number of men the Union committed to this operation and the long-range ramifications of the expedition, the Federal expedition into Florida in 1864 was a success! It was indeed a costly one that fell too short of achieving its full potential, but yet a successful one if one considers a gain for one side as a loss for the other side.

The 1864 Federal expedition into East Florida has been examined by a small group of writers. In most cases, they have given the expedition a brief, general coverage in order to set the stage for a more detailed coverage of the battle of Olustee, the high (or low) point of the expedition. Their emphasis stresses the political motivation for the expedition (as it apparently related to the 1864 presidential election) as its primary initiating cause and then assesses its success or failure in that framework. The Federal expedition, however, had a number of very valid, attainable military objectives which were, in fact, achieved. The political situation existing at the time has been given greater importance than it deserves and has colored the treatment of the expedition. A more comprehensive view of the battle of Olustee can be obtained if it is considered within the larger context of the 1864 Federal expedition into East Florida. In turn, that expedition can more readily be appreciated if placed within such larger contexts as Florida's status within the Confederacy and the relation of that expedition to concurrent events taking place outside of Florida during the Civil War.

Clausewitz defined the enemy's resources as including their fighting forces proper, the country with its physical features and population, and their allies.[2] All things in warfare are interdependent, and a gain for one side is a corresponding, directly proportional loss for the other side—an idea currently termed the "zero-sum game." The 1864 Federal expedition into East Florida could be seen as an early example of a military operation characteristic of modern warfare if its objectives included ones other than military and if it had the potential for influencing results elsewhere and contributing to a final victory that was more than a military victory. Furthermore, a more accurate appraisal of the expedition's success or failure can be made if the wider and long-term ramifications of that expedition can be seen. In the course of the following narrative, an effort is made to examine the 1864 Federal expedition into East Florida within its proper historical setting. Of equal importance is an examination of the status of Florida herself, both within the Confederacy and within the American Civil War. I conclude that the expedition was sound, although too limited in both its concept and leadership, and that, viewed within the parameters of modern warfare, it indeed had great potential for the Union cause.

I would like to thank Samuel Proctor of the University of Florida for his guidance, patience, encouragement, and generosity with his time and assistance. I am grateful to Elizabeth Alexander, Stephen Kerber, and the staff of the P. K. Yonge Library of Florida History, University of Florida, and also to the St. Augustine Historical Society, the Florida Historical Society in Tampa, the Florida State Library at Tallahassee, Charlotte Ray of the Georgia State Archives, and Franklin M. Garrett of the Atlanta Historical Society. All were of great assistance in my research.

I thank my fellow graduate students at the University of Florida for their advice and encouragement in so many ways. I am indebted to Kermit Hall of the University of Florida's history department, who was particularly inspirational in his instruction. Last, I wish to express my sincere thanks to my wife of some thirty years, Tiny Nulty, who graciously endured my struggle to create this manuscript.

Confederate Florida

1

The Jilted Bride

Florida's Early Years in the Confederacy

On the day Florida adopted its ordinance of secession, January 10, 1861, U.S. troops were transferred from Barrancas Barracks to Fort Pickens in Pensacola harbor. There was good reason for the Union to take this precaution. A number of Florida's more ambitious citizens, aided and abetted by such people as the state's U.S. congressmen and the governor, had not waited for such formalities as the secession convention before taking action. On January 5, U.S. senator David Levy Yulee sent a message to "Joseph Finegan or Colonel George W. Call" in Tallahassee stating that the *"immediately* important thing to be done" was the occupation of the Federal forts and arsenals in Florida, giving first priority to taking the naval station and military installations at Pensacola before the Federal government could reinforce them. He continued on to emphasize the need for the earliest possible organization of a "Southern Confederacy and of a Southern Army" adopting, for the present, the existent Federal Constitution.[1] Unfortunately for the South, the political and military organization of the Confederacy was not easily accomplished.

It would take over a year before the Confederacy could move through the various stages of a provisional government to a more formal one. During this progression, a great deal of misdirection, confusion, duplication of effort, critical omissions, and wastage of scarce resources took place. This national situation was repeated on a lower level within the various states that made up the emerging Confederacy, and Florida was no exception. The early burst of patriotic enthusiasm that had led to secession eroded among the harsh realities of mobilization for a war that no one had adequately planned or prepared for, one which was vastly different, conducted on a much larger scale than had ever been experienced by the participants, and lasting much longer than anticipated. The first year under the provisional government was a critical one in deciding the direction of the war. For Florida, it was one of great frustration and disappointment. In a hurry to be one of the first to secede, she found herself as one of the first abandoned by the Confederacy. With little to offer, requiring much, and highly vulnerable, Florida was a liability to both herself and the Confederacy.

Senator Yulee's suggestion to seize Federal installations prior to Florida's secession was not his first challenge to the Federal government. On December 21, 1860, he had requested from the secretary of war a list of U.S. Army officers appointed from Florida, and on the twenty-eighth, in conjunction with Sen. Stephen R. Mallory, Yulee had asked for a detailed listing of the numerical strength of troops garrisoning Federal posts in Florida, including their arms and ammunition. On January 7, Yulee and Mallory again requested the information about the Federal installations and finally received a reply from the Federal secretary of war on January 9 denying them the requested information.[2]

On the same day that Senator Yulee had written Finegan and Call to encourage them to initiate action to seize the Pensacola installations, Governor Perry had sent a letter to a Colonel Duryea (or Dunn) authorizing him to raise a company, proceed in secrecy to the Federal arsenal at Chattahoochee, and seize it along with all arms and ammunition located at that site—with assistance, if needed, available from the Seventh Regiment, Florida Militia.[3] The arsenal was seized the morning of January 6, with a loss to the Federal government of one six-pounder gun, fifty-seven flintlock muskets, 173,476 rounds of musket cartridges, and 5,122 pounds of gunpowder. A desperate ordnance sergeant telegraphed his superior in Washington reporting this seizure and requested instructions.[4] His message was followed by one from the ordnance sergeant in charge of Fort Marion at St. Augustine on January 7, reporting its seizure "by the order of the governor of the State of Florida."[5] Fort Clinch, unoccupied and unfinished and, at least on paper, defending Fernandina, was taken by state troops a few days after Fort Marion was seized.

As early as November 1860, while traveling through Florida, U.S. Army captain M. C. Meigs concluded from his observations of the people and their feelings that there would be attempts on Federal installations in the state, and he so warned General Scott.[6] The Federal commander of the garrison at Key West had echoed this warning, but he received no instructions. While, in fact, orders had been issued by the national government on January 4 detailing reinforcements for both the Key West and Pensacola areas, they would be either too late to be effective or not received in time to prevent takeovers by state troops of some of the Federal installations.[7] On January 12, state troops seized Barrancas Barracks, Forts Barrancas and McRee, and the navy yard at Pensacola. On January 14, upon hearing of the adoption of the ordinance of secession, Federal captain John M. Brannan at Key West moved his force of forty-four men from their barracks into the interior of Fort Taylor. He acted without instructions from Washington, anticipating the orders that, unknown to him, had already been issued but would not get to Key West until almost two weeks after he had acted.[8]

Lt. Adam Slemmer, who commanded the Fort Barrancas garrison, now withdrawn into Fort Pickens at Pensacola, found himself isolated and besieged, awaiting instructions, supplies, and reinforcements in a situation similar to one Major Anderson was in at Fort Sumter in South Carolina. With a garrison of 81 men, Slemmer was in command of a dilapidated fort originally built for 1,260 that had been abandoned and allowed to deteriorate. Prior to moving to the fort, Slemmer had hastily spiked the guns at Barrancas that were bearing on Fort Pickens, while Lt. Henry Erban of the storeship *Supply* managed to do the same to the guns at Fort McRee.[9] Both Slemmer and Erban had made unsuccessful attempts to get cooperation from

Comdr. James Armstrong, in charge of the navy yard, to keep
Federal property from falling into the hands of the rebels.
While Lieutenant Slemmer worked feverishly to upgrade the
defenses at Fort Pickens, troops from Louisiana, Alabama, Mis-
sissippi, and Georgia started to pour into Pensacola as early as
January 11 to augment the local militia.

On January 12, the navy yard at Pensacola was surrendered
by Commodore Armstrong, and the Federal government lost
what was probably its most important naval base on the Gulf.
The Southerners gained an extremely valuable dry dock, extensive and valuable marine workshops, warehouses, barracks, a
well-equipped marine hospital, two powerful forts, 175 cannon, more than 12,000 projectiles, and ordnance stores at
the navy yard variously estimated in value from $117,000 to
$500,000.[10]

On the night of January 12, a group of four, representing
themselves as commissioners of Florida and Georgia, demanded surrender of Fort Pickens. It was refused by Lieutenant
Slemmer. Demands for surrender were repeated on January 15
and 18 and were also refused. While the standoff between the
two sides continued, the defenders continued their feverish
efforts to rehabilitate the old fort in preparation for the expected attack.

At a meeting between President Buchanan and a delegation
of Southern senators in Washington, the Southerners were
assured by the president that an attack on either of the two
currently besieged Federal forts, Pickens or Sumter, before Lincoln's inauguration would only play into the hands of the Re-
publicans. The Federal secretary of the navy, thereupon, sent a
message to Lieutenant Slemmer at Fort Pickens instructing
him not to allow Federal vessels to land at Pensacola. The
trade-off was telegraphed instructions from the Southern senators to the commander of the forces besieging Fort Pickens to
prevent an assault on that fort.[11] While the Federal forces at
Key West prepared for an attack that would never come, and
the Federal forces at Pensacola prepared for an attack that, from
the size of the forces arriving and being trained, appeared imminent, Florida turned her attention to preparing for war.

Progress had been uneven in the time since Governor Perry had requested appropriations for a military fund and authorization from the legislature to reorganize the state military. A number of local militia companies had come into existence in the closing months of 1860, but they were poorly armed at best and probably had more effect on the development of a militant political attitude than they did on the organization of an effective militia.[12] The money requested was appropriated, but no militia-reorganization law was enacted. By the close of 1860, Florida was no more ready for war than were most states, North or South. The first troops to be raised were organized and equipped through private means. A number of irregular groups of vigilantes, regulators, and minutemen had been formed which in most cases had no legal basis and were poorly trained and armed. The governor accepted their offers of service "with alacrity" into the state militia.[13]

In early February 1861, Governor Perry appealed to the general assembly for legislation to enable the increase and to organize the state militia more effectively. The general assembly responded on February 14 with a law that created Florida's Civil War Militia. The state adjutant general was authorized to distribute blank rolls to every captain or lieutenant then holding a commission from the state, and these blanks were to be used to enroll men for six months' service with the forces of the state. The adjutant general was then authorized to divide the men into companies, regiments, and brigades according to geographic area. Companies were to have from sixty-four to one hundred men. Provision was made for election of officers and for establishment of such noncombatant military elements as surgeons and chaplains. The governor was authorized to raise immediately one cavalry and two infantry regiments.[14]

Recruitment for the state militia became increasingly difficult as the year 1861 progressed. On March 1, the Confederate army was formally organized, and the secretary of war informed the various state governors that the Confederate War Department was henceforth authorized to shape the course of military organization in the states. Furthermore, by the act of February 28, the president was authorized to receive twelve-month volunteers, assuming command of all military in matters "concerning outside powers." On March 9, the first requisition for troops was levied by the Confederate government, with Florida to provide five hundred troops.[15] Concurrent recruitment for both state militia and Confederate army forces was fully underway by mid-March 1861. Recruitment was locally based, and men began to assemble at Tallahassee, Apalachicola, Gainesville, Quincy, Marianna, Monticello, Pensacola, Chattahoochee, Fernandina, Jacksonville, and other designated locations.[16]

Despite the hurry and confusion of a short-notice mobilization, units began to take form, and soon a regiment of West Florida volunteers known as the First Florida Infantry came into being. The regiment was mustered into the Confederate army on April 5 and arrived at Pensacola on April 12. Four days before their arrival, the Confederate government put out a second call for volunteers, and Florida was assigned a quota of 1,500. The following day, this levy was amended in the case of Florida to say that the war department "wishes the whole force to be infantry, unless Your Excellency should be able to furnish two companies of artillery."[17] This would appear to be the first time specific types of military units were requested. In the absence of any particular guidelines, units were coming into existence on the basis of what the individual members felt they would like to be rather than what was needed or could be armed and equipped. This was true on local, state, and national levels. As was to be expected, the most glamorous arm was cavalry, and anyone who could avail himself of a horse saw himself as a cavalier.

On April 16, an additional 2,000 men were requisitioned from Florida. Apparently not having received this latest levy, Governor Perry responded to the secretary of war on April 19 with a little concern about the number of troops required for Confederate army service. He informed the secretary that he was currently engaged in raising 1,500 troops (the original levy) and asked whether an additional 500 would be called for. Perry stated that the effective forces for the state did not exceed 13,000 men. The secretary replied immediately that he had called for an additional 2,000 but suggested that if they could not be raised, the requisition on Florida would be revoked, and the troops raised elsewhere. Apparently stung by this last message, Governor Perry replied shortly that he would raise the 2,000 troops as soon as possible.[18]

On May 13, Governor Perry informed the secretary that the troops were almost ready but that he could supply them with only one thousand muskets. After requesting arms for the rest, the governor asked if he could concentrate troops at certain undefended points on the coast and requested officers to drill and instruct the newly mustered troops. Having received no answer by May 17, the governor again requested information as to when and where the troops were wanted. On May 18, Governor Perry informed the secretary that one regiment was available and awaiting orders, with two others ready except for arms and equipment, asking if the secretary could provide these. A note of frustration is apparent in his message, as after stating that several of the companies were encamped at the expense of the officers, he ended his message with the phrase, "Say where wanted and when."[19]

The secretary of war informed Governor Perry on May 23 that the armed and equipped regiment was accepted and detailed for duty in Florida, but the Confederacy could not accept another regiment unless it was armed. On the twentieth, Governor Perry complained to Florida's representatives in the provisional government, J. Morton, James B. Owens, and George T. Ward, that he had raised two thousand troops as requested, but since they were not accepted, he was in a quandary as to what to do with them.[20] On May 29, Governor Perry informed the secretary that he had two regiments organized for the defense of the state and one for Virginia and requested an answer. Finally, on June 1, the now-desperate governor wired the Confederate secretary of war: "I have been telegraphing you since the 13th ultimo relative to the two thousand troops raised under your requisition. We have batteries erected at several points on the coast, requiring at least two regiments to garrison. If Florida is to take care of herself, say so."[21]

Nevertheless, requisitions on Florida for 1,000 men for the

Confederate "Reserve Corps" were sent out on June 30.[22] This last requisition was still not filled six months later. During 1861, the Confederate War Department levied Florida for 5,000 troops. The total number that entered either the state or Confederate military service that year was 6,772, organized into four infantry regiments, one cavalry regiment, nine unattached infantry companies, four artillery companies, and three cavalry companies. Individually, there were 5,491 infantry, 1,150 cavalry, and 331 artillery.[23] The state militia numbered fewer than 1,000 men and included most of the unattached companies. In the governor's message to the Florida House of Representatives on November 27, 1861, he summarized his problems in relation to the state militia. He called attention to the imperfect military organization of the state and stated that a militia system could not coexist with a voluntary system. Furthermore, the official returns from recent elections for military officers revealed that there was not a complete militia regiment and hardly a complete militia company in the state. "The manner in which volunteer companies have been raised has subverted militia organizations. . . . The number of fighting men has not increased but the number of officers has doubled. . . . Hence is seen occasionally a considerable display of swords and buttons and but few muskets and bayonets."[24]

The problems continued under Perry's successor, John Milton. Service in the Confederate army was preferable to that of the militia because of the lure of service for short periods with pay. Cavalry was the most popular branch of services, and when Governor Milton took office, he found himself with many more prospective cavalrymen than he thought necessary. Milton protested to President Davis the authority given by the war department to W. G. M. Davis to raise a cavalry regiment which Milton felt was useless in Florida and an unnecessary expense to the state. "Almost every man that has a pony wishes to mount him at the expense of the Confederate government." He went on to state that, independent of Davis's regiment, he had turned down requests for "ten associates for cavalry companies within the last two days." Milton summed up his argument:

The unnecessary expense for cavalry would supply the means for the proper coast defenses; would enable me to equip companies of light artillery and infantry, which equipments might be preserved to protect the peace which we hope to obtain in the present war. But the hundreds of horses which are now being withdrawn from agricultural industry will be of little avail in war and leave the State without the means of agriculture which will be difficult to supply.[25]

The First and Second Florida regiments had been raised to fill the quota assigned the state under the first call of President Davis. The Third and Fourth regiments were formed in a response to a call for two additional regiments to defend the coast of Florida. The problems Governor Milton had with the Third and Fourth regiments and with what was originally intended to be the Fifth Florida Regiment are indicative of problems many Southern governors were having in raising troops, supporting them, and then agreeing with the central government over their use. The Third Regiment, Col. W. S. Dilworth commanding, was headquartered at Fernandina, with companies spread, at times, as far away as New Smyrna. The Fourth Regiment was raised by Governor Perry for Confederate service with the hope that his friend D. P. Holland would be elected its colonel. Unfortunately for Governor Perry's plans, Edward Hopkins was elected instead, so before leaving office, Perry appointed Holland in charge of an artillery battalion at Fernandina, expecting that this unit might evolve into the Fifth Florida Regiment. The officer commanding at Fernandina, Col. W. S. Dilworth, needed artillerymen and mustered this battalion into service, against specific orders from the war department prohibiting acceptance of units lacking sufficient equipment. Colonel Dilworth further violated a Confederate prohibition against accepting units into Confederate service whose officers had not first been approved by the war department and properly commissioned.[26]

Colonel Dilworth's command and the artillery battalion were the subject of a number of letters from both Governor Milton and Colonel Dilworth to President Davis and the secretary of war. Governor Milton, who liked neither Dilworth nor

Holland, alluded to the insobriety of all but one of the Third Regiment's field grade officers and the illegality of the artillery unit. Colonel Dilworth claimed that politicians were interfering with the war effort and even threatened to take his units across the state line and enlist them in Georgia's military.[27] The problem was complicated by the absence of a Confederate commander in Florida. Gen. John B. Grayson had been assigned to such a position in late August 1861 but arrived in poor health and died shortly afterward. Not until late November did a Confederate officer arrive to take charge. In the meantime, both Governor Milton and Colonel Dilworth felt that they had acceded to the position until such time as a replacement for General Grayson arrived. On October 22, the secretary of war attempted to solve the problem. He instructed Brig. Gen. James H. Trapier, who had been assigned as General Grayson's successor, to go first to Fernandina, which appeared to be a critical target for the Union. Trapier was informed of the problems involving the election rather than appointment of the officers and their incompetency, along with the violations of Confederate mustering procedure. He was advised that the war department would not hesitate to muster the troops there out of service and then in again by new companies.[28]

General Trapier, however, was delayed by the Union attack on Port Royal and did not get to Fernandina as early as originally planned. In the meantime, the secretary of war wrote Colonel Dilworth on October 26 that Holland's artillery battalion would not be accepted in its current state.[29] A letter from the secretary of war to Governor Milton on November 22 informed the governor that General Trapier was going directly to Fernandina and would bring matters into proper order. The same letter contained some good news relating to another problem that had given the governor some concern. The boundary between the military departments of Middle and East Florida was changed from the Chattahoochee River to the Choctawhatchee.[30] The governor had been very concerned about the Middle Florida area and upset over the creation of a military department that did not include the entire area contiguous to the Chattahoochee River to include Apalachicola and Tallahassee. Governor Milton needed some good news because his letters to officials of the central government were beginning to reflect his growing frustration. In a November 19 letter to President Davis, Governor Milton summed up his problems.

> At all important points we are threatened with attack; nowhere prepared to meet the enemy; and when, as governor of the State, I have applied for arms and munitions of war, I have been answered a requisition should be made by the officer in command of the military department, yet none is in command. [Trapier had not yet arrived.] It would have been almost as reasonable under the circumstances to have referred me to the Emperor of China.[31]

Governor Milton went on to report that the citizens of Florida were beginning to despair of being protected by the Confederacy and were losing confidence in their governor. In desperation he pleaded to be issued arms and ammunition, given control over all Confederate forces in the state not part of Gen. Braxton Bragg's command at Pensacola, and allowed to defend Florida as commander in chief. In his closing remarks he stated, "It is highly important that some one should be in command having the experience and common sense among the troops, and to make them available for the defense of the State."[32] The secretary of war replied on November 29 that the belated arrival of General Trapier has "doubtless put an end to the apprehensions you suggest." He continued, "Your excellency may rest assured, and you may assure the patriotic people of your State, that you shall not be overlooked in the efforts for the common defense."[33]

The secretary's assurance did not soothe the governor. In a scathing letter to President Davis written on December 9, Milton started out by citing the existence of a cavalry unit located in Tampa, where it was of no possible use, and subsisting off the state while doing nothing. He said it was just one of many examples and went on to warn:

> Every reflecting man in the country is becoming alarmed at the uncalled for waste of substance of the land at a time when it should be husbanded; and throughout the State the people are

becoming indignant that such bodies of unarmed men and idle horses should be reared up among them, with no prospect but to consume the means of support for the women and children, cripple the usefulness of the armed troops for defense against the enemy, and bring ruin upon the people and disgrace upon the Confederate Government.[34]

Governor Milton then moved to the heart of the problem, which was the conflict between the authority of the state and that of the central government. He wrote, "The worst feature of Black Republicanism was that which threatened to ignore State boundaries and the rights of States as free, sovereign, and independent parties to the compact known as the Constitution of the United States of America." He charged that the raising of troops by the war department "within the limits of a State in disregard of the constituted authority of the State" was overriding "the constituted authority of the States and destroying the last vestige of human liberty." He continued:

When we see a President making war without the assent of Congress; when we behold judges threatened because they maintain the writ of habeas corpus, so sacred to free men; when we see justice and law trampled under the armed heel of military authority, and upright men and innocent women dragged to distant dungeons upon the mere edict of a despot; when we find all of this tolerated and applauded by a people who had been in full enjoyment of freedom but a few months ago, we may be admonished that there may, in time, be danger to us, unless we meet with our opposition at the very threshold of every invasion of the rights of States, whether that invasion be intentional or not.[35]

After June 30, 1861, recruitment, mobilization, and regimental organization became a matter for the central government. No more requisitions were sent to the governors by the war department. The states were divided into military districts, and the officers in charge of each district presented requisitions to the governor and received help from him in raising troops. In states like Florida, which had a state militia, recruitment for both state and Confederate forces from limited manpower resources worked to the disadvantage of both levels of government. The Confederacy's Conscription Act was passed in April 1862, which all but eliminated what state militia still existed. In Florida it was anticlimactic because, over the protests of Governor Milton, a special session of the Convention of the People of Florida, meeting in January 1862, abolished Florida's state militia effective March 10, more than a month before the Confederate Conscription Act was passed. The convention was motivated partially by confidence in the central government and partially by the attractive idea of having lower taxes if there were no necessity of supporting a militia.[36]

For Florida, the timing for the abolishment of the militia was particularly bad. Confederate setbacks in Tennessee called for a reinforcement of that area by all available Confederate units from the lesser important Deep South at the same time that the only troops left to defend Florida from Federal invasion, the state militia, were eliminated. To forestall the complete collapse of state defenses, the executive council passed a short-lived resolution reorganizing the militia. Meeting serious objections to its resolution, the executive council repealed it, and from that time until the end of the war, the governor had to work within the framework of volunteer military organizations.

It was also a year and a half after Florida's secession before the single, homogeneous military system of the new central government brought some sort of limited order into what had been a haphazard, confusing, inefficient, and duplicative process of raising troops. Initially relying on volunteers and supplied by a wide range of sources from private contributions to government issue, Florida officials raised troops with little thought to the needs of the state or central government. Training and arming were a matter of location and good or bad fortune. By the end of 1861, a significant percentage of Florida's available military manpower and military resources was in the service of the central government and destined for employment in areas outside of the state. This situation would cause a continuing rift between the state and central government over the state's military status within the Confederacy, the nature of its contributions to the central government, and the support to be received from that government. As early as May 17, 1861, Gen. Braxton Bragg, commanding the Confederate forces at Pensacola, was being queried by the central government in relation to the numbers of troops he could spare for Virginia.[37] While the First Florida Infantry was not among those recommended for transfer at that time by General Bragg, that unit would be departing the state within a year. This query to General Bragg was an indication that the central government did not consider Florida to be high on their list of priorities. The first Florida unit actually to leave Florida was the Second Regiment of Florida Volunteers, some 927 strong, which departed from Baldwin for Richmond, Virginia, in mid-July 1861. The monthly strength report for the Department of Middle and East Florida (which did not include the troops at Pensacola) for December 1861 stated that an aggregate of 3,972 men were actually present for duty.[38] Within the next year, this figure would drop by half to about 2,000, where it would hold for much of the rest of the war. By the end of the war, Florida contributed over 15,000 men to Confederate service, most of whom had left the state by the end of 1862.

Although rather meager in comparison with the troop strength in other Southern states, Florida's manpower was the most important asset it had to offer the Confederacy initially. The first year of the war in Florida saw a great deal of confusion and misdirection in mobilizing this resource. Starting with secession, both the state and Confederate Provisional Governments displayed a lack of strong leadership and direction over the numbers of troops to be raised; the types of units desired; their training, arming, and staging; the selection of officers; and the type and location of their employment. Although granting that few could foresee the size and type of war this was to be, that the provisional government had to start from zero in getting organized, and that the Federal government would be as determined as it was to put down the rebellion, still we must point out that Florida, like many other Southern

states, wasted time, energy, and both financial and human resources at a very early stage of the war.

The cost of outfitting troops entering both the militia and
Confederate service was a heavy drain on the state's resources.
This situation was further complicated by the financial acts of
the convention and the legislature, which tended to contradict
rather than support each other. In January 1861, the legislature
had provided for the issue of $500,000 in treasury notes and
$500,000 in bonds. The bond issue was countermanded by the
convention, which authorized the governor to borrow the
$500,000 and issue coupon bonds backed by the sale of public
lands to exclude that set aside for education or internal im-
provement. Payment for these lands, however, was to be made
only in gold, silver, or the paper of solvent banks, a catch-22
situation because few, if any, of these forms of currency were in
the hands of the people. The result was that no lands could be
sold, the bonds could not be negotiated, and the treasury notes
were the only resource of the state.[39]

On August 31, the provisional government passed an act re-
imbursing Florida for the money the state had spent in "arming, equipping, and maintaining troops for the service of the
Confederate States of America," in view of the fact that Florida
"has exhausted her treasury and has great need of money to
carry on her military operations." The money was to be issued
to Florida in Confederate treasury notes, *provided* that Florida
deposited with the secretary of the treasury an equal sum in
the bonds of Florida to be issued "under an ordinance of the
convention of said State."[40] Both Confederate and state treasury notes depreciated rapidly toward practical worthlessness,
with the state notes holding a slight edge in the descent.

Even when money was available, arms were difficult to obtain. Procurement of military supplies was conducted in such
cities as Charleston, Savannah, New Orleans, Mobile, and Columbus, Georgia.[41] After midsummer of 1861, arms became
even more difficult to obtain, and the Richmond government
refused to accept unarmed Florida troops into service.[42] Companies of partially armed troops were combined with others

to form fully armed units.[43] The problem of supplying arms was never solved, and as late as May 1862, Brig. Gen. Joseph Finegan appealed directly to the people of Florida for arms, preferably "shot guns, double and single barrel rifles, and muskets."[44]

All troops that left the state for Confederate service were armed, but those remaining were not as well off. Some arms were received in the state by blockade-runners, which stood to make a lucrative profit. The *Gordon*, for example, came into Mosquito Inlet with arms for the Confederacy and was the subject of an immediate dispatch from Governor Milton to the secretary of war on October 29, 1861, stating, "Florida wants arms. She has never received a musket from the Confederate States. The *Gordon* brings sabers and pistols. Can I get some?"[45]

One arms-carrying blockade-runner that did not make it was the steamer *Salvor*, owned by James McKay of Tampa. That ship ran aground and was captured in October 1861 with a cargo that consisted of twenty-one thousand rifles, one hundred boxes of revolvers, six rifled cannon, and a large amount of ammunition. When the steel-clad steamer *Fingal* ran the blockade into Savannah, President Davis immediately got messages from the governors of Florida, Georgia, and South Carolina requesting a part of the arms the ship had brought through the blockade.[46] Governor Pickens of South Carolina, in a June 30 report to the secretary of war, claimed that six thousand arms had been sent to Florida.[47] There does not appear to be evidence in reports from Florida of the arrival of this many weapons from another state.

In early 1862, a cargo of arms and ammunition had been brought into Nassau aboard the steamer *Gladiator*, and its cargo subdivided onto two small fast steamers bound for Mosquito Inlet in Florida. The 10,000 guns that came into New Smyrna destined for the chief of ordnance at Savannah were eagerly grabbed at by all of the weapon-hungry units in Florida that could get to them. Eventually, after all of the special agents dispatched were able to recover as many weapons as they could, Florida ended up some 1,289 weapons richer. Some

552 of the weapons were seized by the Seventh Florida Regiment, soon to leave for Confederate service.[48] This fiasco illustrates how difficult it was to get goods that had run the blockade into Florida from the point of arrival through the state to other parts of the Confederacy. These difficulties included both those of travel over relatively undeveloped facilities and security of the goods from theft. All of the Confederate states were short of armaments, and any news of the arrival of arms traveled quickly. Each individual state was looking out for its own needs and competed with other states and the central government for available assets. Other types of military equipment, including clothing, knapsacks, cartridge belts, canteens, and such, were provided by the state or central government to a limited degree. Many Florida units were equipped with military accoutrement purchased for local units in Florida by committees organized in towns and villages. The results varied widely but were rarely completely satisfactory.

A thread that runs throughout a consideration of Florida's relationship to the Confederacy is the matter of command and control: Who has the authority? Who is in charge? While I touch on these questions in a number of areas, for purposes of clarity it would be well to summarize the situation that existed in Florida during the early years of the war. The seceded states found themselves embroiled in the unique situation of having to reorganize politically under a new central government while assuming new internal functions such as raising military forces, providing for external defense, controlling scarce resources, and financing all of these and any other war-related measures. This was a very difficult period for Florida.

Normally, in war, the executive branch of government becomes more important, assuming increased powers in order to administer more effectively by making rapid decisions on a wide variety of problems that require immediate settlement. Such was not the case in Florida. Beginning with the December 1860 election of the delegates to the People's Convention and the adoption by that group of the resolution that claimed it had the power to speak for the people, authority within the state of Florida fragmented. This extralegal group coexisted and competed with the duly constituted and elected officials of the government, including the governor and general assembly. Complicating the situation was the presence of a conservative governor-elect, John Milton, who had been elected in November 1860 but who would not take office until October 1861, alongside the lame-duck, radical incumbent, Madison Starke Perry. When Governor Milton finally did take office, he found his task complicated by the presence of radical Democrats in both the legislature and the convention. Additionally, in early 1862, the new governor found he had to contend with an executive council that was created by the convention for the purpose of "strengthening the executive department during the exigencies of the present war."[49] What this meant in reality was that the governor was supposed to share his police and war-prosecution powers with the council. While this council was dissolved later in 1862 and did not create or perpetuate any policy of primary importance, it was a slap in the face of the state's chief executive and, along with the convention, a usurpation of his authority.

Governor Milton's relations with the central government were no less complex. The first year of the war was conducted by a provisional government that had to organize itself while trying to determine priorities and policies. Militarily, it had to create an armed force, train and equip it, and then employ it where it was most needed. Such steps took time. In an attempt to resolve various conflicts over military authority within the state of Florida, the Confederacy created a military department embracing Middle and East Florida and, in late August 1861, assigned Gen. John B. Grayson to its command. General Grayson's illness and subsequent death and the assignment of first Gen. Edmund Kirby Smith and then Gen. James H. Trapier delayed the arrival of a replacement for Grayson in Florida until late November 1861. In the absence of an authoritative military representative of the central government, everyone from the governor on down attempted to fill the vacuum.

The governor's main concern was the state and, in particular, the middle portion of the state, where the major portion of the population (including his political support) and most resources were located. The central government, on the other hand, was more concerned about the national situation and, as it currently affected Florida, the portion of the state that formed part of the South Atlantic coast. To complete the picture, various citizens groups and politicians were primarily concerned about their own locales. A major problem which neither the Confederacy nor the Union effectively realized and capitalized upon was that Florida, much like Virginia prior to the Civil War, was effectively more than one state because of its extended east-west geography in strategic, political, economic, and social reality. Parts of the state were more closely bound to portions of other states than to parts of their own state. This fact would provide constant internal and external dissension on matters of defensive priorities. This situation was aggravated by the abandonment of the coastal areas and the withdrawal of Confederate troops from Florida, which left the state to fend for itself.

The direction of the defense of the state, however, was not left to its chief executive. West Florida came under the influence of the Confederate forces at Mobile. Although the governor had recommended his own man to head the military department of Middle and East Florida, Joseph Finegan, a civilian politician from Fernandina, was appointed a brigadier general in the Confederate army and assigned to that command by the secretary of war. General Finegan was a business partner of former senator David L. Yulee and had been recommended by Florida's delegation to the provisional government. Although Governor Milton had requested several times to be designated as the commander in chief of Florida's forces and permitted to defend the state himself, such was not to be the case. The central government insisted on maintaining military command of the area but was unable to provide resources. The chief executive of the state was charged with providing resources but was not allowed to determine how those resources were to be used. The governor was principally concerned with the middle of the state; General Finegan from Fernandina was more concerned with matters there as well as the railroad he had helped build and that his partner David L. Yulee now controlled. It was a very frustrating administration for Governor Milton, who sincerely desired to assist the Confederate government in its endeavors but found himself bypassed and undercut by that government. Concerned about his own state, he was continually hamstrung by competing authorities in his efforts to provide adequately for Florida.

Florida, with over six thousand miles of tidal shoreline, a vast land area, a small population, and a very limited industrial capacity, was probably the most vulnerable of all the seceding states in January 1861. The peninsula could be penetrated in a number of places by water; her coastal terrain was hardly defensible, characterized by numerous islands, flat beaches, and sand dunes bordering inland waterways, which were fed by immense swamps and lakes. Her population was largely concentrated in a belt across the northern part of the state, with only scattered settlements along her coast, and these mainly in the northern portion of the state.

The major railroad system in the state, although limited in mileage, did service northeastern and central Florida well but only went as far west as Tallahassee and did not connect with either the western part of the state or with any other part of the Confederacy. (See maps 1 and 2.) President Davis was eager to have the Pensacola and Georgia line extended from Tallahassee to the Chattahoochee River, where transportation by water could reach Columbus, Georgia—and this line was actually extended as far as Quincy in 1862.[50] Late in 1861, it had been proposed to extend the Pensacola and Georgia to the Georgia state line, where it could connect with the Savannah, Albany, and Gulf Railroad, a project Gen. Robert E. Lee thought of the highest priority.[51] A petition for a government subsidy of eighty thousand dollars by the Pensacola and Georgia to complete this project was refused. However, on February 10, 1862, the Confederate Congress appropriated one million dollars to be used by the president to connect the Richmond and Danville and North Carolina roads, an indication, perhaps, of Florida's lower strategic priority.[52]

In the governor's message of November 17, 1862, Milton had recommended completion of the Pensacola and Georgia to the

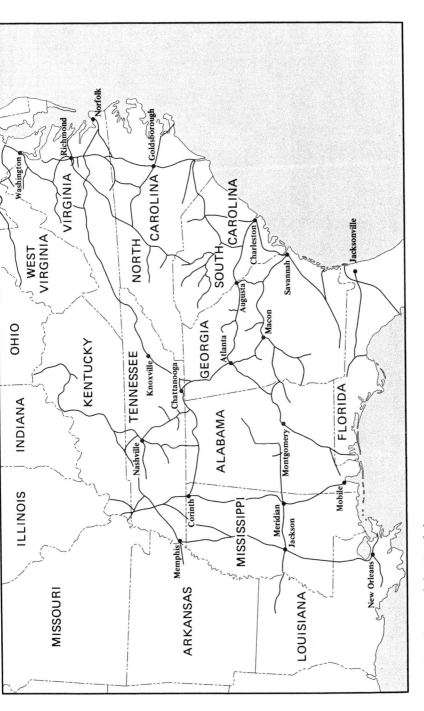

1. Railroad map of the Confederacy

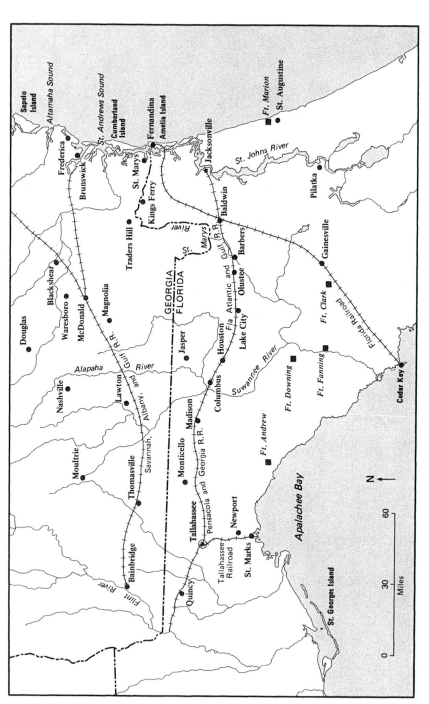

2. Railroads in northeast Florida and southeast Georgia. Redrawn from James Harvey McKee, *Back in War Times* (New York:

Chattahoochee as a "military, political, and commercial necessity." He believed this had priority over a suggestion that a
connection be made at either Houston or Monticello with the
Albany and Gulf Railroad that ran from Savannah to
Thomasville and Bainbridge, Georgia, to the Chattahoochee. A
committee recommended building a connector line from Lawton, Georgia, to Live Oak, Florida, rather than the proposed one
from Monticello.[53] Construction had started on this connector
from both ends, and by the end of 1861, substantial progress
had been made. Although grading was completed on the
Georgia side, rails were not laid until 1863. On the Florida side,
twenty-one of the twenty-two miles had been graded, and ties
laid on eight of those miles, but rails for the entire route were
lacking as well as the construction of a bridge over the Suwannee River. A subsequent political and legal battle between the
state and Confederate government over the conscription of
rails from the Florida Railroad (involving a part owner, former
senator Yulee) prevented the completion of this connector line
until March of 1865, too late to be of any use to the Confederacy.[54]

In 1862, it took two and one-half days to go from Waldo to
Tallahassee, some 150 miles with one-night stops in Lake City
and Madison. The Civil War found the railroad system in Florida unfinished between Tallahassee and Pensacola and between
Tampa and Waldo, although the latter had been graded. The one
railroad in the extreme western portion of the state connected
Pensacola with Alabama but with nothing to the east. Its rails
would be later torn up and used by the Confederacy elsewhere.
Militarily, the Florida railroad system provided the fastest
means by which troops could be concentrated in the northern
portion of Middle and East Florida and between the Atlantic
and the Gulf coasts in that region. The system could also assist, with some difficulty because of the lack of connections
with railroad systems of contiguous states, in the movement of
subsistence supplies or materials that had run the blockade to
the remainder of the Confederacy. Of particular military importance was the town of Baldwin, where the railroad that
went from the Atlantic to the Gulf crossed the line that went

from Jacksonville to Tallahassee. Additionally, any of the towns along the railroad lines that served as collection points for men and material took on an importance out of proportion to their size.

Florida's extended coastline and proximity to Cuba and the Bahamas seemed ideal for blockade-running, but her limited internal transportation system converged on only a few major seaports and was primitive in most of the rest of the state. The contraband that could be brought in would have difficulty getting to where it was needed, either within the state or within the Confederacy. For example, one of the routes taken by supplies brought in by blockade-runners to Mosquito Inlet had the supplies hauled by wagon over rough terrain to the St. Johns River, transported by small steamer up the Ocklawaha to Fort Brooks, carried by wagon from there to Waldo, from Waldo by railroad to Baldwin, and finally, by wagon again between the Florida railroad system at Madison to Quitman on Georgia's railroad system, more than twenty miles apart. A month might be consumed in just transiting Florida.

The Federal forts located in Florida had been designed to provide security against seizure of harbors that could be used as bases by enemy naval forces. The most strategic area in Florida, the Keys, commanded the entrance to the Gulf. The Federal government occupied the forts that controlled the Keys during the entire war. Pensacola was probably the second-most strategic point in Florida because of its excellent anchorage, navy yard, and rail connections with Alabama cities. There were no other significant fortifications on the Gulf coast, but on the northern Florida Atlantic coast were two permanent forts. Fort Marion at St. Augustine was complete and had guns; Fort Clinch at Fernandina was unfinished and had only a few unmounted cannons. At the time they were seized by Florida troops, both forts were not garrisoned but were maintained by military storekeepers. Within the state, the city of Tallahassee was important militarily because of its status as a capital and its closeness to the Chattahoochee arsenal. The town of Baldwin was important because it was the junction of two railroads. Other places of some military importance because of their status as seaports, railroad terminals, access points to inland waterways, or a combination of some or all of these factors, were Jacksonville, Fernandina, St. Augustine, Cedar Key, New Smyrna, Apalachicola, St. Marks, and Tampa. When the secession convention met in January 1861 in Tallahassee, it appointed two powerful seven-member committees to consider the state defenses: the committee on militia and internal police, and the committee on seacoast defenses. The chairman of the committee on seacoast defenses, Joseph Finegan, reported that the committee believed that while the Union would be able to blockade the major seaports of the Confederacy, there was virtually no chance of an attack against any Florida seaport. Nevertheless, they recommended that field batteries be placed to defend the more obviously vulnerable inlets and anchorages and that the responsibility for the planning and organization of local defenses be left to local militia officers. The convention evidently approved the committee's report, but not until April 22, 1861, was the governor empowered to use militia in defense of critical seacoast points within the state and a council authorized to help him in carrying out his emergency duties. A further convention resolution gave the state paper jurisdiction over all former Federal installations within Florida.[55] It was under this authority that the state troops seized Fort Clinch at Fernandina, Fort Marion at St. Augustine, the Chattahoochee arsenal, and all of the Federal military installations at Pensacola except for Fort Pickens. The Federal government reinforcements arrived at Forts Taylor and Jefferson in the Florida Keys barely in time to ensure their retention by the Union.

Confederate general Braxton Bragg, in command at Pensacola of a heterogeneous garrison composed of troops from several seceded states, while unable to wrest Fort Pickens away from its Federal defenders, turned Pensacola into the most thoroughly defended region of Florida.[56] Florida militia units occupied St. Vincent's Island and St. Marks, Apalachicola, Tampa, and Cedar Key. On the east coast, Fort Marion and Fort Clinch were garrisoned. The surplus cannons from Fort Marion were transported to other locations. Scattered militia units

were in the vicinities of Fernandina, Fort Clinch, Amelia Island, Jacksonville, Palatka, and St. Augustine. These militia
units served primarily as coast watchers and drilled, performed
guard duty, and worked at converting sand dunes to defensive
positions.

On May 10, in a letter to the Confederate secretary of war,
George T. Ward, who had led the fight in the secession convention against immediate secession, assessed the strategic situation as he saw it. He believed the Union would mount a land
attack in Virginia in conjunction with a number of naval diversions along the Atlantic and Gulf coasts. Concerned with
these naval diversions, he pointed out the vulnerability of Tallahassee, which was in close proximity to the Gulf—twenty
miles by railroad—and in the midst of the most dense Negro
population and the largest plantations in Florida. He went on
to state that it was impossible to fortify the entire coast and
that it would be far better to concentrate on a few major points
such as St. Andrew's, St. Josephs, Apalachicola, St. Marks,
Cedar Key, Tampa, the mouth of the St. Johns or Jacksonville,
and Fernandina. St. Augustine, he indicated, was already fortified. He estimated Florida's military strength to be about nine
thousand troops, a bit thin for its 1,500 miles of coast and
52,000 square miles. Additionally, "The country is deficient in
arms, but still more in military organization and drill." His
proposed solution was to augment key defensive positions
with a combination of small armed steamers to cruise the
coast acting with local volunteers who were to be enrolled,
trained, armed, and paid by the Confederate government and,
in case of engagement, backed up by "the militia of the country." These local volunteers were to be trained as infantry and
artillery and to be transferred only by the president in an emergency, which, in effect, would take coastal defense out of state
politics.[57]

Militarily, Ward was suggesting a new strategy, anticipating
to a degree the formation by Gen. Robert E. Lee of a mobile
defense as a counter to the Union's naval advantage. He was
anxious about the part being played by local politics in defensive preparations and the lack of central direction. Ward fore-

saw that factors other than military ones would be important
in this war and argued against stripping the coast of citizens
and slaves, disrupting planting and industry. Ward also suggested in his letter that men from Florida would be more willing to volunteer for service with the Confederacy if they were
assured that the Confederacy had provided for the protection of
their homes.[58]

By the latter days of 1860, Florida's preparations for war were
less than ideal. There was a complete absence of central direction, either for Florida's needs or for Florida's contribution to
the Confederacy. The governor, governor-elect, Florida's national and local politicians, the duly appointed officials and extralegal convention committees who had appropriated the
power to "speak for the people," citizen's groups, and self-seek-
ing individuals, among a host of groups of all sizes and influ-
ences, attempted to set policies and priorities, or influence
those who did. Military command within the state was confused. There was a Confederate commander in West Florida at
Pensacola, but no military commander for East or Middle Florida arrived to provide the needed central direction until
November 1861, nine months after the firing on Fort Sumter.
The one contribution of the dying general John B. Grayson was
a report he submitted to the secretary of war after being in
Florida nine days and at Fernandina five days. Grayson cited
what he termed the deplorable condition of the state and then
wrote, "As sure as the sun rises, unless cannon, powder &c., be
sent to Florida in the next thirty days, she will fall into the
hands of the North. Nothing human can prevent it." After
itemizing his needs, he continued, "Florida will become a
Yankee province unless measures for her relief are promptly
made."[59]

By June 1, 1861, the significant military and naval installations in Florida were about evenly split between the Union and
Confederate forces. Figures for Union forces in Florida on June
30, 1861, show a total of 1,939 men distributed between Pensacola and Key West.[60] Florida's state troops held Fort Marion
and Fort Clinch on the Atlantic coast, and the Confederate
Provisional Government held Barrancas Barracks, Warrington

Navy Yard, and Forts McRee and Barrancas. Other positions on the Gulf and Atlantic coasts were held by Southern forces but were relatively lightly defended. Apalachicola had two brass six-pounder fieldpieces, St. Marks and Cedar Key two heavy cannons each, Fernandina and Jacksonville had constructed redoubts, each containing four heavy guns, and Fort Marion at St. Augustine had twelve cannons, of which only four were mounted.[61]

During the summer and fall of 1861, both Governor Perry and Governor-elect Milton gave advice to local and Confederate commanders, wrote extensively to officials of the provisional government at all levels, communicated with other state governors, wrote Florida's representatives to the provisional government, and used their influence with members of both the elected and quasiofficial state leadership groups. In short, they did everything conceivable in an attempt to provide for Florida's military needs as they saw them.

East of Pensacola, the two most likely points of attack by Federal forces appeared to be Fernandina on the Atlantic and Apalachicola on the Gulf of Mexico, some 250 miles apart. A considerable portion of Florida's internal dissension over priorities and allocation of resources had to do with the relative merits of defending these two points. Apalachicola was a gateway to Tallahassee, the Florida planting counties, and the interior of Georgia and Alabama via the Chattahoochee River. Although Apalachicola was originally defenseless, Confederate forces raised in Florida built defenses there and at nearby St. Marks, Cedar Key, and Tampa with guns obtained from Fort Marion at St. Augustine and from outside sources. The local citizens at Apalachicola had taken the first steps toward its defense by setting up a battery on St. Vincent's Island. While they were constructing the battery, the Fourth Florida Regiment's Col. Edward Hopkins and five companies arrived on the island, set up camp, and appropriated all of the guns that former senator Stephen R. Mallory, who had been appointed secretary of the navy in Jefferson Davis's cabinet, had helped the local citizens to obtain. Colonel Hopkins's forces then started work on their own emplacement, which left the approaches to the town defenseless. The local citizens petitioned the secretary of war for help, since they knew the governor was powerless in this situation.

Governor Milton, however, stepped into this situation in a letter to Secretary Mallory. Governor Milton suggested that Colonel Hopkins's regiment, which was spread out between Apalachicola and Tampa, be concentrated and sent to Pensacola for training in exchange for Colonel Anderson's Magnolia Regiment, which, with help from local militia and a few experienced artillerists, could defend Apalachicola. The governor addressed this problems when he wrote, "The officers of the regiments mustered into the Confederate service in the State imagine that they are entirely independent of the State authority, and if it is proper I wish you would request the Secretary of War to issue a suitable general order upon the subject especially in the State."[62] This last, of course, was impossible, but the letter illustrates the conflict between state and central government over control and employment of forces that had been raised within a state and the conflict between those two governments on strategic priorities.

On October 18, Governor Milton wrote directly to President Davis concerning a number of his continuing concerns. The first had to do with the raising of cavalry units in the state by local politicians. Milton believed that the defense of the state should be by batteries of heavy-caliber guns located at key points, with concentrated supporting infantry. He felt that there would never be a cavalry battle in Florida unless the lack of coastal defense, artillery, and infantry permitted an invasion. The governor expressed his concern for Apalachicola and suggested that if given a little help, he would defend Apalachicola with state troops.[63] On October 24, in a letter to the secretary of war, Milton suggested that the military department of Middle and East Florida be so arranged as to include Apalachicola and St. Andrew's.[64]

On October 28, Milton again wrote to the secretary of war, protesting the central government's use of the Chattahoochee River as the dividing line between the two military departments in Florida and now suggested that Apalachicola and St.

Andrew's would be better off in General Bragg's department in West Florida. Governor Milton gave as reasons for this turnaround that Apalachicola and St. Andrew's were more "conveniently connected with Pensacola than any important place in Middle or East Florida." Governor Milton also cited certain conflicts over authority between state and Confederate troops which had taken place (involving Colonel Hopkins) and certain unnecessary expenses which had been incurred because of differences in perceived defensive requirements between state and Confederate authorities. In closing, Governor Milton advised that he was working on a presentation of his views concerning a new military department which would embrace parts of Georgia, Alabama, and Florida adjacent to the Chattahoochee River.[65]

He did present his views a day later, but in a letter to President Davis.

> Now permit me to say that Georgia and Alabama are as much, if not more, interested in the defense of Apalachicola, so far as commerce is concerned, as Florida; therefore, in view of our extended coast, and the almost insurmountable obstacles to its successful defense, I would recommend, most respectfully and earnestly, that a military department be composed of the counties contiguous on both sides of the Chattahoochee River, so as to embrace Columbus, Georgia.

In strong language, Milton deplored the vulnerability of Florida.

> My opinion has been, and is yet, that if General Scott . . . really desired the subjugation of the South . . . the conquest of Florida would have been promptly made. . . . The conquest of Florida, as one of the seven states, would have had a powerful influence upon foreign nations, an inspiring effect upon the minds of his troops, and of the citizens and Government of the United States, and formed a basis for future operations which would have checked Virginia and other States that have not seceded, and dispirited many in the seceded States who apprehended with fear and trembling the consequences of a change of government. . . . As it is, unable to conquer any other State, may not Florida claim their attention?[66]

Governor Milton wrote to Gov. Joseph E. Brown of Georgia on
October 31, 1861, seeking help for his proposal of the tristate
military department.[67] Governor Milton's plan for a mid-Flor-
ida defense never came into being. It served as one more frustration for the governor in his conflict with the central
government over strategic priorities and use of limited resources. Although scarcely considered at all by Governor
Milton in his concern over the defenses of the state, both the
Confederate and Federal governments were much more interested in Fernandina than in Apalachicola.

On November 1, 1861, prior to the Union attack on Port
Royal, South Carolina, General Trapier wrote to Governor
Milton from Charleston in anticipation of leaving for Florida.
After saying he was unfamiliar with the numbers of troops in
Middle and East Florida, he stated that he believed it would
require seven thousand troops of all arms to defend and requested the governor to call up at once a sufficient number of
regiments to make up that force. In view of the problems Governor Milton was having in trying to raise state militia troops
in competition with the recruiting efforts of the Confederate
army officials, this letter probably met with a dubious recep-
tion. General Trapier certainly did not aid the governor's disposition when he wrote, "Fernandina, (or Amelia Island) is
obviously the point most likely to become the object of the
enemy's first attack."[68]

The concern of Governor Milton with Middle Florida and his
lack of concern for East Florida was not lost upon the residents
of the latter, who were beginning to believe themselves being
abandoned by both Florida and the Confederacy. Pro-Union
sentiment was more likely to appear in East Florida than in
Middle or West Florida. State militia brigadier general Richard F. Floyd had requested permission from the governor on
April 11, 1862, to place portions of East Florida under martial
law because he felt that the country bordering the St. Johns
River was infested by numerous and dangerous traitors. Floyd
enclosed a letter from a Captain Pearson commanding the
Ocklawaha Rangers, who had stated, "I regret very much to
have to report to you that at least three-fourth's of the people
on the Saint John's River and east of it are aiding and abetting

the enemy."[69] In General Grayson's letter of September 13, 1861, to the secretary of war detailing the deplorable state of Fernandina's defenses, he enclosed a copy of the following circular which had been posted around the city:

> All loyal citizens of the United States are hereby notified that the Federal troops will take possession of the island of Amelia in a few days, and if they desire to escape the vengeance of an outraged Government they must assemble on the south end of the island. All those found at that point, except the military, will be regarded as good citizens of the United States.
> Assemble on the right.[70]

East Florida had become increasingly apathetic toward the Confederacy and, with the increasingly provincial concern of the governor with Middle Florida and the subsequent withdrawal of Confederate troops from the coast, began to accept the idea of being occupied sooner or later by the Federal government. Mayor H. H. Hoeg of Jacksonville advised the citizens of his town to surrender upon the approach of the enemy and not to attempt to defend the city, "Inasmuch as all the Confederate troops, arms, and munitions of war upon the St. John's River and in east and south Florida generally are ordered away, and that the east and south are to be abandoned."[71]

On November 5, 1861, Gen. Robert E. Lee was assigned to command a new military department embracing the coasts of South Carolina, Georgia, and East Florida.[72] His immediate concern was the Union attack on Port Royal, which took place on November 7. Florida's defense, because of her comparative lack of strategic importance, had long been of low priority. While decisions were being made concerning higher priority locations to be defended, Florida was left to fend for herself. General Lee decided that it was impossible to defend the entire South Atlantic coastline in view of the overwhelming Union naval advantage and therefore concentrated on defending the points he considered critical. Within his department these were the entrances to Cumberland Sound and Brunswick and the water approaches to Savannah and Charleston.[73] General

Lee was well aware of the implications of the Union victory at Roanoke Island, which saw steam-driven Union gunboats carrying rifled cannon defeat Confederate coastal defenses. Technological advances had stripped coastal defense forces of the advantage they had long enjoyed over attacking ships. In view of his limited resources, extended coastline, and the Union naval advantage, General Lee changed the existing coastline defense at the waterline within his department to one of mobile defense. Military units would be withdrawn to the interior and staged in selected locations, from which they could be rapidly dispatched, preferably by railroad, to concentrate in areas threatened by Union invasion.

In connection with the entrance to Cumberland Sound, General Lee dispatched navy lieutenant William A. Webb to Fernandina from Savannah on November 12 to help complete the artillery batteries located there and train men to service the guns.[74] General Lee's ordnance officer, Lieutenant Colonel Gill, inspected the defenses at Fernandina on November 17 and reported that the batteries on Amelia Island were not yet completed, with some guns still to be changed and others mounted.[75] General Lee made a rapid inspection tour of his own from Savannah to Fernandina. Concerned about the defenses controlling the entrance to Cumberland Sound, General Lee ordered navy commander Charles McBlair to Fernandina. On December 18, he ordered the Twenty-fourth Mississippi to Fernandina to augment the Florida forces protecting the batteries on Cumberland and Amelia islands. Lee wanted to ensure that defenses on Georgia's side of Cumberland Sound would be manned.[76]

This concern with Fernandina brought a complaint from Governor Milton to the secretary of war on December 26, 1861, about Confederate defensive priorities. In his letter he wrote, "Thrice the expense has been incurred and thrice the force assembled for the defense of Fernandina, and yet Apalachicola is decidedly the most important commercial city, and, in a strategic point of view, in the hands of the enemy would afford greater facilities for injury to the South."[77] When it was obvious that General Lee had rejected Gulf coast defenses in favor of those on the Atlantic coast, Governor Milton organized his own state troops under his appointee Brig. Gen. Richard F. Floyd to defend the Apalachicola area. After all of Governor Milton's protests concerning the raising of cavalry troops in Florida, it is ironic that the 612-man unit contained two companies of mounted infantry.[78]

General Lee made a second inspection tour of Fernandina in early January 1862. He found shortages of cannon, powder, clothing, and ammunition and made arrangements to have these shipped to Fernandina from Richmond, Augusta, Columbus, and Savannah.[79] He missed seeing General Trapier, who had made his headquarters at Tallahassee. The secretary of war had ordered General Trapier to make his headquarters at Fernandina as "being the only point in your district subject to serious attack by heavy forces." General Trapier, however, had apparently swung over to Governor Milton's thinking concerning the importance of Apalachicola and the middle of the state because he presented a long argument to Gen. Samuel Cooper, the Confederate adjutant and inspector general, on why he should stay in Tallahassee.[80] Before this situation was resolved, more significant events overrode the question of whether Fernandina or Apalachicola was the more important point to be defended and drastically changed Florida's defensive system.

On January 14, 1862, a called session of the Florida convention met to discuss the "financial difficulties" of the state. It considered, among other items, requesting the Florida congressional delegation to seek funding for joining the Pensacola and Georgia Railroad with the Savannah, Albany, and Gulf road in Georgia as a "military necessity," assigning Col. W. G. M. Davis's controversial First Cavalry Regiment to Gen. Albert Sidney Johnston's forces in the west, making money available for the health of the troops at Fernandina, and suggesting that General Trapier either stay with his troops at Fernandina or be relieved.[81] This last resolution caused General Trapier to request that he be relieved from duties in Florida and assigned elsewhere.[82] Additionally, much to the dismay of Governor Milton, two ordinances were passed. One created the four-man executive council. The second, two days later, abolished the state militia, and responsibility for the defense of Florida was assigned to the Confederate government.[83]

A second event with ramifications that bore on Florida's situation was the fall of Roanoke Island, North Carolina, which revealed the danger to remote and isolated detachments and batteries on the coast. A number of such Southern islands were subsequently abandoned, including Cumberland Island, and cannon from the Georgia coastal batteries were split between Savannah and Fernandina. General Lee, however, still felt at this point that Fernandina, Jacksonville, and the St. Johns River were to be held.[84]

The third event, or rather series of events, that would leave Florida almost defenseless was the Confederate disasters at Forts Donelson and Henry in Tennessee, which necessitated the sending of all available troops to the Army of the Tennessee to bolster the sagging Confederate defenses. Accordingly, on February 24, 1862, the secretary of war ordered General Lee to:

> withdraw all such forces as are now employed in the defense of the seaboard of Florida, taking proper steps to secure the guns and munitions of war, and to send forward the troops to Tennessee, to report to General A. S. Johnston, by the most expeditious route.
>
> The only troops to be retained in Florida are such as necessary to defend the Apalachicola River, as the enemy could by that river at high water send his gunboats into the very middle of the State of Georgia.[85]

Governor Milton had seemingly won his battle over defensive priorities within the state, but it was a hollow victory. In a bitter response to the secretary of war, Governor Milton wrote:

> The effect of the order is to abandon Middle, East, and South Florida to the mercy or abuse of the Lincoln Government. It cannot be possible that the order was intended to have such an effect. If strictly obeyed, the forces at Saint Augustine, on the Saint John's River, at Tampa, and at this place have to be ordered to the defenses of the Chattahoochee River or to Tennessee. I

cannot and will not believe that an order to have that effect
would have been issued without previous notice to the executive of the State, that proper measures might have been advised for the protection of the lives, liberty, and property of the
citizens of Middle, East, and South Florida. Moreover, the order,
if executed, would not, with the forces now in Florida, secure
the defenses upon the Chattahoochee, for if the enemy were in
possession of Tallahassee and Saint Andrew's or Saint Joseph's
Bays, they can attack in the rear all batteries which may be constructed on either side of the river.[86]

Governor Milton closed with a plea to retain enough of the six
thousand stand of arms that had just come into New Smyrna
by blockade-runner to equip 2,500 Florida militia in order to
defend the state. While the governor expressed some concern
for the people of East Florida, many residents of Tallahassee
were less considerate. They forwarded a petition to the Florida
congressional delegation recommending that Fernandina be
abandoned and that the Second Florida Regiment be returned
from Virginia to defend Tallahassee and the Chattahoochee
River.[87]

The order to evacuate Amelia Island was received on February 25, 1862, just four days before the Federal expedition to
take Fernandina arrived. The Confederate forces had only been
able to remove eighteen of the thirty-three guns in the fort, and
the Federals captured the remaining fifteen. In addition, five
more were later captured at the mouth of the St. Johns, where
they had been emplaced to prevent Union intrusion into that
river.[88] St. Augustine and Jacksonville were captured by Union
forces within the next couple of days, although Jacksonville
was evacuated by the Federal forces a month later.[89] While the
Union troops occupied Jacksonville, a number of residents professed their loyalty to the Union, believing the Federal forces
were going to stay in the area. However, when the Union troops
left, those who had expressed their loyalty to the Union found
themselves in a very difficult position. They either had to leave
with the Union forces or face retaliation from those loyal to the
Southern cause. The Union occupied Jacksonville four separate
times and evacuated it three times. This pattern created se-

rious credibility gaps concerning the Union's ability to protect those who professed loyalty to the Federal government.

On March 2, General Lee was ordered to Richmond.[90] By the middle of March 1862, the towns on Florida's east coast were under Federal control. Pensacola was being evacuated by Confederate forces, Cedar Key and Apalachicola had been visited by Union raiders, and General Trapier had been relieved and replaced by Floridian Joseph Finegan.[91] Prior to his departure, General Finegan was informed by General Lee that he was to pay particular attention to defense of the interior of the state and the lines of interior communication with both the Apalachicola and St. Johns rivers as of "primary importance."[92] The forces available to Finegan to accomplish this mission were limited, as revealed in a request he made on September 29, 1862, for more troops. The general reported that he had "but nine companies of infantry, five companies of Partisan Rangers, one regiment of cavalry, and two companies of light artillery in service," a total strength in Middle and East Florida of 1,726 present for duty.[93]

Eventually, Gen. P. G. T. Beauregard was assigned to replace General Lee as commander of the Department of South Carolina, Georgia, and Florida. After some movement of the boundary back and forth between the Chattahoochee and Apalachicola rivers, the District of Middle Florida was assigned to the command of Brig. Gen. Howell Cobb, and his district's geographic limits were defined as between the Suwannee River and the Choctawhatchee to include the navigable waters of the Chattahoochee and Flint rivers. General Finegan was assigned command of East Florida, with headquarters to be at Lake City, while General Cobb's headquarters were to be at Quincy. Both generals were told that no forces were available to send to them and that they would have to recruit their own military forces.[94]

Within a relatively short time, Florida's scheme of defense had changed dramatically from a concern over the protection of selected key points along the coast to a last-ditch defense of the interior, using "home guard" and irregular units. Governor Milton wrote a very pessimistic assessment of Florida's situation to the Confederate secretary of war on August 5, 1862.

There is not at this time an organized regiment in this State. Companies are stationed at different places, but at no point in sufficient numbers and with suitable arrangements for defense against invasion by the enemy in moderate force. . . . The enemy command the Saint John's River, and are in possession of Saint Augustine and Fernandina, in East Florida. In West Florida, Pensacola, Apalachicola, Saint Joseph's, and Saint Andrew's Bays are blockaded and entirely unprotected. The highest vote ever cast in this State was 12,898. Eight infantry and one cavalry regiment, besides independent infantry companies enough to form a tenth regiment, have been ordered from and left the State in Confederate service. In the State are one infantry battalion, eight cavalry, two artillery, and three independent infantry companies, in the aggregate not more than 1,600 effective men. Scarcely a man to every mile of coast by which we are exposed to the power of the enemy. . . .

There is not within my knowledge a portion of the State free of skulking traitors, the majority of whom are of Northern birth and claiming to be citizens of Florida.[95]

On both the Gulf and Atlantic coasts, exposed men and guns had been withdrawn into the interior, where their main activity was watching and waiting, operating on interior lines, with occasional small forays into coastal areas.[96] By the summer of 1862, much of the earlier enthusiasm for the Confederacy had been dissipated by the realities of war and blockade. A significant part of the state was occupied or defenseless, the Federal blockade was tightening and its effects were being felt, and there appeared to be more Southern disasters than victories. Apathy was commonplace, and some Floridians seemed receptive to the idea of rejoining the Union. In September 1862, Governor Milton wrote to President Davis, "You are apprised that in Florida a very large minority were opposed to secession, and in many parts of the State combinations existed to adhere to and maintain the United States Government, and even now in some portions of the State there are men who would eagerly seize any opportunity that promised success to the United States."[97]

Florida had been the third state to secede from the Union but was slower than most other Confederate states to organize its defenses. Extremely limited in resources, overwhelmed by an impossible task dictated by geography, lacking in ordnance and skilled military leadership, low on defensive priorities of the provisional government, torn by internal division and lack of central control and direction in mobilization, Florida found herself isolated and disaffected from the rest of the Confederacy in the second year of the war. In addition, Florida experienced internal division: the western panhandle was more closely aligned with the Gulf and the Mississippi Valley than with the rest of the state, and the eastern portion similarly with the Atlantic coast and Georgia. The middle of the state, which had led in the road toward secession, contained the hard-core, patriotic Southerners, while dissident elements and pro-Union sentiment grew in the eastern, southern, and western portions of the state. Florida was a defensive liability to both herself and the central government, making little more than token contributions to the common defense. When the state's contribution of manpower was exhausted, she lost what little importance she had to the Confederacy. Strategically, in view of higher priorities elsewhere, the Confederacy had little choice in her relationships with Florida. The state was assigned responsibility for her own defense under Confederate auspices and left to fend for herself as best she could with no men or weapons to be furnished by the central government. Two military departments were created, one without troops and one headed by a political appointee. For all intents and purposes, Florida found herself abandoned by the Confederacy she had been so eager to join, isolated and vulnerable to the enemy.

Florida would, however, have more of value to the Confederacy to contribute later, and a preview of this was contained in a letter written on October 5, 1862, by Governor Milton to the secretary of war. Governor Milton wrote: "I presume there is no State where, in proportion to the amount cultivated, such abundant crops of corn, peas, potatoes, and sugar-cane have been made, and which will afford a more abundant supply of pork and beef than in Florida. The enemy are appraised of these facts and will avail themselves of the advantages to be derived from our abundance, to the exclusion of the Confederate States."[98] As the major sources of subsistence supplies for the Confederacy were progressively reduced by Union activity, Florida would again receive attention from both sides. Until then, the state was subjected to several years of a combination of Federal raids and a tightening blockade.

2

Blockade and Raid

The Middle Civil War Years in Florida

During 1862 and 1863, the major war activities in and around Florida centered on the Union's continuing tightening of the naval blockade, interspersed with occasional raids by the Federal troops on Southern outposts and ports harboring blockade-runners. The Blockade Board, appointed by Secretary of the Navy Gideon Welles, devised ways and means of improving the blockade's efficiency. The board's broad strategic plan was to maintain the blockade and to seize certain Southern ports as bases for the blockading forces. As a military measure, the blockade had two primary objectives: first, isolate the primarily agricultural Southern states, dependent on the outside world for the necessities of life, from the sources of those necessities; second, prevent the exportation of Southern cotton, the South's main source of income, thereby depriving that government of its revenues for the war and the people of their very means of existence.[1]

The blockade started as a traditional one in which a few large vessels were kept moving at a distance in front of a port. This was effective in keeping the respect of major neutral powers for the blockade. However, a contraband trade emerged, and this required the blockading force to use the innovation of anchoring large numbers of small vessels at entrances to blockaded harbors and keeping vessels close to shore in exposed positions in all sorts of weather.

Four characteristics of this blockade made it unprecedented.

The first was the peculiar formation of the shore, which gave almost a double coastline throughout, penetrated by numerous inlets giving access to a complicated network of channels. Second was the vicinity of neutral ports friendly to blockade-runners. There were four of these intermediary points for trade with the South: Bermuda, Nassau, Havana, and Matamoros; of these, Nassau, only 180 miles in a direct line from Florida, was the most important. Savannah, Charleston, and Wilmington, however, rather than Florida, were the main ports of entry for the blockade-runners, and the run to these points from Nassau was between five hundred and six hundred miles, taking about three days for a one-way trip. Third was the Southern cotton monopoly, which made the blockade a source of irritation to neutrals. Last was the introduction of steam-powered blockade-runners.[2]

Beginning in the spring and summer of 1861, vessels were progressively stationed at such points as Savannah, Mobile, and New Orleans. Later, naval forces gained footholds on the Southern coast with the help of small bodies of troops and converted the blockade into a military occupation. These Union enclaves became the headquarters for the various blockading squadrons and bases for coaling, repairs, and replenishment that reduced the time that ships were "off station." Fernandina, Florida, was selected by the Blockade Board to serve such a purpose, and its acquisition in early March 1862, along with St. Augustine and control over the mouth of the St. Johns, gave the South Atlantic Blockade Squadron bases within its operating area.

The operation of the blockade of Florida was different from that of other states. There were no large commercial centers to draw blockade-runners with valuable cargo nor defended strategic coastal points guarding quick access to the interior. There were, however, numerous bays and inlets where small vessels could enter and remain concealed. It was impossible to shut off all blockade-running completely; the best tactic was for the blockaders to patrol the coast and, when a blockade-runner was discovered ashore, send in small bodies of troops to capture or burn it. The history of the Florida blockade is primarily one

characterized by countless numbers of such minor engagements as boarding parties, cutting-out expeditions, raids on
saltworks, sudden dashes into remote and unfrequented inlets
on dark nights, usually followed by the capture of cotton-laden
schooners or stray boats, with the occasional loss of a man or
two.[3] Few of these engagements were of any significance by
themselves, but their cumulative effect contributed to the
slow strangulation of the Florida economy. The task of the
Union blockaders in respect to Florida was made easier by
the relative lack of importance the state had for blockade-
runners, the increasingly nonmilitary aspects of the cargoes
that were carried, and the inability of the local residents to
replace the ships that were captured or destroyed.

The third report of the Blockade Board gave little attention
to East Florida. Florida had few suitable harbors and few connections with the interior. It was believed that Jacksonville and
St. Augustine could be blockaded in the usual manner, while
the lower coast could be patrolled by two small cruisers which
would continually check its shores and bays. In respect to
South Florida, the board members declared, "It can hardly be
said to be inhabited and is of no great consequence as a convenient place of resort for pirates."[4] Besides being thinly popu-
lated, the area was without any railroad facilities, and cargoes
that came into the lower East Florida ports such as New
Smyrna faced a difficult trip by land and water to get to a railroad.

One more reason for the lack of importance of Florida to
blockade-runners surfaced in a letter written in 1864 to George
A. Trenholm, the Confederate secretary of the treasury. The
secretary's attention was called to the difficulties of blockade-
running into the major ports of Wilmington, Charleston, and
Mobile, and it was suggested that surveys be conducted to find
safer ports in Florida. In his endorsement of the letter,
Trenholm mentioned a basic difficulty with the use of Florida
ports for blockade-running—the entrances to selected bays
were not protected, and after vessels had entered and gone upriver for safety, they could be bottled up by a single blockading
vessel at the entrance.[5] The withdrawal of Confederate troops

from East Florida and the seizure of the ports of Brunswick and
St. Marys in Georgia and Fernandina, St. Augustine, and Jacksonville in Florida gave the Federal navy a strong grip on Florida's portion of the South Atlantic coast. In addition, the
occasional patrols and raids up the St. Johns and St. Marys
rivers and along the coast did a lot to discourage blockade-
runners from venturing into Florida.

Blockade-running in the early part of the war was carried on
by ships of all sizes and along the entire three-thousand-mile
coastline of the Confederacy. With the tightening of the blockade, certain characteristics of ships such as speed, "invisibil-
ity," and handiness along with a draft shallow enough to enable
passage when loaded over sandbars were essential; storage
space was a secondary priority. Early in the war years substantial quantities of arms and ammunition were brought in. As
the war progressed, blockade-running attracted a horde of spec-
ulators and adventurers, and the needs of the Confederacy took
second place to luxury goods, which took up minimum cargo
space but brought maximum profits. Such items as steel rails,
machinery, iron plates, and heavy equipment required too
much space, their weight reduced the speed of the vessel, and
they could be sold to the government only at fixed prices. Luxury goods took less space, weighed less, and could be sold to
the highest bidder. Furthermore, the people who both demanded and could pay for these goods were located in the major port cities. Payment was demanded in gold or cotton. The
Confederacy was thus hurt two ways: it was not getting badly
needed war materials, and its financial resources were being
drained, with the resultant damage to Confederate securities
leading to inflation. There were some examples of successful
profit-making through blockade-running in Florida such as the
partnership of Capt. John McKay and Jacob "Jake" Summerlin
in running cattle out of Charlotte Harbor to Havana.[6] However,
the successful operators in the blockade-running business
dealt in higher-priced merchandise and converged on the larger
centers of trade. These men had little interest in the outcome
of the war; their main objective was to make as much money as
possible in the shortest time.[7]

Blockade-running in the first year of the war was amateurish. Later, the effective pattern that developed was for large ships from Europe to bring goods to transfer points, where the goods would then be transshipped on to smaller vessels which carried them into the Southern ports. The two shipments of arms that came in to New Smyrna followed this route. The largest transfer point was Nassau, which was only 515 miles from Charleston, 570 miles from Wilmington, and 180 miles from Florida. Next was Bermuda, 675 miles from Wilmington and 775 miles from Charleston. In the Gulf, Havana was the chief depot.[8] The nearness of the Federal base at Key West, the strictness of the Gulf blockade, and the fall of New Orleans, along with all of the other factors mentioned, centered the attention of blockade-runners on Savannah, Charleston, and Wilmington, and away from Florida.

In one study of blockade-running through Georgia and Florida ports during the Civil War, the author concluded that in terms of its contributions to the war effort of the South and the material needs of its far-flung civilian populace were concerned, blockade-running through the Georgia and East Florida ports may be written off as an insignificant effort.

> The extant records disclose that successful runs between these ports and foreign sources were so infrequent after 1861, and the cargo capacities of most of the vessels that ran from the beginning until the end of the blockade were so small, the game was not worth the candle. They also make it clear why neither the Confederate Government, hard pressed as it was for arms, munitions, and equipment for its forces in the field, nor the Georgians or Floridians, whose appetites for lush profits were as keen as those of their neighbors in the Carolinas and Gulf states, ever attempted large-scale operations through any of the Georgia or East Florida ports.[9]

Marcus W. Price's study shows that from the date of the proclamation of the blockade, only 225 vessels were known to have run in or out of these ports, making in all some 1,302 attempts. This figure compares with 2,960 from Gulf ports and 2,054 from Carolina ports. The vast majority of the attempts from Georgia and East Florida were made in 1861, with only 54 attempts in 1862, 60 in 1863, 63 in 1864, and 2 in 1865.[10] When it is realized that most of these attempts were made by small schooners and sloops, it is clear that the size of the activity was very small indeed. The blockade of the coast of Florida was effective; what did manage to get through was of little consequence to either Florida or the war effort. Just as important, the desired effect of waging economic warfare was achieved; Florida was cut off from the imports she had come to rely upon and was unable to export those items she produced that were the basis of her economy. The war was brought home to Florida by the blockade.

As the blockade tightened and the Confederate troops were reduced and withdrawn into the interior, the Federal forces found some success in raiding coastal localities. Some of these raids were small-scale search-and-destroy types whose objectives were saltworks (whose lights, by the way, assisted blockade-runners in navigation), beached blockade-runners, small caches of supplies, or individuals and groups. A number of these raids, however, were of a larger scale. The success of these raids may have led Federal leaders to consider favorably the Federal expedition into Florida in early 1864.

On January 16, 1862, almost six weeks prior to the seizure of Fernandina, the Federal blockading ship *Hatteras* attacked Cedar Key, the Gulf terminus of the Florida Railroad. A landing party from the ship entered the town and destroyed the wharf of the Florida Railroad Company, its depot, several railroad flatcars, the telegraph office, and seven small vessels in the harbor.[11] Two Confederate companies defending the town had just been sent to Fernandina in expectation of an attack at that location, leaving a lieutenant and twenty-two men from the Fourth Florida Regiment to protect Cedar Key. The Confederate report of the action noted the existence of pro-Union supporters in Cedar Key.[12] When the Union forces occupied Fernandina on March 4, the Union possessed or controlled both terminuses of the Florida Railroad.

The Union occupation of St. Augustine and Jacksonville shortly after Fernandina was taken also revealed the presence of a number of pro-Union sympathizers, some of whom wanted to bring in cotton and other products for shipment to the North for sale.[13] In the report by Union general Horatio G. Wright of the occupation of Jacksonville, he informed his headquarters that the rebels had burned seven sawmills, some four million feet of lumber, the railroad depot, a large hotel (the Judson), some private houses, and a gunboat under construction.[14] The commander of the South Atlantic Blockade Squadron, Capt. Samuel Francis DuPont, reported to his superior that "the sawmills, with others in this country, were of Northern enterprise and capital, by which these people of Florida had their endless forests turned into gold."[15] The search for lumber set up another Union raid, one however that was costly to the Federal forces.

It had been reported to Flag Officer DuPont that a large cache of live oak was hidden in the vicinity of Mosquito Inlet. This area was already receiving Federal attention because of its use by blockade-runners, particularly in the recent arrival of two shipments of arms. Commander C. R. Rodgers of the *Wabash* had written Flag Officer DuPont from St. Augustine on March 12, "I am led to believe that Mosquito Inlet, upon which Smyrna is situated, has been much used for the introduction of arms from the Bahamas."[16]

His suspicions were well founded, as the steamer *Caroline* (or *Kate*) had run in two cargoes of military supplies from Nassau, and the steamer *Cecile* another.[17] The Union gunboats *Penguin* and *Henry Andrews* were sent to locate the lumber and conduct a reconnaissance of the area. On March 23, 1861, a landing party led by the captains of both ships was ambushed on its way back from a land reconnaissance, and both captains were killed along with two or three of their men. Two other sailors were wounded and captured. The *Henry Andrews* under a new captain was sent back on March 25 to recover the bodies of the two naval officers killed in the raid and to locate the lumber. The bodies of the two Federal officers were returned under a flag of truce by Capt. Pickett Bird of the Third Florida, elements of which had conducted the ambush; copies of their mission to locate the lumber were still on their bodies. The new captain of the *Henry Andrews* had no trouble locating the lumber.[18]

While the Union forces had occupied Jacksonville, a number of Federal gunboats had run up and down the river, the *Ottawa* to Orange Mills, some eighty miles upriver, and the *Ellen*, some miles farther. This Union-gunboat patrolling of the St. Johns River was continued even after the Federal troops had evacuated Jacksonville, which increased the difficulty for anything that had been run through the blockade moving with any speed through Florida because of the position of the river in relation to transportation routes. It also resulted in the capture of a number of vessels used in blockade-running, including the yacht *America*, which had been sunk in Dunn's Creek and was raised and recovered by Federal lieutenant Isaac Stevens.[19]

In response to intelligence reports that the Confederate forces were reinforcing East Florida and the feeling that too many Federal troops were tied up in occupation duties along the coast, Maj. Gen. David Hunter, commanding the Department of the South, on April 2, 1862, ordered the evacuation of Jacksonville. At that time, there were some 2,570 Federal troops between Fernandina and St. Augustine, with 1,400 in Jacksonville.[20] This action drew some opposition. Brig. Gen. Horatio Wright, commanding the troops in Jacksonville, wrote to General Hunter: "The necessity for withdrawal of the troops from Jacksonville is to be regretted. A considerable number of the inhabitants had avowed themselves publicly in favor of our cause, and encouraged by the proclamation issued by General Sherman to the people of East Florida, had been active in their efforts to organize a State and city government."[21]

The proclamation referred to was issued on March 20, 1862, by Gen. Thomas W. Sherman and called for assemblages of loyal people to gather and swear their allegiance to the United States. They might then "organize your government and elect your officers in the good old way of the past."[22] Flag Officer DuPont was highly upset at hearing of the evacuation. On March 6, both DuPont and General Sherman had received similar letters from Assistant Secretary of the Navy Gustavas Fox telling them to take Fernandina because "the moral effect on

Florida and the return of that State to its allegiance was vastly more important than the capture of Savannah."[23] DuPont wrote to Fox on April 3, 1862, that Florida could have been taken by General Sherman in "six weeks with a cavalry regiment and 5,000 troops," repeating an idea DuPont had stated three weeks earlier to Fox. DuPont further informed Fox that he was getting letters every day from loyal citizens in Jacksonville and St. Augustine worried about their relations.[24] In a letter written on May 22, 1862, DuPont quoted a conversation with Captain Drayton, who expressed the opinion that "he fully believes East Florida would have organized itself into a State if Jacksonville had not been abandoned—it was silly beyond measure, and when I think two weeks after the forces were withdrawn, General Hunter let sixty officers go on leave."[25]

Apalachicola was attacked by a Federal landing force on April 2. Confederate troops evacuated the town, and it was considered a no-man's-land until the end of the war. On May 20, a Union landing party was attacked at Crooked River in West Florida with some loss on the Union side. On June 15, a small detachment from the *Kingfisher* landed near St. Marks and burned several houses and the lighthouse.[26] Tampa was shelled on June 30 and July 1 and was attacked by a landing party on October 16. This type of activity continued until the end of the war.

Confederate general Finegan had received instructions to protect the Apalachicola and St. Johns rivers. In compliance with these orders, in September 1862, Finegan caused gun batteries to be constructed at Yellow Bluff and St. Johns Bluff on the St. Johns River to prevent Federal gunboats from using that river. The Union response was a combined operation the following month involving six gunboats and 1,500 men. The troops were landed in the rear of the Confederate gun positions, causing them to be evacuated without a fight by the defending force with a loss to the Confederates of six eight-inch guns and two four-inch guns along with sundry small arms and military equipment.[27] Jacksonville was briefly occupied, but since the only purpose of the expedition had been to reopen the St. Johns for the Union gunboats, the troops withdrew after achieving their purpose and returned to their base at Hilton Head.

Between January 23 and February 1, 1863, the First South Carolina Volunteer Regiment (black), under Col. Thomas Higginson, made an expedition up the St. Marys River, which forms part of the border between Florida and Georgia. Their mission was primarily for recruitment of blacks for regiments being formed in the Department of the South. With only limited success in recruitment, some commercial products were brought out. The raid by black troops, however, had a strong psychological effect upon the residents of the area and the rest of the Deep South when it became known.

Jacksonville was occupied for the third time on March 3, 1863, by a combination of white and black troops. The primary objective of the raid was recruitment for the black regiments and, as Gen. Rufus Saxton phrased it, "To occupy Jacksonville and make it the base of operations for the arming of negroes and securing in this way possession of the entire State of Florida."[28] The Federal troops raided and plundered the countryside, meeting more resistance this time than before because of increased Confederate forces in the area. Perhaps making history, Confederate general Finegan had a thirty-two-pounder rifled gun mounted on a railroad car and run up to a point where it could throw several shells into Jacksonville, with unknown effect.[29] A series of skirmishes took place with little progress made toward either recruitment or increase of pro-Union support. General Hunter ordered the third evacuation of Jacksonville, which was carried out on March 31, 1863. In a letter written on April 4, 1863, by Gen. Rufus Saxton to Secretary of War Stanton, notwithstanding the actual results of the expedition, the general claimed:

> The operation was in every way successful, and had it not been withdrawn, would in a short time have cleared the State of Florida of their troops and secured large amounts of cotton and other valuables for the Government. . . .
> I shall urge upon the commanding officer of this department the importance of reoccupying Florida as soon as the Charleston

expedition is over. . . . With the Saint John's River as a base of operations the entire State can be readily occupied by negro forces and restored to the Union. Had the expedition been allowed to remain in Florida I am confident that its success would have fully equaled your expectations.[30]

The evacuation of Jacksonville by the Federal troops was marred by fires that sprang up suddenly in parts of the city and by a number of private homes that were looted by hoodlums among the departing soldiers. The black troops were initially blamed, but news reporters who were present along with Col. Thomas Higginson of the First South Carolina Volunteers maintained it was done by white troops in the part of the city in which they had been quartered.[31] The burning of Jacksonville, along with similar happenings in Georgia and South Carolina, was the subject of a strongly worded letter General Beauregard, commanding the Confederate Department of South Carolina, Georgia, and Florida, sent to General Gillmore, the new commander of the Federal Department of the South. After listing numerous examples of the destruction of civilian property, Beauregard went on to castigate the Federal government for its use of "members of a servile race" as soldiers, citing Napoleon's refusal to use volunteering Russian serfs as an exemplary action to be followed.[32]

Federal forces returned to Mosquito Inlet in late July 1863, in an operation noteworthy because ships of both the South Atlantic and East Gulf blockading squadrons combined in the raid. Four ships swooped into the inlet and got close enough to shell New Smyrna and destroy the local hotel, the Sheldon House, owned by a family whose sons were blockade-runners. A landing party was sent in, and several small vessels were caught in the area and either taken or destroyed along with their cargoes of cotton. Sporadic sniper fire was received and returned in heavy volume. An observer reported that the steamer *Oleander* fired her guns all day on July 26 and expended 280 shells "wastefully" on the twenty-seventh.[33] It was certainly retaliation for the ambush of the naval party looking for the lumber cache the previous year.

With the departure of the Federal troops from Jacksonville at the end of March 1863, the Federal raids in Florida reverted to the smaller-scale operations that had taken place prior to the expedition in September 1862 to seize the Confederate gun emplacements at the entrance to the St. Johns River. Florida again became a backwash of the war, awaiting the day when developments might reawaken military interest in the state.

3

Renewed Interest in Florida

After the initial activity around Pensacola, and as the course of the Civil War unfolded, Florida found herself relegated to a position of unimportance by both sides. Both the initial attempt to take Fort Pickens and the early emphasis on coastal defense were superseded in priority by events elsewhere. The Confederate setbacks in Kentucky and Tennessee required immediate reinforcement of that area to prevent disaster; the most available troops were engaged in coastal defense. Florida scraped the bottom of the barrel to provide at least her share of the needed troops, which left her almost defenseless against the blockade and raiding forces. The North, after ensuring retention of Fort Pickens and control of the Florida Keys, picked up Fernandina and St. Augustine relatively cheaply and were thus able to establish a series of bases along the extended Florida coast for the blockading forces.

As far as the Union strategic planners were concerned, the Union's prime interest in relation to Florida was the establishment and tightening of the blockade. This was effectively achieved by the end of 1862. A series of raids by limited Federal land forces had been conducted with reasonable success, but no major land operation had been envisioned, in view of the expected paucity of results. Toward the end of 1863, however, a number of developments suggested that a Federal military operation having multiple objectives might be successfully and profitably conducted in Florida. Maj. Gen. Quincy A. Gillmore, commanding the Federal Department of the South, proposed such an undertaking. The initial objectives he listed in his request for permission to mount this expedition included opening the area to commercial exploitation, cutting off a source of commissary supplies for the Confederacy, preventing the Confederacy from removing rails from one area for use elsewhere, and recruiting blacks for the Federal army. Later, he added the objective of restoring Florida to the Union. An examination of the development of military, economic, and political factors affecting Florida by late 1863 reveals strong reasons for renewed interest in Florida and sheds light on the immense potential the Federal expedition into Florida in early 1864 possessed.

After losing the opportunity for exploitation presented by the success of the Port Royal attack in November 1861, Federal forces opposite Charleston and Savannah had been stalemated for some time. By late 1863, the combination of the large numbers of troops involved in the siege of these two cities, the lack of tangible evidence of progress in this region to date with no expectation for a change in this situation in the immediate future, the success of Federal forces elsewhere, the problems associated with troops in relatively static defensive positions for long periods of time, and the ambition of Federal leaders created a search for other opportunities within the Department of the South. The availability of naval transports provided the options of rapid transportation and surprise. Militarily, there were no targets available as important and as vulnerable as the railroad junctions and port cities of Georgia, South Carolina, and North Carolina had been in 1861. On the other hand, the series of raids conducted by Federal forces in Florida in 1862 and 1863 had revealed how poorly defended Florida was and particularly how vulnerable she was to combined operations involving land and sea forces. From a purely military point of view, the most important objectives for a raid into Florida were recruitment of blacks for the Federal army, cutting off of the enemy's source of commissary supplies, and both disrupting the rail system and preventing the removal of parts of it to locations where it would be more useful to the Confederacy.

The Act of July 17, 1862, empowered the president of the

United States to receive into the military and naval service "persons of African Descent." Prior to that act, a number of experiments had been made in various parts of the country using blacks as Federal soldiers, which had met with both approval and criticism. After the act legitimized these efforts, wide-scale recruitment and employment of black soldiers took place. By the end of the war, some 178,975 black troops were in Federal service; 99,337 were recruited from Confederate states, including 1,044 from Florida, roughly one-tenth of the black adult male population of that state.[1] This figure may be even higher because of the early practice of assigning recruits gathered on a raid into a state such as Florida to established black regiments from the North such as the Fifty-first Massachusetts or ones formed within the Department of the South such as the First or Second South Carolina. In the Union's Department of the South, success of recruitment of blacks by black units was evidenced as early as November 1862, when an expedition commanded by Lt. Col. Oliver T. Beard along the coasts of Georgia and East Florida left St. Simon's "with sixty-two colored and returned to Beaufort with 156 fighting men (all colored)."[2] Beard explained the process simply, "As soon as we took a slave from his claimant, we placed a musket in his hand and he began to fight for the freedom of others." The expedition also succeeded in destroying about twenty thousand dollars' worth of horses, wagons, rice, corn, and other Confederate property and brought off, in addition to the recruits, sixty-one women and children.[3]

These first troops in the Department of the South were formed into the First South Carolina Volunteers, the first organized black regiment in the Union army, commanded by Col. Thomas Wentworth Higginson, an abolitionist and old friend of John Brown's. On January 23, 1863, Colonel Higginson and his regiment were given a mission of raiding up the St. Marys River for the twin purposes of recruitment of blacks and seizure of lumber. Forty thousand bricks, 250 bars of railroad iron, some lumber, a flock of sheep, and some contraband were brought back.[4]

This raid was followed by a second one led by Colonel Higginson in March 1863. His forces this time included both the First and Second South Carolina Volunteer Negro regiments. The Second South Carolina was commanded by Col. James Montgomery, who had achieved some attention fighting on the side of the free-soil forces in Kansas. The regiment was short of troops, and while Colonel Montgomery had recruited some blacks from Fernandina in February, most that were available had already joined the First South Carolina. A trip to Key West had netted him 130 volunteers.[5] It was hoped that more could be obtained in the area of the St. Johns. Gen. Rufus Saxton believed that Jacksonville would be a center to which the numerous blacks in the area would flock. The intent of the expedition was not lost upon Confederate general Finegan, commanding East Florida, who reported that it appeared the Union was establishing Jacksonville and perhaps one other point farther up the St. Johns River as collecting points to attract runaway blacks. Finegan warned:

> that the entire negro population of East Florida will be lost and the country ruined there cannot be a doubt unless the means of holding the St. Johns are immediately supplied. . . . The entire planting interests of East Florida lie within easy connection of the river; . . . intercourse will immediately commence between negroes on the plantation and those in the enemy's service: . . . and this intercourse will be conducted through swamps and under cover of night, and cannot be prevented. A few weeks will suffice to corrupt the entire slave population of East Florida.[6]

General Saxton, reporting on the effect of the raid to Secretary of War Stanton stated, "It is my belief that scarcely an incident in this war has caused greater panic throughout the whole Southern coast than this raid of colored troops in Florida."[7] While the results of both expeditions in terms of numbers of blacks recruited for Federal service was not impressive, its effect on the local residents, as General Saxton had suggested, was tremendous. Slaveholders withdrew into the interior of the state with their slaves. Confederate captain John J. Dickison was ordered to remove into the interior all free Negroes and any without apparent owners.[8] The ever-present fear of a slave insurrection was fueled, and this fear spread throughout the lower South.[9] From the Federal point of view, these raids by black troops were highly effective, and they continued for the remainder of the war. At the same time, examples of the bravery exhibited by black units at such battles as Port Hudson and Battery Wagner convinced skeptics of the fighting abilities of blacks.

In January 1864, Gen. Quincy A. Gillmore requested General Halleck to send to the Department of the South some of the new black units being formed to "garrison the posts from which I draw the troops" for the expedition into Florida.[10] It would appear that at this time General Gillmore had been planning to use seasoned troops in his operation. The outcome of the 1864 Federal expedition into Florida might have been different had this request been granted. However, General Gillmore's request for black troops was denied, as the needs of the Department of the Gulf were judged to be more pressing for the new units. General Halleck, though, in discussing the objectives of General Gillmore's proposed expedition, wrote, "If it is expected to give an outlet for cotton, or open a favorable field for the enlistment of colored troops, the advantage may be sufficient to justify the expense in money and troops."[11]

General Gillmore had additionally requested permission to consolidate his black regiments such as the South Carolina regiments and designate them as "United States Colored Troops" because the men in the units were drawn from several states. He felt that this mixture interfered with recruiting in Florida and Georgia.[12] On December 22, 1863, General Halleck granted this permission in a letter that also informed General Gillmore that no reinforcements were available to his department.[13] In the instructions that were forwarded to General Gillmore in relation to black troops was the authority to enlist and organize all the black troops that could be recruited within his department, including recruits from Key West and the states of Georgia, Florida, and Alabama.[14]

General Gillmore was further authorized to appoint boards of examination for officers for these black units; determine the organization of these units in terms of arms, such as infantry, cavalry, or artillery; and determine their organization by size, such as regiment, brigade, and division. Finally, all units thus recruited and organized were to be designated "United States" troops.[15] Florida had proven to be a fertile area for recruitment of blacks and remained a strong possibility for further recruitment by General Gillmore to fill his own black regiments. According to Governor Milton, there were sixteen thousand slaves in East and South Florida.[16] In Middle Florida there were some forty thousand.[17] General Gillmore's superiors considered such recruitment an appropriate military objective for a raid. Prospects for achievement of this objective in early 1864 seemed good.

On September 14, 1861, the president of the Pensacola and Georgia Railroad wrote a letter to the Confederate secretary of war in which he pointed out the strategic importance of building a connecting rail link between the Pensacola and Georgia line in Florida with the Savannah, Albany, and Gulf line in Georgia.[18] When completed, this link would give the Confederacy rail connection between Savannah on the Atlantic and either Cedar Key or St. Marks by way of Tallahassee on the Gulf. The letter stated that the Pensacola and Georgia had under contract and ready for track-laying the portion of the connection running from its line to the Georgia border and requested money from the Confederacy to buy the needed iron for the track, which was available in Savannah. Shortly after the eastern part of Florida had been added to General Beauregard's command, he had called the attention of the Confederate War Department to the gap that existed between the rail systems of Georgia and Florida as an obstacle in the way of rapid concentration of forces.[19] By February 1862, Union forces held or controlled both ends of the Florida Railroad Company, which ran from Fernandina to Cedar Key. In March of that year, the Confederate army received orders to take up the Florida Railroad Company rails and those of another rail line and use them to build a new strategic link that would connect the Georgia and Florida rail systems.[20]

This move had Governor Milton's support, but the efforts to remove the rails were stymied by former senator David Yulee, part owner of the road, who put private financial interest over Southern patriotism. A number of letters were written by Governor Milton to such people as General Finegan, General Beauregard, and Secretary of War Seddon to get Yulee to allow the removal of the rail—but to no avail. In his letter to Secretary Seddon, Governor Milton wrote, "Shall what is necessary to the defense of Florida be ordered agreeably to the views expressed by those highest in authority and to whom the welfare of the State has been decided, or shall the State be left defenseless, in complement to Mr. Yulee's and Gen. Finegan's opinions?"[21] Secretary Seddon and General Beauregard both retreated from making a decision that would have assisted Governor Milton. Meanwhile, David L. Yulee resorted to a state circuit court in obtaining an injunction to prevent the army from removing the rails.[22] This caused a delay in the removal of the rails, and the connecting link was not completed until 1865.

At the end of 1863, although the Union held or controlled the various coastal railroad terminals in the state, the internal rail transportation was being used by Southern forces to move men and materials around. Key points in this system were the rail-junction town of Baldwin and the various towns along the right-of-way that were used as collection points by Southern commissary agents. Additionally, of military interest would be the railway bridge on the Pensacola and Georgia line that crossed the Suwannee River west of Lake City and, if it were finished, the proposed railway bridge on the connector line north of Live Oak that headed toward the Georgia State line. Destruction of the bridge west of Lake City would disrupt lines of communication between East and Middle Florida; destruction of a bridge built on the connector line would preserve the gap between the Georgia and Florida rail systems, as an obstacle to Confederate communications between Florida and Georgia.

One additional matter concerning Florida railway systems and motivation for a Federal expedition into Florida is relevant. While David L. Yulee was the principal Southern stockholder in the Florida Railroad Company, Northern investors owned the majority of the shares of stock. With the commencement of war, Yulee was in complete control, as Confederate legislation made his Northern partners enemy aliens. The chief Northern stockholder, Marshall O. Roberts, joined together with Eli Thayer, who was planning an emigration movement to Florida similar to the one he had organized to the Kansas Territory. Thayer hoped to settle parts of Florida with twenty thousand volunteers, who would wrest Florida away from the Confederacy. Both Thayer and Roberts were interested in Union occupation of the northern portion of Florida; Thayer for settlement purposes, and Roberts to regain control over the Florida Railroad Company. Important to Roberts were two confiscation acts the Federal Congress had passed which made various classes of Confederate property subject to seizure by the U.S. government. The two men combined to put pressure on the Federal government to occupy parts of Florida. The passage of the Direct Tax Act was a double-edged sword because of the dual nature of the ownership of the railroad. Failure to pay taxes on it could result in confiscation by the Federal government. Roberts and the other New Yorkers hired L. D. Stickney, a Federal tax commissioner, who was to pay the taxes on the railroad and look out for their interests. Simply stated, however, L. D. Stickney paid attention only to his own interests. Stickney made arrangements to sell the iron he was supposed to protect in New York, and he also failed to pay taxes on the railroad as he was hired to do, which resulted in the sale of the railroad to other parties.[23]

By the end of 1863, Roberts and his associates were putting pressure on the Federal government to protect the rest of the railroad. At the same time, Yulee was trying to prevent the Confederate government from using its power to confiscate needed war materials to remove the rails of the Florida Railroad Company from Florida, even if this was detrimental to the Southern war effort. Both Northern and Southern groups of investors tried to influence the military strategy of their governments, feared the destruction of their property by troops, and faced loss of their investment if enemy forces held the railroad.[24]

In late 1863, seizure of the Florida rail system was a valid military objective for a Federal expedition. Seizure of the system would paralyze internal transportation, disrupt communications between East and West Florida, fragment and compartmentalize the military forces within Florida, interrupt shipment of commissary supplies to the Confederacy, protect Northern commercial interests, and prevent the Confederacy from removing scarce and desperately needed rolling stock and rails to more strategic locations within the Confederacy. Capitalizing on the superior Union naval advantage, approach to within a short distance of the key rail junction of Baldwin could be made by water by way of both the St. Johns and St. Marys rivers, while other portions of the system could be reached within a short time by mobile forces. Any reinforcement by Confederate forces would require time because of the nature of transportation in that part of the country. The number and dispersement of the Confederate forces in Florida at the end of 1863 made significant resistance to such an undertaking unlikely. Use of the rail lines by the Federal force to extend its influence further would be greatly facilitated by seizure of whatever locomotives and rolling stock were currently in existence.

The Union successes in the spring of 1862 were devastating to the logistic support of the Confederate war effort. The blockade tightened, depriving the Confederacy of most of its coasts and harbors; the border areas and the Mississippi Valley were wrenched away. A large area of the Confederacy became a no-man's-land, subject to sporadic destruction. The breadbasket areas from which the Confederacy could draw provisions were sharply reduced, and with minor changes, the Confederacy operated within these limits for the next two years. (See map 3.) "The privatations of the Confederate armed services in subsequent months and years stemmed in large parts from the defeats in the Spring of 1862."[25] In the summer of 1863, supplies from Texas were cut off when the Mississippi came under Federal control. As the principal sources of meat at this time were either occupied by the Federals or cut off by them, the Confederacy increasingly turned to Florida as the best source remaining.[26]

Complicating the matter of availability of commissary sup-

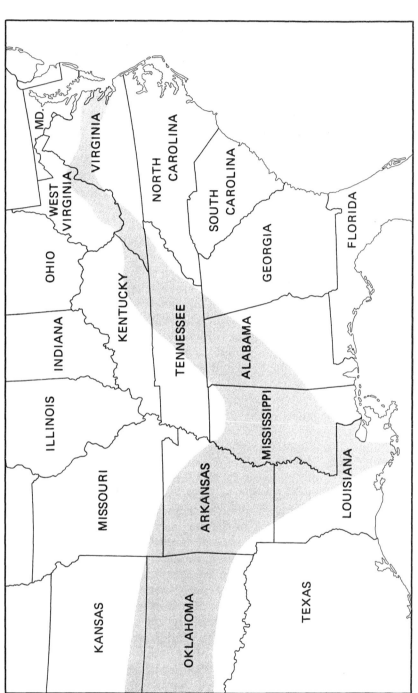

3. Areas of the South under Federal control, 1862

plies for the Confederacy was transportation of those supplies from where they were to where they were needed. One student of Civil War logistics wrote, "By the end of 1863, there was no room except at intervals for anything but government freight on the main lines. Since Virginia and North Carolina had been stripped bare of provisions, General Lee's Army of Northern Virginia was now being supplied from South Carolina and Georgia and the roads to the South of Richmond were being overworked." Starting with the winter of 1863–64, General Lee's army, at the end of a supply pipeline that extended five hundred to nearly one thousand miles from southern Georgia through South Carolina, had scarcely two or three days' supply of food on hand. A surplus could not be accumulated, and with time, supply on hand became even scantier. By the end of the summer of 1864, the railroads, even if working at full capacity and unhampered by Federal operations, could not bring up enough supplies to feed the men and horses half-rations. If he had the time and the patience, General Grant might have won in Virginia by just sitting back and letting General Lee try to maintain his army logistically in the field. According to Charles W. Ramsdell, the problem, however, was not lack of food; there were adequate supplies in Georgia, Alabama, and Florida. The basic fact was that the rail system simply could not carry enough of it. "When this region was cut off and the remnant of the feeble roads wrecked by General Sherman's destructive march through Georgia and the Carolinas, the stoppage of all supplies followed and the long struggle was over."[27]

The commissary supplies available might not have been as plentiful as Ramsdell suggested. By August 1864, the Confederate secretary of war was desperately calling for the farmers of South Carolina and Georgia to furnish supplies, particularly corn and forage, because those commodities had been exhausted in North Carolina and Virginia. In October of that year, it was reported to Col. L. B. Northrop, the Confederate commissary general, that the whole Confederacy was "completely exhausted of supplies," with only enough meat rations for a few days, and there were forty-eight days until the new big crop.[28] North Carolina had been sending its surplus to Virginia, while the surplus of Alabama, Georgia, and Florida had been designated for Bragg's army in Tennessee and Beauregard's men on the Atlantic coast.[29]

As early as October 1862, after a raid up the St. Johns River, Federal navy commander Maxwell Woodhull, after commenting on the growing scarcity of cattle for the Confederacy from other sources, reported:

> The whole dependence of the Confederate government to feed their army now rests on this state [Florida]. I have it from reliable sources that its agents are all over the state buying up all the cattle obtainable, paying any price so that they can get the animals. The only dependence the people of Georgia and Florida have for their sugar is that raised along the banks of this river [St. Johns]. The greatest blow of this war would be the entire destruction of the sugar crop and the small salt-works along the shore on the coast of this State.[30]

On December 23, 1863, Federal brigadier general D. P. Woodbury, commanding the District of Key West and Tortugas, included the following note in a letter to his parent headquarters, the Department of the Gulf: "Two thousand head of cattle are reported to be driven out of Florida every week for the rebel armies. Probably half of these are driven from Middle and Lower Florida."[31]

General Woodbury enclosed an extract from an article entitled "Instructions to Commissary Officers and Agents" taken from a November 7 issue of a Florida newspaper (unidentified) that read: "The utmost promptness, energy, and industry are required of every agent and his assistants to secure all the surplus supplies of the country; otherwise the armies in the field cannot be fed. As Florida is now, next to Georgia, the most productive State remaining to the Confederacy, much depends upon the activity of the Government agents within her bounds." The endorsement to this letter by the commander of the Federal Department of the Gulf, Maj. Gen. N. P. Banks, contained the observation, "If the supply of beef in Florida be of importance to our army, a force should be sent there sufficiently large to scour the country."[32]

There was no doubt that by the end of 1863, Florida was economically more important to the Confederacy than it had been
in 1861. Confederate general John J. Jackson wrote to General
Cooper in 1864:

> The most valuable portion of Florida is the middle counties of
> the Peninsula—Alachua, Marion, and other counties in that
> vicinity. Its productive capacity is very great and the character of
> its supplies is of inestimable value to the Confederacy. The
> sugar and syrup there produced cannot, I believe, be supplied by
> any other portion of the Confederacy. From official and other
> data I learn that the product of army supplies will amount an-
> nually to 25,000 head of beeves, equal to 10,000,000 pounds;
> 1,000 hogsheads of sugar; 100,000 gallons of syrup, equal by ex-
> change to 4,000,000 pounds of bacon; 10,000 hogs equal to
> 1,000,000 pounds of bacon; 50,000 sides of leather; 100,000 bar-
> rels of fish (if labor afforded), equal to 20,000,000 pounds of fish.
> Oranges, lemons, arrow-root, salt blockade goods, iron, etc.
> Counting the bacon at one-third pound and beef and fish at one
> pound to the ration, there are of meat rations 45,000,000—
> enough to supply 250,000 for six months.[33]

The number of cattle in Florida has never been clearly established. In October 1862, the state comptroller reported to the
governor that the number of cattle in Florida was as follows: in
East Florida, 383,717; in Middle Florida, 174,378; and in West
Florida, 100,514, for a total of 658,609.[34] While these figures
are much greater than those reported in the Eighth Census,
William Watson Davis believes they were taken from 1860–61
returns and were actually much under the figures for 1863, as
large droves had been driven from Georgia into Florida.[35] One
piece of evidence of the number of cattle collected for the Confederacy from at least one part of Florida is a summary statement of commissary stores made out by Maj. A. G. Sumner,
who headed the commissary district headquartered at Long
Swamp, Florida. His statement shows a purchase of 10,142
head of cattle for his district for the year ending December 31,
1863.[36]

While there is question about the number of cattle, there was
no question about the need for the cattle. The first cattle herds

obtained by the Confederate government were those found in the northern part of the state near the railheads and the various population centers. As these sources became exhausted, attention turned to Middle and South Florida. The Confederate commissary officer in Florida, Maj. P. W. White, reported in 1863 to Governor Milton that "we are now collecting by detailed men nearly all of the cattle now supplied our armies . . . three-fourths of the Beef Cattle are now furnished from Manatee and Brevard Counties."[37] One of the pioneer Florida cattlemen, Jacob Summerlin, Jr., whose herds were reported to range from Fort Meade to the Caloosahatchee River, is credited with furnishing the Confederacy with some twenty-five thousand head of cattle in the first two years of the war, for which he was never paid.[38]

The cattle from the wire-grass prairies of the Caloosahatchee, Myakka, Peace, and Kissimmee rivers followed the old military trails or cut new trails as they were driven northward through Fort Meade, Bartow, and Brooksville to Payne's Prairie near Gainesville and from there to the railhead at Baldwin. The cattle drives averaged some fifteen to twenty miles a day, and the trip normally took about forty days. From Baldwin the cattle were shipped to Georgia and South Carolina. Some cattle were driven to holding pens along the railroad at places like Madison, Stockton, and Sanderson, while others were driven directly to Savannah by way of Trader's Hill. One estimate supported General Woodbury's claim that as many as two thousand cattle a week were coming to the Confederate army off the Florida ranges.[39] As late as October 3, 1864, Maj. H. C. Guerin sent a telegram to Maj. Pleasant W. White from Charleston stating that Gen. H. J. Hardee wanted three thousand head of cattle per month.[40]

Concerned about an interruption in the shipment of beef to his army, General Beauregard's commissary officer sent an agent to investigate the cause of the delay. The report submitted by Maj. C. McClenaghan to Maj. H. C. Guerin, dated October 29, 1863, is illuminating in terms of the problems of shipping beef from Florida. It was reported that the reason for the interruption was not, as had been supposed, the presence of commissary agents from General Bragg's army competing for the beef but local shipping conditions. It was noted, however, that General Bragg's requisitions were twice as many as General Beauregard's and that Florida was sending one-third of its shipments to Charleston and two-thirds to Atlanta. The local problems delaying shipment included those times of the year when the cattle were spread out and not in large herds, the scarcity of drovers, and the high level of ground water, which made driving cattle difficult. Additionally, there was the increasing difficulty of finding adequate grazing land along the routes over which other cattle had been driven because the grass along the way had been either damaged or consumed. Problems of pasturage would be aggravated in the winter months because of expected damage to the grass from frost, which would result in further delays.

Looking at possible solutions to this problem, the writer of the report believed that if modifications were made in the rail system, time could be cut off that now consumed in the driving of the cattle 175 or 200 miles. He suggested using the rail from the Fernandina and Cedar Key line (the Florida Railroad Company) running north from Baldwin to complete the connection from Live Oak to No. 12 on the Savannah, Albany, and Gulf line in Georgia. He wrote, "This road is already graded, and the cross-ties are on the ground, so all that is required is the iron, and I am informed practical civil engineers say that the road can be put in running order in six weeks, if they had the iron."[41] Cattle could then be driven within thirty miles of Gainesville over frostfree land, and it would then be but sixty hours by freight to Charleston. In addition to reporting on the delay in the shipment of beef, Major McClenaghan called his superior's attention to the sugarcane that was grown in South and East Florida, estimating that some 700,000 pounds of sugar and large quantities of syrup and molasses could be made available.[42]

In November 1863, Florida's chief Confederate commissary officer, Maj. P. W. White, put out what was meant to be a confidential circular. It contained an appeal to the citizens of Florida to contribute as much as possible of their food products because they were desperately needed by the Confederacy. To support his request, he included in the circular excerpts of letters he had recently received from other Confederate commissary officers who were relying upon Florida for their supplies. Two were from General Bragg's commissary officer, Maj. J. F. Cummings. In an early message, Cummings called for all the cattle Florida could immediately send. Apparently not getting an adequate response, an excerpt from a later message written on October 5, 1863, stated, "All other resources are exhausted . . . we are now dependent on your State for beef for the very large army of General Bragg." An excerpt from a letter written from Savannah on October 10, 1863, by Maj. M. B. Millen, the chief commissary officer for Georgia, stated, "Starvation stares the Army in the face . . . I have exhausted the beef-cattle, and am now obliged to kill stock cattle." Maj. H. C. Guerin, South Carolina's chief commissary officer, wrote, "We are almost entirely dependent upon Florida, our situation is full of danger from the want of meat."[43]

The plea to keep the circular confidential was disregarded, and it ended up being posted on trees, posts, and at crossroads all over the state. It was in evidence in Lake City in early January 1864, and a copy was picked up by Federal troops at Baldwin in early February. It subsequently was printed in its entirety in the February 20, 1864, issue of the *New York Herald*. While sometimes suggested as a possible reason for the Federal expedition in 1864, none of the Federal commanders seems to have mentioned it. Southerners thought otherwise. General Beauregard stated, "The paper needs no comment. . . . I am assured it was one of the main causes of the expedition to Jacksonville and thence towards Lake City."[44] When Confederate general J. Patton Anderson assumed command of the Confederate forces in eastern Florida in March 1864, after the battle of Olustee, one of the first things he did was to request a copy of Major White's circular.[45] In view of the dependency of the Confederacy upon Florida as a significant source of commissary supplies, any interruption of the shipment of those supplies would have an almost immediate negative effect on the Confederacy. This effect would be felt particularly in General Bragg's and General Beauregard's armies. One of Federal general Gillmore's objectives for the proposed expedition was to cut off those commissary supplies being shipped from Florida.

The year 1864 was a presidential election year, and the Republican party was composed of two basic factions, Conservative and Radical, differentiated by attitude toward the seceded South. Whoever won this election, it was assumed, would prosecute the war to its successful conclusion and dominate the reconstruction of the South. As 1863 came to a close, the two men most mentioned for the Republican nomination were Abraham Lincoln, the incumbent, and Salmon P. Chase, his secretary of the treasury. Chase needed to build a political base, and one area where he could make progress toward that end was Florida; the means by which he could do so was the Direct Tax Law of 1862. This act provided for the appointment of Direct Tax commissioners, who were to assess real property in rebellious areas, advertise the taxes due, and then sell at public auction the property of delinquent owners.[46] The tax commissioners could function only in Federally occupied territory, and so a major goal of Chase and his agents was to extend the control of Federal armies wherever it was possible. One such area was Florida, and Chase was aided in this endeavor by the men he appointed as Direct Tax commissioners in Florida in September 1862. These included Harrison Reed, later governor of Florida during reconstruction; John S. Sammis, a local businessman who had been forced to leave Florida because of Union sympathies; and the opportunist Lyman D. Stickney. From the beginning, Stickney was aware of the ambitions of the secretary of the treasury, and he knew he stood to profit from any success Chase achieved, particularly if Florida could be separated from the Confederacy and become a source of electoral votes.

The question of how possible it would have been for Florida to have been split off from the Confederacy and returned to the Union was addressed some years after the war by former Confederate general Samuel Jones.

Florida appeared to offer better prospects of success in such an undertaking than any other Southern State. Its great extent of

coastline and its intersection by a broad and deep river, navigable by vessels of war, exposed a great part of the State to the
control of Union forces whenever it should be thought desirable
to occupy it. The exigencies of the Confederate service had in a
great measure stripped Florida of troops. If a column of Union
troops could penetrate the country westward from Jacksonville,
occupy a point in the interior, and break up communications
between east, middle, and west Florida by the destruction of the
railroad and bridges about the Suwannee River, the Southern
Confederacy would not only be deprived of a large quantity of
the food drawn from east and south Florida, but a *point d'appui*
would be established for any of the inhabitants who might be
disposed to attempt the organization of a State acknowledging
allegiance to the United States.[47]

L. D. Stickney's initial attempt to become a political power
in a rapid political reconstruction of Florida by a rump government of Florida Unionists brought him into contact with Eli
Thayer and that gentleman's plan to settle Florida through a
mass migration of "free labor" from the North. In September
1863, Eli Thayer presented a proposal to Abraham Lincoln that
called for a new military department, the Department of Florida, with himself as military governor and Brig. Gen. James A.
Garfield as commander of a thirty-thousand-man Federal
army.[48] Allied to the idea was the use of the blacks currently in
Florida to protect his soldier-colonists and using portions of
Florida as a refuge for freedmen. Stickney's interest was in the
advantages that would accrue to him as a tax commissioner in
a Federally occupied Florida. Thayer's plan to settle Florida
with blacks and Northern volunteers met rejection from President Lincoln and Secretary Stanton, and he was unable to get
much support in either the House of Representatives or the
Senate. In the later years of the war, it was all but forgotten.
Extension of Federal control over Florida would have to come
by other means.

   In September 1863, Stickney traveled to Washington and had
a meeting with Chase. Stickney stated that the pressing need
was for military conquest and informed Chase that this could
be done by five thousand troops, and the commander of the

Department of the South, Major General Gillmore, was favorable to the idea of a Florida expedition. Furthermore, Stickney was looking to get a brigadier general's commission for Col. H. C. Plaisted, the commander of the Federal forces at Fernandina (Stickney's base of operations), and a separate military department for Stickney's friend Gen. Rufus Saxton, who was with the Department of the South. The suggestion was that these arrangements would give the Chase forces a tighter grip on the state.[49] In December, Stickney wrote Chase about a long talk he had with General Gillmore, who was agreeable to helping make Florida a free state. Stickney reveals his scheming nature as he continues: "I think it very important indeed for *you* that Gen'l Gillmore be identified with the Florida conquest. He is anxious to win distinction according to the Republican programme. At the same time, I do not think the Senate ought to be in a hurry to confirm him as a Maj-General. Wait until the Delegation in Congress from Florida ask his confirmation for his services in conquering the rebels of their state."[50]

President Lincoln issued his Proclamation of Amnesty and Reconstruction on December 8, 1863. This proclamation stated that in any seceded state, if 10 percent of the number of voters of that state who had voted in 1860 took an oath of loyalty to the United States, the president would recognize a newly created state government. Stickney staged a "Union meeting" in St. Augustine on December 19, 1863, in order to lay the foundation for a Chase organization in Florida that would be ready to take advantage of the expected military conquest. In fairness to Chase, who appears to have been used by Stickney, Florida was not of major importance to him. Chase was interested in restoring the Union and in stamping out slavery; it was easy to believe the many reports that Stickney and his associates kept sending him from Florida reporting optimistically on the large numbers of Floridians ready to rejoin the Union.

Certain resolutions made at the St. Augustine meeting were not in keeping with Lincoln's amnesty proclamation. Nevertheless, after the meeting L. D. Stickney wrote John Hay, Lincoln's personal secretary, claiming that the meeting had been in response to Lincoln's proclamation. He then asked John Hay to come to Florida and be the state's representative in Congress. John Hay discussed the matter with President Lincoln, who appointed Hay a commissioner with instructions to "go to Florida and engineer the business there."[51] L. D. Stickney had anticipated President Lincoln's interest in Florida and appeared to be hedging his bets by playing for both sides. At the same time, Lincoln undoubtedly was aware of Stickney's connection with Chase and had confidence in Hay's ability to handle Stickney.

On December 15, 1863, General Gillmore suggested his Florida expedition and gave as his objectives recovering the most valuable portion of the state, cutting off a rich source of the enemy's supplies, and recruiting black troops.[52] No mention was made of any political objectives. On January 13, 1864, President Lincoln wrote to General Gillmore:

> I understand an effort is being made by some worthy gentlemen to reconstruct a loyal State government in Florida. Florida is in your department and it is not unlikely that you may be there in person. I have given Mr. Hay a commission of Major and sent him to you with some blank books and other blanks to aid in the reconstruction. He will explain as to the manner of using the blanks, and also my general views on the subject. It is desirable for all to cooperate; but if irreconcilable differences of opinion should arise, you are the master. I wish the thing done in the most speedy way possible, so that when done it will be within the late proclamation on the subject. The detail labor, of course, will have to be done by others, but I shall be greatly obliged if you will give it such general supervision as you can find convenient with your other more strictly military duties.[53]

President Lincoln's letter was the basis for many later misconceptions regarding the Olustee campaign. It contained no extraordinary request for a change in Gillmore's plans and, in fact, did not even mention any proposed military operations in Florida. One may even get an overall impression that the reconstruction was to take place in areas already under Federal control. To establish the proper significance of the political motivations for the Federal expedition, it is necessary to examine the correspondence relating to this area closely. In his reply to this letter, Gillmore clearly indicated that he understood that his future duties would include an increased emphasis on reconstruction. "I am led to the impression . . . I am expected to initiate, guide, and control such measures as may be necessary under the Presidential Proclamation of December 8, 1863 to restore the State of Florida to its allegiance. . . . The plan now being pursued by General Banks in Louisiana impresses me very favorable, and can doubtless in its principal features be both easily and speedily applied to Florida."[54]

When John Hay recorded his arrival on January 20 at General Gillmore's Headquarters at Hilton Head, South Carolina, he wrote that the general "seemed perplexed rather & evidently thought he was expected to undertake some immediate military operations to effect the occupation and reconstruction. . . . I told him that it was not the President's intention to do anything to embarrass his military operations—that all I wished from him was an order directing me to go to Florida & open my books of record for the oaths, as preliminary to future proceedings."[55]

General Halleck had written to General Gillmore after Gillmore had presented his original proposal for a Florida expedition and alluded to the fact that the objective of that expedition had not been fully explained. Gillmore replied to Halleck after a week's delay with the following letter dated January 31, 1864.

In reply to your letter of the 22nd instant I beg leave to state that the objects and advantages to be secured by the occupation of that portion of Florida within my reach, viz, the richest portions between the Suwannee and Saint John's Rivers, are: First. To procure an outlet for cotton, lumber, timber, turpentine, and the other products of the State. Second. To cut off one of the enemy's sources of commissary supplies. He now draws largely upon the herds of Florida for his beef, and is making preparations to take up a portion of the Fernandina and Saint Mark's Railroad for the purpose of connecting the road from Jacksonville to Tallahassee with Thomasville on the Savannah, Albany and Gulf Railroad. Third. To obtain recruits for my colored regiments. Fourth. To inaugurate measures for the speedy restoration of Florida to her allegiance, in accordance with instructions which I have received from the President by the hands of Maj. John Hay, assistant adjutant-general.[56]

In this letter, General Gillmore had added a political objective (the restoration of the state to the Union) and an economic objective (the opening of a port in Florida) to the objectives he listed in the original request for permission.

At the end of 1863, the restoration of Florida to the Union was a distinct possibility. As early as 1862, the president had appointed military governors in the states of North Carolina, Louisiana, Tennessee, and Arkansas. Louisiana had even gone so far as to elect representatives to Congress, and they had been seated.[57] There had been considerable evidence of loyalty to the Union given by residents of the Federally occupied St. Augustine, Key West, Fernandina, and, until the first Federal evacuation, Jacksonville. It was highly probable the required loyalty oaths could be obtained from enough Floridians if they were assured of protection.

One of General Gillmore's added objectives for the Florida expedition had been the opening of an outlet for Florida's commercial produce. Port Royal, South Carolina, had been made a partially open port on June 1, 1862, but the blockade continued for other ports in the Department of the South until Fernandina was opened on December 1, 1864. The administration of the trade and blockade regulations was under army control until May 1863, when it was turned over to the Treasury Department. Goods were not prevented from getting into Florida by the treasury blockade; the problem was for Florida to export its products, which would help revive the civilian economy and keep the local residents from becoming dependent upon the military. Under Treasury regulations, products for export had to be brought to Port Royal first. This practice wrecked the economy of those parts of Florida held by Union forces.[58] The only real hope for those so affected was for the Department of the South to open a port in Florida to help its economy; it was this that General Gillmore proposed to do as one of the objectives for his expedition.

General Banks's combination of military and economic success in Louisiana was common knowledge. When the army controlled trade, it allowed sutlers to be post traders, and it licensed other traders. After the Treasury Department took over, sufficient cargoes came in as "military necessities." Colonel Plaisted, the Union commander in Fernandina, had been recommended for promotion by Treasury Department Direct Tax Commissioner L. D. Stickney. Stickney and Plaisted had been to see General Saxton, and they worked out a plan of action. If a separate department was created, it was their intention to name Stickney's partner in Fernandina, William C. Morrill, as post sutler. Morrill, who had originally come to Florida as a musician with the Ninth Maine, would then be the only one who could bring goods to Amelia Island, and all other traders and regimental sutlers would have to buy from him.[59] Suffice to say that there were enough carpetbaggers like Stickney and his partners around to ensure that cooperative military leaders would profit from the exploitation of areas controlled by the Federal government.

By the end of 1863, there was sufficient reason for the Federal government to take an interest in Florida. It was a source of recruits for the black regiments in the Department of the South, it represented a major source of commissary supplies for the Confederacy, and the Confederacy planned to move scarce rails from the area to more strategic locations. Additionally, there was a strong possibility Florida could be severed from the Confederacy and restored to the Union, and a port in Florida might be opened to alleviate both the local economy and enhance certain people in the right positions. Troops were available, transportation was available, and the area was vulnerable—a minimum risk had good prospect of returning a maximum gain.

4

Surprise and Success

The Landing and Exploitation

On February 4, 1864, Gen. Quincy A. Gillmore reviewed the assembled units that were to make up the Federal expeditionary force. That evening, orders were issued to Gen. Truman Seymour to embark them without delay upon naval transports furnished by the chief quartermaster. Moving quickly to comply were Col. William Barton's brigade, composed of the Seventh New Hampshire, Seventh Connecticut, and the Eighth U.S. Colored Troops; Col. James Montgomery's black brigade, containing the Fifty-fourth Massachusetts, Second South Carolina, and Third U.S. Colored Troops; and Col. Guy Henry's mounted brigade, made up of the Fortieth Massachusetts Mounted Infantry and the Independent Battalion of Massachusetts cavalry; and three artillery batteries—Langdon's light battery (four pieces), Elder's horse battery (four pieces), and one section of James's Rhode Island Battery (two pieces). Selected to follow in a second echelon were the Forty-seventh, Forty-eighth, and 115th New York infantry regiments. The men were to carry six days' rations, knapsacks, haversacks, and blankets, and not less than sixty rounds of ammunition. The orders to embark specifically limited the number of wagons per unit, ordered camp equipage left under security, and stated that only a small quantity of medical supplies need be taken. Ambulances were to be supplied by the medical director, and the hospital steamer *Cosmopolitan*, with a full supply of medical stores, was to follow the command within a few hours.[1]

The orders suggested an action of short duration, a rapidly

Scenes from the 1864 Federal expedition from *Harper's Weekly.* Courtesy of the Florida State Archives, Tallahassee.

moving expedition, with an expectation of minimum casualties. A bit unusual, however, was the fact that all of the brigades were to be commanded by colonels, normally regimental commanders, although there were a number of experienced brigadier generals available within the Department of the South. Included in the task force were several newly formed units which had never been under fire; Gillmore, however, had originally planned to take only veteran units, replacing them in their siege positions with inexperienced troops. Gillmore had also hoped to be able to mount more of his raiding force, but the horses he had requested were not furnished. Seemingly minor matters at the time—the limited size of the mounted force, the presence of green troops, and the lack of senior experienced leaders—would prove critical to the level of success of the Federal expedition.

Embarkation day was cold, wet, and windy. Maj. John Appleton of the Fifty-fourth Massachusetts expressed the idea that it was "not a nice day for an excursion," hoping that the start of the operation would be put off until the following day.[2] Seymour was instructed to try to get most of his task force to sea before daybreak on February 6, with the objective of having the entire force rendezvous off the mouth of the St. Johns River by daybreak on Sunday, February 7. Upon arrival, Seymour was expected to cross the bar on Sunday morning's high tide, ascend the river to Jacksonville, effect a landing, and push forward a mounted force as far as the junction of the two railroads at Baldwin. Col. Henry R. Guss, commanding the Ninety-seventh Pennsylvania, which was garrisoning Fernandina, Florida, was to interdict the landing area by tearing up the tracks on both railroads beyond Baldwin after the train came into Jacksonville on February 8. It was hoped that either the surprise landing or the torn-up tracks would result in the seizure of a train.[3] (See map 4.)

While the location of the landing was a surprise, the Union move was not unexpected. As early as January 14, 1864, Gen. P. G. T. Beauregard, commanding the Department of South Carolina, Georgia, and Florida, had reported to Gen. Samuel Cooper that he suspected an imminent movement by the Federals. The officer responsible for keeping watch on the Union fleet in the waters of Port Royal and the Broad River had reported to him that some thirty-five vessels had gone to sea in a fog on the afternoon of the fourteenth. Concurrently, there

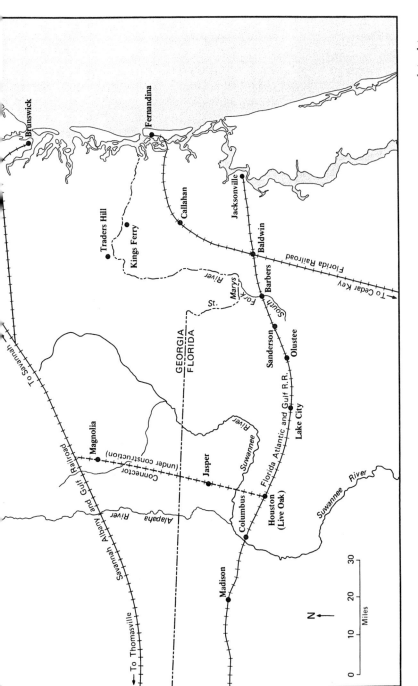

4. Federal area of operations, northeast Florida. Detail of 1870 railroad map, courtesy Georgia Department of Archives and History, Atlanta.

had been a reduction of activity on the part of the Union forces on the adjacent islands. General Beauregard immediately warned Gen. J. F. Gilmer at Savannah of a possible Union move and alerted the proper staff officers to hold rail transportation ready on the Charleston and Savannah Railroad. Beauregard moved his headquarters to Savannah on January 16, anticipating a Union attempt on that city. Since there was no indication by February 3 of a Union movement in the direction of Savannah, he returned to Charleston but left orders with Gen. J. F. Gilmer to hold the Sixty-fourth Georgia Volunteers, the First Florida Battalion, and a light battery in readiness for a possible move on short notice to Florida.[4]

Maj. T. B. Brooks of General Gillmore's staff appeared at Mayport, a small fishing village at the entrance to the St. Johns River, the evening of February 6 onboard the steamer *Island City* and informed the navy ships blockading the mouth of the river there was to be a major expedition in that area the following day. At his suggestion, pickets were placed to prevent advance warning of the landing. Four men, classified as "refugees," were then hired by the major to go inland on Saturday night to cut the telegraph wire from the city and burn a railroad bridge. The gunboats *Ottawa* and *Norwich* furnished the arms, rations, and turpentine for the mission. A proposal to send the *Norwich* farther upriver immediately to trap the blockade-runner *Saint Mary's* in McGirt's Creek was opposed by Major Brooks on the grounds it might interfere with the operation. At 6:30 P.M., the *Island City* proceeded upriver to Trout Creek, dropped the four-man raiding force off in a canoe, and returned to Mayport some three hours later.[5] There is no record of whether the raiders' efforts were successful.

At daylight on the seventh, the ships carrying the Federal expedition began arriving in the objective area. Because of the ebb tide and the need for assistance from tugs, only thirteen of the transports were able to cross the bar that morning.[6] The *Maple Leaf,* with General Seymour aboard, came in at 8:50 A.M., and within a short time plans were made aboard the gunboat *Ottawa* for the twenty-mile approach to Jacksonville. The gunboat *Norwich* was to precede the transports at a distance upriver, stopping at a Mr. Palmer's place to learn what force, if any, was in Jacksonville.[7]

The *Norwich* got underway at 10:10 A.M., with the transports following some six miles behind her. Palmer's was reached at 2:05 P.M., where it was learned that only about twenty men were in town and the expedition was not expected. The *Norwich* continued on, arriving off Jacksonville at 3:20 P.M. with the closest transport, the *Maple Leaf,* at that time in sight of Commodore's Point. The *Norwich* steamed in close past the wharves to the upper end of town for a quick reconnaissance and then returned, at which time, about 3:40 P.M., several of the transports were made fast to a dock and the troops aboard debarked. One of the transports, the steamer *General Hunter,* took fire from some enemy pickets in a wooded area on the outskirts of town, wounding Elijah Norris, the second mate of the *General Hunter.*[8] Immediate pursuit of the rebel snipers was ordered, and the first troops to land, black soldiers from the Fifty-fourth Massachusetts, took off on the double in compliance; they were soon joined by Company C of the First Massachusetts Independent Cavalry. After a chase of some two miles by the black infantry troops, the cavalry took over and continued for another three miles. Eleven prisoners were taken, including two signal officers and their equipment and a number of horses and mules.[9] Capt. Gustavas Dana, Seymour's chief signal officer, was with the cavalry and was able not only to save some of the communication equipment for Federal use but also to get a copy of the code being used by the Confederate operators. Additionally, a thirty-pounder cannon loaded with "broken glass, cow shoes & nails" and pointed in the direction of the Federal advance was overrun and taken before it could be fired by the gunners.[10]

Debarkation of the troops continued, and preparations were made to push on to Baldwin in the morning. Jacksonville reflected the effect of its recurring Union occupations and evacuations, as many of the houses were burned or demolished. Of the three thousand people who composed its population at the time of the 1860 census, only some twenty-five families remained in the town, mostly women and children. Surprise had been achieved, with the first indication of the Federal landing being the arrival of the *Ottawa,* followed in quick succession by the transports. Perhaps discretion was the better part of valor, noted a member of the Fifty-fourth Massachusetts, because, "As we neared the pier, a few handkerchiefs were waved at us from some of the buildings near the water. Every person in the place claims to be Union."[11] The landing forces had just missed a train which had come in and departed on the seventh. It was believed, however, that the rebels were going to tear up the rails the following week for shipment to another part of the Confederacy. Whatever the truth of this was, a news correspondent present believed that the expedition was going to push forward rapidly to prevent any further damage to the railroad. He closed his account with the assessment, "Every thing thus far has gone on in the most prosperous manner. The State abounds in cattle, and provisions are not scarce."[12]

The location of the Federal landing was reported as quickly as possible to Confederate authorities. General Finegan telegraphed General Beauregard on February 7 (received on the eighth) that five Federal gunboats and two transports had made their appearance in the St. Johns; the following day General Finegan sent word that eighteen vessels (gunboats and transports) had arrived at Jacksonville and troops were landing.[13] General Beauregard found himself with a complex problem to solve. A threat was being made on Florida, a major source of the Confederacy's subsistence supplies for both Beauregard's forces and the Army of Tennessee. At the same time, he was responsible for the defenses of Charleston and Savannah and currently facing severe manpower shortages because terms of service had expired for a large number of his troops. To make matters worse, he had been requested by higher headquarters to send men from his coastal defenses to reinforce General Bragg's Army in Tennessee. General Beauregard immediately notified Gen. Samuel Cooper of the Federal landing and stated that he believed the purpose was to cut off subsistence supplies from that area. He informed General Cooper that he wished to send forces to Florida but needed reinforcements to protect Savannah and Charleston, as five thousand state troops from Georgia and South Carolina had just been discharged.[14]

In the meantime, General Beauregard ordered General Gilmer, at Savannah, to send the troops he was holding in an alert status to Florida to report to General Finegan and informed Gilmer that Col. A. H. Colquitt's brigade was being sent to him "for exigencies."[15] Gen. W. M. Gardner, the commander of Middle Florida, was ordered to send General Finegan, the commander of East Florida, every soldier he could spare.[16] General Finegan was notified on February 8 that reinforcements were being sent to him from Middle Florida and from Savannah; he was told, "Do what you can to hold enemy at bay and prevent capture of slaves."[17]

General Beauregard apparently had little confidence in the ability of the Confederate leadership in Florida to handle the problem. At 8:30 A.M. on February 9, General Beauregard requested that General Cooper send a "competent officer of sufficient rank" such as Lt. Gen. D. H. Hill to command in South Carolina, as "I may be required in Georgia or Florida at any moment." He also suggested that Maj. Gen. Howell Cobb, former commander of Middle Florida, be ordered to the department. General Cooper's return endorsement, however, suggested that "Major-General Gilmer is the next ranking officer and should succeed to the command." At 3:15 on February 9, Beauregard again wired General Cooper, suggesting that if there was an objection to sending D. H. Hill, "Major General McLaws would be equally acceptable."[18] General Beauregard then wired General Hill, telling him that he had requested his services and asked, "Can you aid in the matter?"[19] This was followed by a message to Maj. Gen. Howell Cobb addressed to "Atlanta, Ga., or wherever he may be" informing him that Beauregard had applied for him to command two districts in Florida. Beauregard asked Cobb also, "Can you aid in the matter?"[20] In between his frantic attempts to get a senior officer to his department so as to free himself to go to Florida, General Beauregard went directly to the Confederate secretary of war on the ninth, appraising him that he had sent two infantry regiments and a battery of artillery to General Finegan from Savannah. He had replaced them and the recently discharged Georgia state troops at Savannah with Colquitt's brigade and asked if a brigade could be sent to Florida from some other department. Beauregard informed the secretary, "Our supplies in that State becoming indispensable. I suppose enemy's movement is a feint to draw troops from South Carolina and Georgia."[21]

On the day the Union forces landed at Jacksonville, General Finegan, the Confederate commander of the Department of East Florida, was at his headquarters at Lake City, some sixty miles from the landing site. To oppose the 6,000–7,000 Federal troops that had landed, Finegan had available to him two battalions and three independent companies of infantry, seven companies of cavalry, and two batteries of artillery, comprising (using strength figures reported at the end of January 1864) some 89 officers and 1,178 men. This force was dispersed in small, isolated units from Fernandina and Mosquito Inlet on the Atlantic coast to Tampa on the Gulf and the Suwannee River. This dispersion of forces had been necessitated by the threat posed by the occasional Federal raids that had been taking place the previous two years such as the ones at Cedar Key, Mosquito Inlet, and on the St. Johns and St. Marys rivers. General Finegan immediately took measures to concentrate those Confederate forces presently in East Florida. Capt. A. A. Ochus, commanding Bay Port, was ordered to march to Gainesville and from there by rail to Baldwin; Capt. J. Q. Stewart was ordered to move his company by forced march to Otter Creek on the Florida Railroad, and from there by rail to Baldwin; Capt. S. W. Mays, commanding No. 4, was to leave ten men there and move to Baldwin; Captain McNeill was to send half of his company to No. 4, relieving the ten men left there, who would then rejoin Captain Mays; and Capt. M. J. Clarke would move his company at Crystal River by forced marches to Baldwin.[22]

On February 8, Union brigadier general Alexander Schimmelfennig, with parts of the First and Second brigades and Foster's brigade of General Vogdes's division along with six pieces of artillery, crossed to Kiawah and Seabrook islands on the South Carolina coast to make a demonstration aimed at distracting the enemy's attention from the Florida expedition. The next day the Union forces advanced, crossing the Haulover

Cut to John's Island at daylight, driving in the Confederate pickets with some loss and taking prisoners. Although suspecting that it was a diversionary move, General Beauregard was forced to take it seriously. He held the three and one-half infantry regiments of Col. Alfred Holt Colquitt's brigade ready to reinforce Gen. H. A. Wise, who appeared to be facing some 4,500 Federal troops. As additional backup, Beauregard brought in other Confederate troops from Sullivan's and James's islands on the South Carolina coast.[23] At this phase of the Union operation, the demonstration was a strong success, giving the Federal forces in Florida a great numerical superiority over their opponents.

General Gillmore's troops had full control of Jacksonville by the night of the seventh, occupying defensive positions on the western part of the city in preparation for an expected rapid thrust inland at daybreak. During this occupation an incident took place that caused a bit of tension between the land forces and their naval support. In General Gillmore's February 9 report of the landing to General Halleck, he stated, "Upon our approach the enemy abandoned and sunk [sic] the steamer *Saint Mary's* and burned 270 bales of cotton a few miles above Jacksonville."[24] Apparently General Gillmore laid claim to the *Saint Mary's* in a letter (not found) to Admiral Dahlgren because the admiral replied rather heatedly to it in his own letter on February 12. The admiral took issue with General Gillmore's claim that the army's rapid move into the interior had caused the rebels to destroy the vessel and that the prize rightfully belonged to the army.[25]

What was at issue was the awarding of captured blockade-runners as prizes, a practice which could bring the captor(s) financial gain. The admiral enclosed with his letter one written by Acting Master Frank B. Meriam of the steamer *Norwich*, which stated the facts as the navy saw it. After determining that General Gillmore did not plan to move his troops inland on the night of February 7, Meriam had anchored the *Norwich* at 6:30 P.M. as close as he could get to the entrance to McGirt's Creek and then stationed a picketboat at the mouth of the creek. Meriam saw General Gillmore the next day and asked when the troops intended on moving forward. Gillmore's reply was, "This afternoon if the horses come up." Meriam, again that night, put a picketboat in the mouth of McGirt's Creek. At 3:30 A.M. on February 9, the picketboat sounded an alarm but was not located by its mother ship because of the heavy fog which had settled in. When the picketboat finally returned to the *Norwich* at 6:15 that morning, the officer in charge of it reported that he had fired at a boat which he had heard but could not see in the fog. Meriam soon found that the *Saint Mary's* had been boarded during the night, the cotton burned, and the ship sunk. Meriam arrived back at the sunken vessel at 1:00 P.M. but found no trace that anyone had been there between the time it sank and his arrival. Later a small rifled gun was found on shore, and some of the ship's boats were found in a creek. Meriam was convinced that if his picketboat had not been in the creek, the *Saint Mary's* would have escaped up the river.[26] There is no record of how the problem was resolved between the two services, but the incident illustrates the factor of financial gain that expeditions of this type made possible for Union leaders.

The rapid thrust inland by the Union forces did not start at daybreak on February 8, as planned, but at 3:00 P.M. The intention of the Union forces, at that time, seems to have been to conduct a rapid raid into the interior to disrupt Confederate internal communications, seizing or destroying whatever was of value to the enemy, and reconnoitering the local situation. The extent of penetration was to be to the south prong of the St. Marys River, some thirty to thirty-five miles from Jacksonville.

When the movement toward the interior took place, the Union forces departing Jacksonville were divided into three columns, each taking a different route. Col. W. B. Barton, now commanding a new brigade made up of the Forty-seventh, Forty-eighth, and 115th New York regiments, was on the Lake City and Jacksonville road; Col. Guy V. Henry's mounted force on a parallel road to the left; and Col. J. R. Hawley, now commanding Colonel Barton's former brigade made up of the Seventh Connecticut, Seventh New Hampshire, and joined by the

Eighth U.S. Colored Troops, on a road to the right. These roads converged at a junction three miles above Jacksonville. It had originally been planned to march the infantry three miles past that road junction, bivouac for the night, and then move on in the morning to attack Camp Finegan. The infantry reached the junction after dark, where it was thought advisable to stop, but Colonel Henry with the cavalry and artillery continued to move inland. Although it was anticipated that contact with the rebels would be made at a small creek two miles from Jacksonville, Henry's column traveled some five miles before any contact was made. Walt Whittemore of the *New York Times* accompanied the mounted raiders and penned this impression of the ride:

> A night's ride, with the darkness so dense we could not see our horse's heads, through a hostile country which affords advantages for guerrillas, over a road the bridges of which the enemy had destroyed, and so forced our troops to ford the streams, would not be esteemed a pleasant adventure by our timid friends at the North. Every one, however, was in good spirits, and did not care how rapidly he rode, provided he could soon come up with the enemy.[27]

The raiding force passed rapidly an abandoned four-man picket post, continuing their ride for another half mile until they came in sight of the Confederate campfires at a reserve picket post. A charge by the advance guard of the Union raiding force captured five pickets at the post and a sixth later who was wounded and had run into the woods.[28] After picking up the enemy's horses, the column rode on for another ten minutes before coming within sight of Camp Finegan. Union scouts reported that there were some 200 cavalry men formed up in line of battle awaiting the Union advance. The Confederate defenders were elements of the Second Florida Cavalry, under the command of Lt. Col. Abner McCormick. Colonel Henry elected to bypass the camp with his force and hit instead an artillery camp believed to be some four miles farther at Twelve-Mile Station. After the Union advance guard reported the location of the camp, Colonel Henry and Maj. Atherton Stevens moved forward to scout the position. They observed about 150 men sitting around the fires in the act of preparing food to eat, with horses and mules still harnessed and the wagons partially loaded with the officers' baggage. Obviously the artillerymen had not been warned and had taken few precautions regarding their own security.

Colonel Henry returned to his command and advanced the Independent Battalion quietly to within twenty yards of the camp. The Fortieth Massachusetts's mounted infantry were formed in line of battle directly in front of Captain Elder's horse artillery. With Colonel Henry and Major Stevens in front, the buglers blew a loud blast, and the Union forces charged. Although it was reported that the cavalry dashed into the middle of the camp and surrounded it on all sides, most of the rebel troops managed to escape into the woods at the first sound of the bugles and under cover of darkness. Sgt. A. J. Clement of Company M, the Independent Battalion, Massachusetts's Cavalry, participated in the charge. About midnight his unit arrived on a little rise overlooking the artillery camp. When the charge was about to take place, he recalled that Colonel Henry ordered the bugler to sound the charge twice and shouted to the men these words, "If ever you yell in your lives, boys, yell now!" And in the language of the official report of that event, "They charged with a yell that still lingers in the ears of those who heard it."[29]

The mounted raiders captured two three-inch rifled guns belonging to Capt. H. F. Abell's Company B, Milton Light Artillery, and two six-pounder brass smooth-bore guns belonging to Capt. J. L. Dunham's Company A, Milton Light Artillery. Additional military equipment belonging to one or the other of the companies was also taken; however, a train that was expected was warned off by a telegraph operator. It was the last message the operator was able to get off, for "Major Stevens walked into the room and seized the fellow by the throat as he was on the point of sending another message. In a few minutes his instrument was knocked to pieces and the wire cut."[30]

Captain Abell placed the blame for the loss of his two three-inch rifled guns, one of his caissons, a forge, and a battery wagon on the poor condition of his horses. General Finegan's endorsement to Abell's report of the incident confirms at length the existing problem of disease among the Confederate artillery horses and the fact that Abell's horses had been scheduled for removal to Lake City for treatment when the Federal expedition intervened. Captain Abell's report also included notification of the loss of an additional three-inch gun belonging to his unit the following day at Baldwin, when it was captured by the advancing Federal cavalry.[31]

Captain Dunham placed the blame for the loss of his two six-pounders on the railroad. When word was received of the Federal landing, the unit's baggage and property had been moved to the railroad depot at Pickett's (Ten-Mile Station). On the evening of February 8, Lt. Col. Abner McCormick, Second Florida Cavalry, sent back word to the battery to move a section of guns up immediately to the rear of a battle line he was establishing on the west side of the drill field at Camp Finegan. Although present, Captain Dunham was not in command of the unit at the time, having been on sick leave for over a month. He passed the order on to Lieutenant Bates, then commanding, who moved the guns forward. Captain Dunham accompanied the move to Camp Finegan, where he was told to halt the artillery and form on the left of the line. Three of the guns being brought up, however, had already passed the proposed line of battle. When they were finally halted and returned, Lieutenant Colonel McCormick told Lieutenant Bates to move back toward Baldwin. As the baggage and company property were at Pickett's, the battery returned there instead to await the cars that were supposed to pick up the unit's property before moving on to Baldwin. After waiting a while, the men, except for the guard, were allowed to sleep, and the horses were unhitched awaiting the arrival of the cavalry and the infantry. At about 11:00 or 11:30 that night, they were aroused by a sergeant from Company B, Milton Light Artillery, riding through the camp shouting, "Save yourselves if you can; the enemy is right upon you!"[32]

Besides the loss of the two guns, Captain Dunham reported losing eighteen men, twenty-three horses, twenty-two mules, one battery wagon, five other wagons, and a forge. General Finegan's endorsement to Dunham's report states that it appeared that Lieutenant Colonel McCormick failed to notify the artillery company of the advance of the enemy.[33] With artillery pieces in short supply in Florida, the lost five pieces could be considered a severe loss. It would loom even larger within a few days.

Meanwhile the Federal infantry, after a short halt, scrapped their original plans of an overnight stay at the road junction and instead continued on to Camp Finegan. James H. Clark, with the 115th New York, was part of the night approach march to Camp Finegan. "We made a hard march—mostly on a double-quick—through swamps and woods, fording creeks and scaling piles of logs and brush, until the point of attack was just ahead." The Federal troops managed to surprise and capture the pickets protecting the camp before they could give warning. However, after almost surrounding the camp, something alerted the Confederate soldiers, and a great number were able to escape into the swamps. The Union troops took possession of the camp and Confederate equipment that was left there, including an abundance of food supplies. Clark left a vivid picture of the scene.

> The rebel camp was filled with fat turkeys, chickens, ducks, and geese; and as soon as arms were stacked the order charge hencoops was given, and the soldiers soon swept away all poultry from before them until the feathers flew in all directions. Such a cackling and gobbling was never heard in eastern Florida, and the rebels secreted in neighboring swamps must have enjoyed the midnight serenade, to say the least. The camp was abandoned in great haste.
>
> We found hogs hanging up just dressed; kettles of beef steaming over the fire; plates of warm hominy and liver on the table; and papers and books strewn in every direction. Rebel officers hardly stopped to dress, and left coats and swords behind for the dreaded Yankees.[34]

It is obvious from Clark's description that the Confederates were not expecting the Union advance and had not set out ade-

quate security. The 115th New York spent part of the next
morning scouring the swamps and woods for the camp's defenders, who "appeared to be perfectly panic-stricken, and
large numbers of them surrendered without firing a gun or
making the least resistance."[35] After finally calling off their
search, the infantry regrouped and moved toward Baldwin,
some fifteen hard road miles away.

Colonel Henry's mounted force left the artillery camp at
Pickett's at 4:00 A.M. on February 9, leaving one company to
guard the property. At the various places where the road
crossed the railroad, tracks were taken up either to prevent the
rebels from getting supplies or to keep them from sending
troops to Henry's rear. This ten-mile portion of the ride was
uneventful, as no resistance was encountered, and Colonel
Henry entered Baldwin at 7:00 A.M. Baldwin, for all of its strategic importance as a rail junction, contained only fifteen
buildings, the largest of which was the railroad station. Here,
another telegraph operator and three instruments were seized.
The Union forces also captured three railroad cars, two full of
corn and one containing Captain Abell's three-inch gun along
with a caisson. In the railroad depot was found a large quantity
of supplies and "cotton, rice, tobacco, pistols, and other property valued at a half million dollars." Breakfast at the hotel was
paid for by some enterprising Union troopers with Confederate
money that was found in the trash in the depot.[36] Possession of
the site of the junction of the only two major railroads in Florida gave the Union the ability to curtail transportation severely
in the state, thus achieving one of the major objectives of the
expedition. While the size and condition of Baldwin was in no
way indicative of its actual military importance, one Confederate official charged with procurement and movement of commissary supplies from Florida to the rest of the Confederacy
described it within a few days to the senior Confederate army
commissary supply officer, Col. L. B. Northrop, as "the key to
the Peninsula."[37]

From Camp Finegan, General Seymour reported to General
Gillmore on February 9 that he had arrived at that location the
day before and had with him the Forty-seventh, Forty-eighth,

and 115th New York regiments. He had sent Colonel Henry with the Seventh Connecticut, the Third U.S. Colored Troops, and the Eighth U.S. Colored Troops on to Baldwin. In his assessment of the situation, he called attention to the difficulty of resupplying a raiding force beyond Baldwin by wagon and suggested haste in getting a train sent forward from Fernandina for that purpose, as it appeared doubtful one could be captured by the forward element. He closed with the remark, "If you want to see what Florida is good for come out to Baldwin."[38] General Gillmore and part of his staff joined General Seymour at Baldwin later in the day on the ninth.

Meanwhile, Gen. Alexander Schimmelfennig, conducting the Union's diversionary attack in South Carolina, had remained on John's Island on February 10; the next day he pushed forward some three miles, making contact with the enemy's pickets and probing the Confederate lines with artillery fire.[39] By so doing, he continued to occupy part of General Beauregard's attention, forcing him to hold Colonel Colquitt's brigade in the Savannah area.

Before leaving for Baldwin on February 9, General Gillmore had been at Fernandina that morning with Col. Henry R. Guss, who commanded the troops garrisoning the town, the Ninety-seventh Pennsylvania Volunteers. At 8:30 that morning Major Galusha Pennypacker with 290 men of the Ninety-seventh had departed Fernandina for a raid on Camp Cooper, crossing to the mainland over the railroad bridge. A half hour later, Capt. DeWitt C. Lewis with another twenty-five men of the Ninety-seventh, a detachment of sailors, and two howitzers left Fernandina aboard the U.S. brig *Perry*. A two-pronged attack on Camp Cooper had been planned with the *Perry* and the steamer *Island City* moving to the mouth of the Nassau River, and then up that river for about fifty miles until opposite Camp Cooper, to cooperate in the raid with Major Pennypacker's forces traveling by land.

Major Pennypacker, with help from a Mr. E. G. Grisham and two black guides, Prince and Charles, moved overland to Lofton Creek, approaching Camp Cooper in the early morning hours of the tenth. Shortly after 3:00 A.M., scouts reported the camp a mile ahead. Pennypacker deployed the men of the Ninety-seventh so as to hit the camp from three sides. The attack took place at dawn as planned but, except for a few security guards, the Union forces found the camp empty. It had been occupied by Maj. Robert Harrison and three companies of the Second Florida Cavalry, who had left Camp Cooper two days earlier for Camp Finegan.

Two of the Ninety-seventh Pennsylvania's companies were sent to make contact with Captain Lewis aboard the steamer, but this rendezvous almost turned into a tragedy. The troops were wearing captured Confederate gray as a lark, and the spotters aboard the Federal vessels thought at first they were about to be attacked. The truth was discovered in time to prevent anyone's getting hurt. The two companies were then embarked aboard the steamer for the trip back to Fernandina. Major Pennypacker had, meanwhile, already left with the remainder of the force to return home. Pennypacker's raiders had traveled a circuit of some fifty miles in twenty-four hours in a well-planned and well-executed, coordinated attack, only to come up empty-handed.[40] Had the raid been conducted two days earlier, it might have been more than worth the effort, in view of events yet to come.

On February 8, 1864, Company C (Beauregard Volunteers) Sixth Georgia Regiment, left Charleston, South Carolina, for Lake City, Florida. Partly because of the gap of twenty-six miles between the Georgia and Florida railroad lines, they did not arrive at Lake City until February 15. General Beauregard had long been concerned about this gap between the railroads in the two states within his department. As early as 1862, in a letter written to Judge Thomas Baltzell in Charleston, South Carolina, he had called attention to this gap as a handicap to rapidly concentrating troops from Savannah or the interior of Georgia for the defense of Middle Florida.[41] Passing through Madison, Florida, a member of the Sixth Georgia described a dinner prepared for his unit by the ladies of that town.

Learning that we were *en route* for the defence of the "Land of Flowers", and [would] parry the threatened blow now aimed at

their homes, and that we would pass through their town, they
had prepared for us a sumptuous dinner of such viands as they
knew would be heartily relished by hungry soldiers. After dinner, in behalf of our command, the accomplished Bennett Stewart, of Company "G" of our Regiment, tendered the thanks of
the command to the ladies for this manifestation of their appre-
ciation of our services in their behalf. He assured them that their
homes should be protected at all hazards, and the enemy driven
from their State.[42]

On February 9, General Gillmore ordered Col. Joseph C. Abbott's Seventh New Hampshire forward from Jacksonville to
report to General Seymour's advance force.[43] The following
morning, Colonel Henry's mounted brigade resumed their raid,
leaving Baldwin at nine o'clock heading westward. The column
moved cautiously now, being wary of ambushes, but met no
opposition. They continued to take rebel supplies along the
railroad right-of-way. Four miles out of Baldwin, they found
thirteen bales of cotton; farther on, approaching Barber's Station, they entered a building next to the railroad and discovered
a thousand barrels of turpentine and five hundred pounds of
bacon. At eleven that morning, Colonel Henry's troops entered
Barber's, where the main body halted and formed a defensive
hollow square while an advance guard of four men moved forward to see if the rebels had set up a defensive position at the
South Fork of the St. Marys River, some three-quarters of a
mile ahead. Approaching the river, the four ran into an ambush
the Confederates had set up, and one man was killed and two
wounded.[44]

Colonel Henry dismounted one company of the Fortieth
Massachusetts as skirmishers, with instructions to pay particular attention to the right of the road, where the con-
formation of the river exposed the left of the Confederate line
to the Union fire. The Independent Battalion was then sent
charging down the road to the bridge, which was discovered to
have been destroyed. The men continued on, fording the river
at that point. When most of the Independent Battalion had
forded the river, the Confederates withdrew, leaving a number
of horses behind. The *New York Times* correspondent reported

that some 150 rebels opposed the Union advance; the Southerners lost 2 killed and 3 wounded, the Union 4 killed and 13
wounded. Some fifty horses and a number of sabers, carbines,
and pistols were captured.[45] Clark of the 115th New York
claimed that at least one of the Union dead had been murdered.
The man was a sergeant, one of the Union wounded who was
lying down unable to help himself. Clark claims the Confederates came back and put six more bullets into his body.[46]

The Confederate force opposing the Union advance was the
Second Florida Cavalry. Capt. Winston Stephens, commanding
Company B of that unit, reflected a pessimistic note when he
penned these words to his wife on the day after the skirmish:

> I write you these few lines to allay the anxiety you may feel on
> my account. We have so far been able to elude the enemy,
> though we have at times been surrounded and from appearances
> we thought our prospect was fair for a Northern prison. Our
> command consists of 256 infantry and 56 men in the cav-
> alry. . . . I don't know if we will be able to get out of it without
> being captured. . . . We are having hard times and plenty of it. I
> think the enemy are some ten thousand or more.[47]

General Finegan reported that the Union force was met at
the "Little Saint Mary's" by Maj. Robert Harrison and two
companies of cavalry who were marching from Camp Cooper
to Lake City and "being unaware of the force of the enemy,
gave them battle at a strong point." General Finegan reported
Confederate losses at two killed and two wounded and Union
losses, as reported by a spy, as fifteen killed and thirty
wounded.[48] Major Harrison's troops had departed Camp
Cooper on February 8, two days before the surprise raid on
that camp conducted by Major Pennypacker and the Ninety-
seventh Pennsylvania Volunteers.

The *New York Times* correspondent reported that the Confederate troops had been told that the Union force did not
number more than three hundred and could easily be prevented
from fording the river.[49] In addition to horses and weapons, one
thousand pounds of sugar marked for Baldwin was found near
the railroad. Barber's, some thirty-six miles from Jacksonville

on a bend of the St. Marys River, was named after a local cattle farmer who was reputed to have paid taxes on some thirty-seven thousand head of cattle. His living quarters, however, belied his alleged wealth. The *New York Tribune* correspondent noted: "He lives in the most wretched style, in a filthy house, without a vestige of refinement, comfort, or decency. This is the style of the inhabitants along this route—'crackers,' 'sand-hillers,' and 'clay-eaters,' who seem to have but one idea which they share with the brute creation—the desire to find something to eat." The general nature of the *Tribune's* coverage of the expedition up to that point was highly optimistic. Thirteen cannon had been captured, considerable commissary supplies confiscated, a respectable number of prisoners taken, numerous "refugees were streaming into the federal lines" (a number of which were willing to take an oath of loyalty to the Union), and a sawmill was set up in Jacksonville capable of supplying the whole department with inexhaustible supplies of lumber.[50]

On February 10, the day of the skirmish at Barber's Ford, General Finegan was continuing to concentrate his troops in Florida. From Lake City he ordered the following:

1. Lt. Drury Rambo, at Wellborn, was to leave twenty men with the horses at that location and report with the balance of his men to Captain Dunham at Lake City.
2. Captain Dunham was directed to prepare his two howitzers for immediate duty and, taking what men he needed from his own and Captain Abell's companies, report to Maj. A. Bonaud.
3. Major Bonaud was to move his battalion along with a section of Captain Dunham's artillery, Captain Crawford's infantry company, and all the cavalry present in Lake City to the west side of the St. Marys River to a location between where it was crossed by the railroad and Barber's bridge. His orders were to prevent any further advance of the enemy and report anything of consequence. He was to keep his men in camp and be ready to form line of battle "at any moment."[51]

Maj. G. W. Scott and his cavalry, along with Captain Crawford's Independent Infantry Company, were to report to Major Bonaud. Maj. P. B. Bird, Sixth Battalion Florida Volunteers, was to move at once to Waldo, gather his men and supplies, and then move to Sanderson to await orders. Capt. Charles Cone, Cone's Independent Cavalry, was to report to Major Scott. Scott was to move to Sanderson and there join Major Harrison's cavalry companies.[52] Major Scott's unit had been inspected on the day these orders were issued, and a large number of weaknesses had been revealed. One company had no rifles, only sabers; other companies were also only partially armed. There was a shortage of cartridges, and saddles were so poor that they hastened the breakdown of the horses.[53] The loss of horses and equipment by Major Harrison's force defending the crossing of the Little St. Mary's when added to this inspection report suggests that the Second Florida Cavalry was not in the best of shape for combat, a fact that might have had a bearing on their performance at the battle of Olustee.

General Gillmore informed General Seymour on the tenth that it was expected that a working locomotive would be available within a few days for logistic support. Furthermore, General Gillmore was going to send several companies from Colonel Montgomery's Second South Carolina as scouts up the river for a few days and had ordered three companies of engineers to Baldwin, where, under Lt. Peter S. Michie, work would commence on a defensive position. The message contained this order, "You will push forward as far as you can toward the Suwannee River."[54]

That same day, General Gillmore acknowledged Admiral Dahlgren's message, which notified him of the admiral's planned departure with most of the naval support. General Gillmore expressed the idea that the three gunboats that would remain in the St. Johns were ample, believing that the enemy were too panic-stricken at the time to make any resistance in East Florida. Gillmore included the statement that he planned to be fifty miles from Jacksonville that night.[55] In a separate message, General Seymour was informed that, as previously agreed, four companies had been ordered to Camp Finegan, and the Fifty-fourth Massachusetts moved up to Ten-Mile Station.[56]

Colonel Henry's mounted Union raiding force, striking westward from Barber's at one o'clock in the afternoon, arrived at Sanderson, a village a little larger than Baldwin and forty miles from Jacksonville, about 6:00 P.M. Three large buildings were in flames as the raiders entered the town, who missed by fifteen minutes a train from Lake City which had picked up some government stores. One of the burning buildings had contained three thousand bushels of corn—a second, two thousand barrels of turpentine and rosin, and the last, commissary stores. Two hundred bags of salt and fifty bushels of oats were also recovered.[57] Sanderson appeared to be one of the more important collection points for Confederate supplies that were located along the railroad.

After a short rest, the raiders headed westward out of Sanderson at two o'clock in the morning in the direction of Lake City and by eleven A.M. were within three miles of Lake City, without having met any Southern resistance. Continuing to advance, the Union mounted force shortly made contact with a deployed Confederate battle line in a belt of woods. Captain Elder's horse artillery went into battery, and the Fortieth Massachusetts and the Independent Battalion were sent forward as skirmishers to feel out the enemy position. Lt. John Porter Fort, First Georgia Regulars, was in charge of the Confederate line, with orders to draw the Union forces closer. He remembered that it was a foggy morning and that the Union troops approached to within seventy-five to one hundred yards before either side could see the other. Both sides then commenced firing. When the fog lifted and the Union forces could see the Confederate line of battle, Fort reported that they "retreated with haste."[58] The *New York Times* reporter, with the Union forces, described the Confederate line as one mile in length. While one company of the Fortieth broke the left of the Confederate line, Colonel Henry felt that his forces were inadequate to hold back the Confederate right and so decided to await the arrival of more infantry.[59]

The Union troops retreated slowly at a walk, covered by the Independent Battalion. Sergeant Clement of the Independent Battalion remembered that darkness was rapidly falling and the horses were jaded, with food short for both men and mounts. The raiding force had gone far beyond their original destination of Baldwin and, in view of an impending rainstorm, which soon arrived, Colonel Henry decided to fall back a few miles for the night. The night was spent in a torrent of rain. Colonel Henry sent a message to General Seymour that night asking for further orders and stating his opinion that he could get to Lake City if one more infantry regiment was added to his advance force. The problem was he had outdistanced his infantry support, now roughly thirty-four miles away. The situation was complicated further by the difficulty of keeping the advance mounted force supplied. Without a working locomotive, all supplies were being brought up to Sanderson by wagon, a slow and tedious accomplishment. It was finally decided that Henry's advance force would fall back to Sanderson, to which point several infantry regiments had been advanced. Rebel deserters reported that General Finegan was making preparations that Thursday evening to evacuate Lake City, sending the government property located there back to Madison, and that his stand before Lake City was designed to conceal that activity.[60]

James H. Clark of the 115th New York remembered that cold, rainy, miserable night, but he recalled that it was not only the Union forces who were suffering. "Three of the 'Johnnies' being rather 'hard up' for grub, and not very bitter advocates of treason, came to the edge of a piece of woods and waved a couple of white rags as tokens of peace. Some of the boys went up to them, took away their guns, and escorted them to camp, where they took the oath of allegiance."[61]

Confederate general Finegan reported the Lake City engagement to General Beauregard in a message dated February 13, 1864, claiming that he had removed from Sanderson the large amount of commissary and quartermaster supplies that had been there before the Union troops arrived, with the exception of some 1,500 bushels of corn which the Confederates had burned. In his assessment of the situation, he described the threat posed by the size of the Union force, particularly its cavalry and its ability to raid into the richer interior counties to run off blacks and destroy subsistence supplies. He reported the Union's fortification of Baldwin and a position on the St. Marys and requested more cavalry units to counter the Federal raiding potential. He certainly got Beauregard's attention when he wrote, "The beef from the peninsula will of course be suspended until the enemy is driven off."[62] Unfortunately, General Beauregard was limited in his resources and on February 11, instructed General Finegan not to expect further reinforcements from Georgia. Finegan was not to fight "unless compelled or certain of success. In such case maneuver to delay enemy."[63]

At the point where Colonel Henry's mounted troops faced General Finegan's Confederate troops before Lake City, the Union forces had a better than two-to-one advantage in manpower and artillery, and a significantly greater advantage in mobility. Had Henry's men and their mounts been in better condition, the Southern forces could have easily been bypassed, and Henry could have continued on with little or no opposition to destroy the railroad bridge over the Suwannee. The possibility also existed of raiding Lake City and capturing or destroying the supplies accumulated there, perhaps even capturing the locomotive so desperately needed by the Federals.

General Seymour reported the results of Henry's skirmish at Barber's to General Gillmore in a letter from Baldwin dated 7:00 A.M. the eleventh. He advised his senior that Henry had been at Sanderson the night before and was pushing on toward Lake City that morning. The 115th New York was presently located at Barber's; the Forty-seventh New York, Forty-eighth New York, Seventh New Hampshire, and two guns were en route from Baldwin to Barber's. Seymour then went on to say that the proposed movement on Lake City was not possible because of transportation difficulties and recommended the advance force be withdrawn at once with only Jacksonville and Palatka to be held. He was convinced that Florida would not come back into the Union "until more important successes elsewhere are assured" and that "the Union cause would have been far better benefitted by Jeff. Davis having removed this railroad to Virginia than by any trivial and non-strategic success you might meet."[64] In view of the success to date of the expedition, this assessment of the operation was a bit of a surprise.

Seymour's chief signal officer, Capt. Gustavas Sullivan Dana, later reported on an incident that had happened the night before Seymour's letter was written.

> We reached Baldwin on the 10th and General Gillmore came out that night and talked all night with General Seymour keeping us poor staff officers who were trying to catch 40 winks on the floor with our saddles, awake. I judge from what I heard that neither general had much faith in the success of the expedition and that it was purely a political move, intending to drive the rebels to the west side of the Suwannee River giving us the whole east part of the State which was to be protected by gun-boats patrolling the Suwannee and Saint Mary's Rivers, and thus enabling the larger part of the State to have a vote in the coming presidential election.[65]

If Captain Dana's observations are true, both Generals Seymour and Gillmore were taking a very narrow view of the objectives of the expedition. Furthermore, General Gillmore had really not understood, or chose to disregard, President Lincoln's and John Hay's instructions to the effect that restoration of the state was not to change the original objectives of the expedition. Although every indication pointed to the military success of the expedition because of its daring, its leaders now became overly cautious.

Apprehensive about the advance of Union forces past Sanderson, Gillmore informed Seymour on February 11 that eight companies of the Fifty-fourth Massachusetts had been sent to Baldwin and advised him, "Don't risk a repulse in advancing on Lake City, but hold Sanderson unless there are reasons for falling back when I don't know." This was followed by a second message to Seymour by courier from Baldwin that same night which contained the suggestion, "If your advance meets serious opposition concentrate at Sanderson and the South Fork of the Saint Mary's and, if necessary, bring Henry to the latter place."[66] General Seymour replied from Baldwin by telegraph, which had been installed that day between Baldwin and Jacksonville, that he had just received Gillmore's message and that Seymour's command had already left for Sanderson. It continued that there was no news from Henry, Col. Benjamin C. Tilghman (Third U.S. Colored Troops) was at Baldwin, Col. Charles W. Fribley (Eighth U.S. Colored Troops) was at Pickett's, no Negroes had come in, and Baldwin was the place to fortify.[67] In a concern for more security, General Gillmore ordered the Fifty-fourth Massachusetts to Baldwin (less two companies which were to be retained in Jacksonville) and directed Colonel Montgomery to send three companies of his Second South Carolina Regiment to either Doctor's Lake or Green Cove Springs, crossing places on the west bank of the St. Johns River, to try to capture rebel pickets that might be stationed there.[68]

General Beauregard saw something in the Federal expedition that, unfortunately for the Federals, the Union generals did not see for themselves. General Beauregard wired General Gilmer at Charleston at 12:30 P.M. on February 11 that the enemy's present movements indicated an effort to concentrate from both sides of the peninsula of Florida at Tallahassee. General Gilmer was informed that General Beauregard "did not approve pressing to concentrate at a point in rear of Finegan to prevent junction and maneuvers to strike blow on either fragment."[69] A half-hour later, General Beauregard sent the following message to Brigadier General Gardner, commanding Middle Florida, at Quincy, Florida: "Important to know whether enemy made a landing in force about this time on Gulf Coast of Florida, Saint Mark's especially. Have measures taken to secure and forward earliest possible information soon as possible."[70] Regrettably for the Union, Florida was split between the Department of the South (Gillmore's command) and the Department of the Gulf (in which Tallahassee and St. Marks fell). Later, Union general Asboth from the Department of the Gulf would suggest:

In my humble opinion, a combined movement toward Tallahassee from the Atlantic via Jacksonville and Lake City, and
from the Gulf via Saint Mark's, would have proved more disastrous for the rebels, and I would most respectfully request to be
enabled to establish a permanent post at Saint Mark's; it would
afford another safe base of operations toward the interior of Florida, protected, as it is, by blockading vessels of Admiral Far-
ragut, anchored near the light house, 7 miles seaward from Saint
Mark's.[71]

A letter on March 8, 1864, from Union brigadier general
Woodbury, District of Key West and Tortugas, to his parent
command, the Department of the Gulf, contained information
about the efforts of a Commander Harmony who was attempting to organize a group of Southern deserters to burn the railroad bridge over the Suwannee River on the railroad between
Jacksonville and Tallahassee. This group had already mounted
a forty-five-mile raid on the "largest salt-works in the Confederacy—395 kettles and 52 boilers, having the capacity to
make about 1,600 bushels daily."[72] On April 4, 1864, General
Asboth of the Department of the Gulf, in reporting that "since
our reverse in East Florida the rebels have become more enterprising in their movements and more bitter in their persecu-
tions of all who show sympathy for the Union," suggested:

To prevent the entire ruin of those unfortunate Union families
and secure us the control over West Florida, it would be desirable that at the next advance of the Federal Forces in East Florida a combined movement be made also in West Florida, by
adequate forces from Barrancas, Boggy Bayou, opposite East
Pass, Washington Point, the head of the Choctawhatchee Bay,
and Saint Mark's, the terminus of the Tallahassee Railroad.[73]

These observations came too late to be of use. Since General
Finegan, immediately after the Federal landing on February 8,
had stripped Middle and East Florida of all the Confederate
troops available and concentrated them at Lake City, a Union
thrust from the Gulf at that time would have had a high probability of success. It might also have broken up somewhat the

concentration at Olustee that General Finegan finally did manage to put together by February 20, had its timing been coordinated with the troop landing at Jacksonville. Whatever might have been, Beauregard saw the danger a two-pronged attack on the state presented; the leaders of the Federal expedition did not.

Governor Milton wired Confederate Secretary of War Seddon on the tenth asking for at least five thousand troops to "save Florida," finishing with the urgent plea, "Without prompt help all will be lost."[74] On the morning of the eleventh, Beauregard forwarded Governor Milton's message requesting the five thousand troops to General Cooper at Richmond, commenting that "immense loss of subsistence for armies and of property seems inevitable" but that he would be risking loss of Savannah and Charleston if he were to send any more troops from his command. He pleaded for two brigades to be sent to Florida temporarily from northwest Georgia or North Carolina. Early that afternoon, Beauregard followed this message to Cooper with another that detailed his situation.

> General Finegan reports enemy about to attack him near Lake City. Rapidity of movements indicate Tallahassee as the objective point, probably to form junction with forces from the Gulf. I have ordered two and a half additional regiments and one light battery to Florida, to prevent loss of that State; but have much weakened Savannah and railroad to that city. If one brigade could be sent here and another to Savannah, I would send immediately balance of Colquitt's troops to General Finegan. A prompt answer is desired, as well as for 2 general officers I applied for few days since.[75]

While the Union leaders were convincing themselves that the expedition was a mere political ploy, the various Confederate leaders close to the scene of action, including Governor Milton and General Beauregard, saw its real potential. It posed a very serious threat to a major source of subsistence supplies to the Confederacy, to the stability of the slave population, to the maintenance of Florida as a part of the Confederacy, and to a very thinly spread Confederate Atlantic coast defense handicapped by a primitive transportation system. Furthermore, to meet that threat, General Beauregard had been forced to weaken his defenses around Savannah and Charleston, requested help from Richmond at a time he had been asked to furnish men to the Army of the Tennessee, was forced to use valuable transportation assets to move troops to Florida, and was losing troops from South Carolina and Georgia by expiration of enlistment. In assessing the threat posed by the Union forces, no mention was made by the Confederate leadership of any political implications regarding the 1864 Federal presidential election, a motive much overrated in evaluating the expedition. From the Southern point of view, the Federal expedition had an importance much beyond that assigned to it by its own leaders.

The Lake City engagement was the critical point in the expedition that spelled its success or failure. Instead of exploiting the benefits they had gained by superior mobility and surprise and continuing the momentum they had achieved, the Federal leaders turned overly cautious. The full potential of the expedition was lost on the men who conceived and executed it because of their limited ability to realize its ramifications in terms of higher-level strategy. At a time when daring and innovation were called for, the Union commanders were irresolute, conservative, overly cautious, and inflexible in their conduct of the expedition.

At 7:00 A.M. on February 12, General Seymour sent a message from Sanderson to General Gillmore informing him that he had ordered Colonel Henry's advance force to fall back to Sanderson and suggested that Colonel Fribley's Eighth U.S. Colored Troops be sent permanently to garrison Palatka.[76] At about the same time, General Gillmore ordered General Seymour to concentrate all of his forces at Baldwin "without delay" and alerted Seymour to a possible danger from a mounted force that was reported to be heading in the direction of Seymour's right flank on the St. Marys River. Colonel Tilghman with the Third U.S. Colored Troops at Baldwin was directed by General Gillmore to send scouts to the ford of the St. Marys River, and Seymour was informed of this action by a separate message.[77] At 1:00 P.M., Gillmore replied to Seymour's 7:00 A.M. message concerning Henry's being ordered back, making the unwarranted assumption that such action had been taken by Seymour because the enemy was too strong to the front. Gillmore called for more information on the enemy and advised that he was going to garrison Palatka on the St. Johns River with the command garrisoning St. Augustine under Colonel Osborn of the Twenty-fourth Connecticut. Seymour was directed to keep a force well out in front of him toward Sanderson.[78]

With the return of Henry that same day, Seymour's confidence in the expedition seems to have returned. In an early afternoon message to Gillmore he related that Henry, Elder, and he were in agreement that the Union forces should hold only the South Fork of the St. Marys for the present. He gave as his intention the consolidation of his position on the South Fork along with one at Callahan while conducting a raid on Gainesville by a portion of Henry's force with the objective of trying to capture a train. He requested that troops be sent to control the bridge at Middleburg and that other troops be concentrated at a location where they could be supplied, pending a move forward by Seymour, at which time he would call them forward to Barber's. In a postscript, Seymour asked Gillmore to have the naval force at Fernandina destroy all the ferryboats in the St. Marys as far up it as they could reach, and in the event an advance by his forces was made, it was suggested that a demonstration be made against Savannah. Last, he stated that he expected Capt. John Hamilton's Light Battery E, Third U.S. Artillery, which had recently been ordered to Jacksonville, and whatever regiments that were to be assigned to him be sent up to Baldwin.[79] Meanwhile, Col. Francis Osborn at St. Augustine was ordered by General Gillmore on the twelfth to move the Twenty-fourth Connecticut, less two companies and the veterans who were due to go north on leave, and proceed to Picolata on the St. Johns for temporary duty.[80] Gillmore's plan to hold and fortify a Federal enclave marked by a line from Fernandina to Baldwin to Palatka to St. Augustine appeared to be taking shape.

General Beauregard, still caught in a dilemma over the conflicting problems presented by the Florida expedition and the defenses of Savannah and Charleston, decided to resolve the issue by calling the Union bluff represented by Union general Schimmelfennig's forces on John's Island. On the night of the eleventh, General Beauregard ordered a heavy fire of all of his batteries bearing on Morris Island as if to cover an assault. Whether this was effective or mere coincidence, the Union troops withdrew back to Kiawah that night in obedience to orders. While on John's Island, however, the Union forces discovered a book containing all the signals sent from Folly Island by the signal telegraph, correctly showing that the rebels had the key to the Union system of signals.[81] The pullback of Federal forces at this time to their previous positions allowed General Beauregard to release Colonel Colquitt's brigade with the Chatham Artillery attached to leave for Florida, where they arrived in time to play a key part in the battle of Olustee. While these Confederate reinforcements were traveling to Florida, Seymour was about to waste a crucial week in senseless delay. Had the momentum of the Federal expedition been maintained, the demonstration in South Carolina would have been considered successful. As things turned out, it was too little and too late. For the Confederate forces, it was now a race against time.

On February 13, Colonel Henry received his orders to conduct a raid on Gainesville with the mission of capturing or disabling trains supposed to be at that location. He was expressly instructed that "all public property that cannot be removed will be destroyed, but private property will be scrupulously respected." It was hoped that minimum alienation of the local citizenry would facilitate the political objective of seeking restoration under the Ten Percent Plan. After hitting Gainesville, and on his return to Baldwin, he was to detach a small force to be sent to Middleburg.[82] In order to increase the firepower of his mounted infantry, the left wing of the Seventh New Hampshire, a regiment which, like the Seventh Connecticut, was armed with seven-shot repeater Spencer rifles, was ordered to exchange their weapons with the Fortieth Massachusetts Mounted Infantry.

Near the end of the war Col. Joseph Abbott, commanding the
Seventh New Hampshire, spoke of the matter in a letter to the
adjutant general of New Hampshire. Colonel Abbott stated
that he had protested, but in vain. Three hundred of the men
were recruits and had barely been instructed in the use of the
carbine but not at all in the use of the rifle. Forty-two of the
Springfields were pronounced unserviceable by the brigade inspector the day after they were received. "The men were dis-
pirited, the officers were annoyed and chagrined, and the whole
effect of the proceeding could not have failed to be embarrass-
ing to any officer." Colonel Hawley, the commander of the brigade to which the Seventh New Hampshire was attached, was
also held in low regard because the exchange was not made
with Hawley's own regiment, the Seventh Connecticut. The
regimental historian of the Seventh New Hampshire reported
that there was not a bayonet among the Springfields and
thought that in one company, Company I, thirty were unserviceable; in Company D, nineteen were deficient in lock, ham-
mer, or rammer and "consequently were no more use to our
soldiers than an equal number of fence stakes."[83] Although
half of the regiment was armed with these almost useless
weapons (and included among that unit were some three hundred new recruits), the Seventh New Hampshire within the
week would be assigned a critical position in the Union lines at
the battle of Olustee under Colonel Hawley as brigade commander.

With good reason to be optimistic over the success to date of
the expedition, General Gillmore sent a progress report on February 13 which included his immediate plans to the Union
general in chief, Major General Halleck. He informed General
Halleck that he intended to construct defensive positions
suitable for 200- to 300-man units at Jacksonville, Baldwin,
Palatka, and perhaps one or two other important points. He
estimated that 2,500 men, in addition to the two regiments
that had been permanently stationed in Florida (one at St. Augustine and one at Fernandina), were sufficient to control Florida along with the artillery that had been captured. General
Gillmore also included a recommendation he had made to the

secretary of the treasury that the port of Jacksonville be declared open in order "to see the lumber and turpentine trade on the Saint John's revived by loyal men." This message contained the essence of General Gillmore's plan for Union operations in Florida. General Gillmore closed, stating that he would return to Hilton Head the next day, leaving General Seymour in charge. In a postscript, Gillmore enclosed a copy of Confederate major White's "confidential notice" concerning Confederate food shortages and commissary requirements in Florida.[84]

On February 13, Capt. G. E. Marshall, with a picked force of forty-nine men from Companies G, H, and K of the Fortieth Massachusetts, left Sanderson for Gainesville, arriving there at two o'clock the following morning. The importance of Gainesville was touched on by former Confederate cavalryman Lawrence Jackson, who described it as a depot for supplies and blockade goods and a supply source for most areas east of the Suwannee River. Cattle were driven through this area after pasturing on the grasslands to the south, and a large number of wagons and teams were normally to be found in the vicinity.[85]

Captain Marshall's men had skirmished all night on the way to Gainesville and upon arriving put out pickets and sentries to prevent warning being given of the presence of the Union force. It was learned from a local black that a Confederate cavalry force was near, and a Confederate picket of two men was surprised and captured. A Confederate messenger, however, did get away and made contact with Capt. W. E. Chambers's Company C, Second Florida Cavalry, at Newnansville, where the unit had stopped on its way to Lake City. Captain Marshall, with about forty minutes' advance notice and with the aid of a number of blacks, erected a fortification made out of 167 cotton bales, barricading the egress roads leading through the town. Behind these cotton bales were placed the Union troopers armed with the seven-shot Spencer rifles.[86]

Lawrence Jackson recalls that after getting word about the presence of the Yankees in Gainesville, Captain Chambers's cavalry company ate their dinner and then leisurely came back to Gainesville, stopping along the way many times. About four miles from Gainesville, the Confederate cavalry linked up with Lt. Col. Louis G. Pyles, who headed a group of old men and boys. It was decided to approach the town by two roads, the cavalry on one, and Pyles's troops on the other. The force under Pyles never showed up, and the cavalry made a charge on the barricaded Union forces, where they were repulsed by the superior Union firepower. The Confederate forces withdrew and did not return until the following morning after the Federal force had departed. Trooper Lawrence recalled that his unit followed the Yankees, who took with them quite a number of Negroes, halfway to Waldo and then halted. "We had in Chambers's command about one hundred and twenty of as good soldiers as there are in the army and the Yankees had about fifty all told. The outcome was anything but creditable to the officer in command of the Confederate forces."[87] The *New York Tribune* correspondent reported that thirty-six Negroes were brought to Jacksonville from Gainesville, of which thirty-three enlisted.[88] General Seymour's report of this raid, dated the seventeenth, noted that no private property was destroyed or molested and that the public subsistence stores were distributed among the inhabitants. "Probably $1,000,000 worth of property fell into our hands, but it could not be removed and it was considered advisable to destroy it."[89]

After the Gainesville raid, the Confederate forces were convinced that the raiding force would hit Lake City next. To meet that threat, newly arriving units from Georgia were hastily utilized. The Chatham Artillery had been moved from Charleston on the eighth to Savannah, where they remanned their old encampment at White Bluff. As part of the troops released by Beauregard, the unit moved on the morning of the twelfth to the depot of the Florida, Atlantic, and Gulf Coast Railroad, where it boarded trains for Valdosta, arriving at four in the afternoon on the thirteenth. From there the battery traveled at night overland, due to the gap between the Florida and Georgia rail lines, arriving at Madison, Florida, on the morning of the fourteenth. At Madison, it again entrained, arriving at Lake City at three in the morning on the fifteenth. The Chatham Artillery and the Sixth Georgia were immediately ordered to a blocking position some twelve miles south of Lake City, where a strong line of pickets had been established to prevent the Federal force from hitting Lake City and destroying the bridge at Columbus. They remained in place until the seventeenth, when they were recalled to Lake City and directed from there to report to Olustee.[90]

While the raid on Gainesville was taking place, a two-pronged Union raid was underway toward King's Ferry and the Georgia line. Elements of Henry's mounted brigade supported by infantry were to leave from Barber's, while a second force composed of elements from the Ninety-seventh Pennsylvania supported by gunboats was to leave from Fernandina. Colonel Henry's force, which included the 115th New York infantry, three companies of the Independent Battalion's cavalry, and one gun of Captain Elder's horse battery, left on the morning of the fourteenth toward Callahan Station near the Georgia line to "scour the country," destroy the railroad, and burn some ferryboats. The remoteness of the area was highlighted by a noon stop for lunch at the house of a veteran of the Indian War who had never seen greenbacks and who "beheld for the first time in four years the flag of his country."[91] The Union troopers marched some twenty-five miles the first day, mostly through swamp and water. Leaving their blankets and coats under guard the next morning, the force continued on to Callahan, where they accomplished their mission, driving off some Confederate cavalry and destroying two ferryboats and the telegraph station before returning to their previous night's camping spot.[92]

The following morning, they started on the return trip, with rations scarce and the men worn out. Clark later recalled the men's feet were bleeding and "every soldier declared that they could not go a single inch farther." A stop was made and a council of officers held to decide whether to continue or stop. The decision was made to continue because of the danger of stopping. The force returned to Barber's that night in poor condition. Clark recalled, "Our march had been so rapid, that the cavalry and artillery horses were worn out, and many had dropped dead along the road."[93] This force would have just two days to recuperate before making the long march to Olustee.

The objectives of the raiding force from Fernandina were more extensive. On the fifteenth, Major Pennypacker, with three hundred men from the Ninety-seventh Pennsylvania, departed Fernandina for Woodstock Mills and King's Ferry Mills on the St. Marys River with the mission of seizing lumber that was stored there and a mill gearing to be used in the Department of the South.[94] After moving some thirty-three miles without detection, they arrived at King's Ferry Mills about sunset at about the same time as did the raiding force coming from Barber's. The following day the men of the Ninety-seventh started to build rafts with the lumber. Maj. T. B. Brooks, of General Seymour's staff, arrived on the sixteenth with another two hundred men of the Ninety-seventh aboard naval transports (one of which, the *Harriet Weed,* carried three guns) and the mortar schooner *Para.* The Fernandina raiding force and its supporting vessels stayed at King's Ferry Mills until the twentieth, finding some 700,000 board feet of prepared pine at the ferry and, about six miles farther up the river, an additional 800,000 board feet. Half of this lumber had been rafted, towed, or carried on the decks of steamers down to Fernandina within five days.[95]

While at the mills, Major Pennypacker sent Captain Lewis and Company F on a raid over on the Georgia side of the river to cut the telegraph communications between Savannah and Tallahassee. This line had been cut before in one or two places, but communications had been resumed by new and temporary connections that had eluded discovery. Captain Lewis's men followed the telegraph line for fifteen miles from Trader's Hill before discovering a point where a wire branched off into a hollow tree so close to the line as almost to defy detection. The wire led from the roots of the tree into a swamp and from there by a concealed route to reconnect beyond the part that had been destroyed. Major Pennypacker's Pennsylvanians were also able to capture a notorious guerrilla identified only as Captain Wilds. When in Union custody, the man denied being who his captors claimed he was, but on the testimony of one of his former slaves, who said, "You tink [sic] I don't know you when you own me so long," he recanted.[96] Major Pennypacker's highly successful raid was cut all too short by the news of Olustee, and he returned with his men to Fernandina.

Following the military dictum of reinforcing success, orders were issued at Union headquarters for the Department of the South on Folly Island, South Carolina, on February 14, detailing the First North Carolina Volunteers, Fifty-fifth Massachusetts, and Hamilton's battery to report to General Seymour at Jacksonville. The two infantry regiments were not at full strength, however, as a number of men with smallpox or exposed to the disease were retained, along with one medical and one line officer from each regiment.[97]

On the same day the Union reinforcements received orders, General Beauregard's headquarters at Charleston directed General Gilmer at Savannah to send Col. Robert H. Anderson's Fifth Georgia Cavalry from Green Pond to Florida via Trader's Hill. This unit entrained aboard the Florida, Atlantic, and Gulf Coast Railroad, but the special train was delayed because its fuel gave out, and the men had to detrain, go into the forest, and cut wood to fire the engine. Further delayed by the march across country from Valdosta to Madison, the Fifth Georgia Cavalry did not arrive until the day after the battle of Olustee.[98] They might have furnished the Confederate side at Olustee with a major advantage, particularly in the pursuit. Later, on the afternoon of the fourteenth, another order from General Beauregard to General Gilmer directed that Colonel Colquitt's brigade be sent to General Finegan at Lake City "as soon as possible by the shortest route."[99] General Finegan was then directed to request more artillery from General Gardner, commanding Middle Florida, should he feel the need for more; Gardner was told at the same time to have light artillery ready for Finegan's request.[100]

On February 15, General Order No. 24 of the Union's Department of the South was issued. It invited "Loyal people, and such as desire to become so," to return to their homes in East Florida, where it was the "intentions of the United States Government, and wholly within its power, to afford them all needful protection." The order went on to admonish all officers to "enforce in the strictest manner, and under the severest penal-

ties, all existing orders and regulations forbidding the destruction or pillage of private property."[101] The entire Federal
operation, in fact, was being conducted under the strictest lim-
itations on any conduct that might alienate the local Floridians. One correspondent accompanying the expedition
criticized this "kid gloves" policy for not allowing the army to
levy contributions upon the country for the support of the
army. He cited the example of a captain recommended to be
dismissed from the service because he had allowed his men on
"extreme outpost duty" to kill a pig for their supper.[102] One
can only wonder how Gen. William T. Sherman would have
operated under this policy in Georgia or whether the 1864
Federal expedition would have been more successful had they
been permitted to "live off the land" and not be tied to supply
by wagon while waiting for a working locomotive.

Another general order created the District of Florida, to include the portion of Florida within the responsibility of the
Department of the South, and placed this district under command of General Seymour.[103] This was the move that tax commissioner L. D. Stickney had desired for his friend Gen. Rufus
Saxton, with the intention of mutually profiting from that appointment.

On February 16, General Seymour sent a message to General
Gillmore, who was now back at his headquarters at Hilton
Head, South Carolina, in which he demonstrated a complete
comprehension of the plan of operations for Florida that General Gillmore had so recently described to General Halleck.
Speaking of "a strong movable column to push in advance of a
well-secured base and to be kept constantly active," General
Seymour expressed concern over the question of who was to
command the advanced force. Although no displeasure with
Colonel Henry had been officially recorded, General Seymour
expressed belief that the position should be one held by an officer of approved judgment and experience and suggested such
a man was Col. M. R. Morgan, a native Southerner from the
Subsistence Department who could be appointed a brigadier
general when given the assignment. General Seymour then
completely reversed a strong statement he had made only a day

or so earlier when he expressed the idea that the "people of this State, if treated kindly by us, will soon be ready to return to the Union" and stressed the necessity for a printing press so that he could communicate with the local people.[104]

The following day General Seymour notified General Gillmore that he was moving westward from Baldwin with three additional infantry regiments he had called forward and requested elements of three other regiments be moved up from Jacksonville. He informed Gillmore he would no longer wait for a locomotive or additional supplies, and he was planning to advance "with the object of destroying the railroad near the Suwannee that there be no danger of carrying away any portion of the track." Seymour urged that a demonstration be made in the vicinity of Savannah to deter Confederate troops being dispatched from there. He reported on the troop dispositions he had made to support his own movement and noted again his critical need for both a locomotive and a printing press. He stated in his letter that he expected to be in motion by the time General Gillmore received his message.[105]

Upon receiving General Seymour's communications, the shocked Gillmore immediately sent him a note, to be hand-delivered by his chief of staff, Brig. Gen. J. W. Turner, suspending the forward movement and ordering the Union troops back to Baldwin. General Gillmore called attention to his plan of operations and the last instructions to Seymour. These were to "hold Baldwin and the Saint Mary's South Fork, as your outposts to the westward of Jacksonville, and to occupy Palatka, Magnolia, on the Saint John's." Colonel Henry's mounted force was to be kept in motion "as circumstances might justify or require." Gillmore cited Seymour's earlier statements about the futility of the operation and the chances for restoring Florida to the Union. Gillmore indicated that he was confused over what Seymour was doing and ordered Seymour to comply with the instructions he had received before Gillmore had left Florida.[106] Unfortunately for the Union, General Turner's ship ran into bad weather, and he did not arrive with General Gillmore's letter until after the battle of Olustee had been fought and lost.

General Seymour's command decision to advance is highly

controversial and is surrounded in mystery. When General Turner was later questioned by the Senate Committee on the Conduct of the War and was asked if this advance were considered as really a breach of orders, he replied: "General Gillmore did not intend or expect to have General Seymour advance." Seymour had made that decision, according to Turner, because he believed the people were ready to come back into the Union. He did not anticipate a large force in front of him and believed the destruction of the Suwannee River railroad bridge would prevent enemy forces from coming into Florida.[107]

Col. Joseph R. Hawley, regimental commander of the Seventh Connecticut and acting commander of one of General Seymour's four brigades at the battle of Olustee, later wrote of a meeting "a night or two before the battle" that General Seymour had held with "six or eight" of his officers. According to Hawley, the officers felt that it would be virtually impossible to hold a position in the middle of the state, "having for its line of communication a rickety railroad with one engine running sixty miles back to the base at Jacksonville." They believed that the Confederate forces could trap the Union forces by allowing them to advance one more day and then interdict the railroad that connected to Jacksonville. Most officers favored using the St. Johns River as the main western line, but "Seymour thought it his duty to go on."[108]

Another theory as to why Seymour changed his mind so suddenly has to do with a plan for military action in South Carolina he had submitted to U.S. senator Ira Harris from New York State on January 12, 1864, one month before the Florida expedition. The plan suggested an amphibious landing on the South Carolina coast, a march inland of some forty miles, and an attack on the key railroad junction at Branchville, South Carolina. Seymour believed that this operation would divide the Confederacy by driving a wedge between Gens. Robert E. Lee and Joe Johnston. The Branchville rail junction would be fortified, and if the Confederates attacked, they would be at a disadvantage.[109] General Seymour was echoing the offensive-defensive strategy envisioned by the former railroad executive, Gen. George B. McClellan, who foresaw the importance of rail

junctions as strategic targets and the advantage that rifled guns
had given to the defense. The plan had a good probability of
success at the time of the Port Royal attack in 1862 but would
have been a bit more difficult in 1864. Gen. Robert E. Lee and
Gen. P. G. T. Beauregard had reorganized the Southern coastal
defenses into mobile defenses, giving special attention to the
use of railroads and their defense.

When he sent his plan to Senator Harris, General Seymour
suggested that General Gillmore would favor it. Since there
was no endorsement by Gillmore, apparently Seymour was acting without official approval. Seymour did suggest that Harris
bring the plan to the attention of President Lincoln but asked
that "these views might, if you please, be expressed as your
own."[110] It would seem that General Seymour was being motivated to some extent by his own personal ambition.

Assigned to the Florida expedition, Seymour may have become disenchanted with the prospect of being involved with an
operation that was smaller in scale and less strategically important than the one he was proposing for South Carolina. In
his letter to Senator Harris, he belittled a Florida expedition,
claiming that the state would fall by itself into Union hands
when General Johnston was defeated.[111] He also expressed this
opinion later in substance to General Gillmore. Finding himself in Florida with no immediate prospect for more glorious
fields of battle, General Seymour seemed to be applying the
same strategic reasoning that he had used in the Branchville
operation proposal to the situation in Florida. If the railroad
bridge over the Suwannee at Columbus could be destroyed, it
would separate East and West Florida. Seymour may have also
heard that there was a possible second bridge crossing the
Suwannee River in the vicinity of Sulphur Springs. Supposedly
it was not complete, but it was on the proposed rail connector
line between Lawton, Georgia, and Live Oak, Florida. The
connector-line route had been graded and its crossties laid, but
it needed rails. If rail became available to the Confederates, the
connector line could have been in operation within six
weeks.[112] The existence of even an incomplete connector rail
line, particularly one crossing the Suwannee River relatively

close to the bridge at Columbus, may also have tempted General Seymour to risk an advance. The opportunity not only to separate East from West Florida but also to ensure the separation of Florida from Georgia by rail made that area of the Suwannee strategically important.

Whether Seymour was aware of the existence of the connector line is not known, but General Gillmore had mentioned to General Halleck that one objective for the Florida expedition would be to prevent the Confederates moving rail to the connector line.[113] Seymour did believe that some rail from Florida might be removed to Virginia and used to supplement lines there. This had to be prevented. Perhaps General Seymour became convinced that if he did not advance to prevent the removal of the rail, the rail might be used to build a connector line that would parallel the line headed north out of Branchville. This would render that rail junction less strategically important and, equally so, the plan that General Seymour had given to Senator Harris.

General Seymour might also have felt that his career was languishing in comparison to those of fellow officers. Although he had graduated from West Point in 1846, he was subordinate in command to General Gillmore, who had graduated from West Point three years later. Seymour had served with distinction as an artillery officer in the Mexican War and against the Seminoles in Florida in 1856–58. He was at Fort Sumter during the bombardment in April 1861, commanded a division at Malvern Hill in the Peninsula Campaign, and was brevetted a lieutenant colonel for his actions at Second Manassas. He also distinguished himself at the battle of South Mountain and was brevetted a colonel for his performance at Sharpsburg.[114] He was transferred to Charleston Harbor in November 1862, where, under a master plan conceived by General Gillmore, he was the field commander charged with the abortive attack on Battery Wagner in July 1863. In that engagement, the North lost 1,515 men, while the South lost only 181. Military analysts have charged him with being too slow to order supporting units into the attack, a charge that would be repeated in relation to his conduct at Olustee.[115] Perhaps, after a series of distinguishing performances early in the war, General Seymour found himself bogged down for two years performing the tedious requirements of seige duty in a military area that was a sideshow to more momentous events and with only a bloody failure to show for his efforts. Anxious to recoup the fortunes of his personal military career after the disaster at Battery Wagner, he blundered into an even worse one in Florida.

There does exist one description of Seymour's behavior during the period of the 1864 expedition that is interesting in light of what eventually happened. John Hay wrote: "Seymour has seemed very unsteady and queer since the beginning of the campaign. He has been subject to violent alternations of timidity & rashness, now declaring Florida loyalty was all bosh, now lauding it as the purest article extant, now insisting that Beauregard was in front with the whole Confederacy & now asserting that he could whip all the rebels in Florida with a good brigade."[116]

Confederate reinforcements, in the meantime, had been converging on Lake City. Four days after the Federal landing, and at the time of the Lake City skirmish with Henry's raiders, General Finegan had only 600 infantry and cavalry with two guns. Two days later, on the thirteenth, he had 2,250 infantry and cavalry and 10 guns; by the nineteenth, he had amassed 5,200 infantry and cavalry and three batteries containing twelve guns, roughly equal to the Federal force he would face the following day.[117] Anticipating an engagement, Finegan selected a location near Olustee Station which seemed to offer the best defensive position between the South Fork of the St. Marys and Lake City because the combination of swamps and bodies of water restricted approach movements to a narrow front. Work began on February 13. On the seventeenth, Lt. M. B. Grant, Confederate Engineers, arrived after a two-day trip from Savannah. Grant's professional evaluation of the terrain was that it offered little assistance to a defense or obstacle to an advance because of its flatness and lack of significant streams. The only natural features that a defense could take advantage of were the various ponds or bays that were scattered throughout the area.[118] (See map 5.)

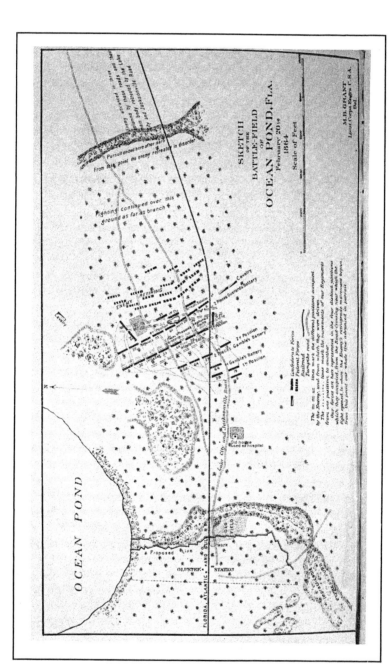

5. Grant's sketch of the Ocean Pond battlefield. Reprinted from *ORA* XXXV, pt. 1, p. 338.

When Grant arrived, he found Finegan's small army en-camped on a line extending from Ocean Pond on the left to a large cypress pond on the right. In the absence of any other engineering officer, Lieutenant Grant was put in charge of con-structing a defensive position upon which he started after im-pressing slaves and tools for a work force. Although working hard to make the defensive emplacement formidable, Lieuten-ant Grant had strong doubts about the value of such a position, believing that even if it were complete, it might deter a direct attack but, because of the nature of the terrain, could be turned by a detour of a few miles.[119] Grant's efforts were pretty much in vain, as the defensive works were neither completed nor used when the battle of Olustee took place some two and one-quarter miles in front of the position.

The concentration of Confederate troops was remarkable, considering the different points they came from and the dis-tances some of them traveled. The presence of the four infantry regiments brought by Colquitt from Savannah was a major rea-son for the Confederate success at Olustee. Once released by Beauregard after being held in reserve because of the Union demonstration in South Carolina, the brigade barely arrived be-fore the Union advance. Maj. George C. Gratten, the brigade's adjutant general, reported that Colonel Colquitt left Savannah the morning of February 16, 1864, with four regiments of his brigade—the Nineteenth, Twenty-third, Twenty-seventh, and Twenty-eighth Georgia regiments (the Sixth Georgia having al-ready moved forward). The brigade was transported by the Flor-ida, Atlantic, and Gulf Coast Railroad to Station No. 9, arriving there in the night. The next morning they commenced march-ing across the country to Madison, Florida, taking no baggage except cooking utensils and such as the men could carry in their knapsacks. The brigade halted in the evening at a river some ten or twelve miles from Madison and went into camp. About twelve o'clock at night Colonel Colquitt received a dis-patch from General Finegan stating that the enemy were ad-vancing and requesting him to move as rapidly as possible. Colonel Colquitt immediately ordered his command forward, reaching Madison the next morning at sunrise after having marched over thirty miles in twenty-four hours without leaving a man by the roadside. Trains of cars were in readiness at Madison and moved as soon as the troops could be put aboard. As the brigade passed through Lake City, it was joined by the Sixth Georgia Regiment, arriving at Olustee Station the same evening, February 18. There it was learned that the reported advance of the enemy consisted of a body of cavalry which had turned toward the south, after destroying some depots and other items. The entire day after arrival at Olustee was quiet, "and the troops enjoyed a good opportunity to rest."[120]

The day before the battle, General Finegan had the two brigades at Olustee Station organized as follows (strength figures used, showing the number of companies and the total number of troops, are those reported for the units on January 23, 1864, and are used only to give an impression of the approximate size of the units on the day of the battle):

First Brigade—Col. A. Colquitt
Sixth Georgia, 10 companies, 618
Nineteenth Georgia, 10 companies, 591
Twenty-third Georgia, 10 companies, 590
Twenty-seventh Georgia, 10 companies, 605
Twenty-eighth Georgia, 10 companies, 538
Sixth Florida Battalion, unknown

Second Brigade—Col. G. P. Harrison
Thirty-second Georgia, 10 companies, 1,036
Sixty-fourth Georgia, 10 companies, 746
First Georgia Regulars, 10 companies, 800
First Florida Battalion, unknown
Guerard's Battery, 1 company, 104

Reserves
Fourth Georgia Cavalry, 10 companies, 933
Second Florida Cavalry, unknown
Florida (Leon) Light Artillery, unknown
Chatham Artillery, 1 company, 111
Florida (Milton) Light Artillery (−), unknown[121]

It should be noted that the Florida Fifth Cavalry arrived on the twentieth, having been in Gainesville the night before, and was in poor shape after its forced march to get to Olustee. It would be committed late in the battle. Both the Georgia Fifth Cavalry and Captain Dickison's unit of the Second Florida Cavalry arrived after the battle was fought. On the morning of the battle, Finegan had available at Olustee eight regiments and three or four battalions of infantry (some question exists whether the Second Florida Battalion was present), two regiments and one battalion of cavalry, and three batteries of artillery. In strength, 4,600 infantry, less than 500 cavalry, and three batteries of artillery containing twelve guns.[122] General Seymour, by the evening of the nineteenth, had arrived back at Barber's, where he had concentrated eight infantry regiments, one mounted infantry regiment, a cavalry battalion, and three batteries and one section of artillery—in all, some 5,500 officers and men and sixteen guns.[123]

Both sides were approximately equal in strength, although both commanders would fight the battle thinking they each were heavily outnumbered. Neither commander took any significant steps to gather current information on the strength or disposition of his opponent. On the evening of the nineteenth, General Finegan was committed to the occupation and defense of a partially completed line of entrenchments at Olustee Station. On the same evening, General Seymour was preparing to make a sudden advance against an enemy believed to number four or five thousand located at Lake City and then push his mounted force forward to destroy the railroad bridge over the Suwannee River, some thirty miles beyond Lake City. Neither was preparing to fight a battle of the size that would take place the next day, or even considering the location where it did take place as a possible site for an engagement.

5

The Battle of Olustee

The First Stage

Before seven in the morning of February 20, 1864, under a clear sky with the golden sunlight starting to filter through the pines, the Union forces departed Barber's Ford in a column of brigades headed westward on the Lake City and Jacksonville road. Col. Guy V. Henry commanded the advance guard, made up of the Fortieth Massachusetts Mounted Infantry with the First Massachusetts Independent Cavalry attached and Battery B (four pieces) of the First U.S. Artillery (Elder's horse battery). Col. J. R. Hawley's brigade followed, composed of the Seventh Connecticut, Seventh New Hampshire, Eighth U.S. Colored Troops, and Battery E (six pieces) of the Third U.S. Artillery. Next in line was Col. W. B. Barton's brigade, containing the Forty-seventh New York, Forty-eighth New York, 115th New York, and Battery M (four pieces), First U.S. Artillery, with one section from Battery C (two pieces) of the Third Rhode Island Heavy Artillery attached. The trains and medical vehicles followed, and the rear was brought up by Col. James Montgomery's brigade, made up of the First North Carolina, Colored, and the Fifty-fourth Massachusetts, Colored.

Colonel Henry's mounted brigade soon outdistanced the marching elements. Strangely, from the speed of their advance and the comparative lack of security precautions, the brigade seemed to have no expectation of meeting the enemy in force. One observer who was present noted that speed rather than security seemed to be the rule; much of the artillery and many of the guns were unloaded as the Union troops advanced. They were perhaps lulled into complacency by the constant repetition of the enemy's advance guard retreating before them, as had been happening since they had left Jacksonville. "Our policy had been to dash after them, and capture and scatter as many as possible. We had met with no repulse and few casualties. Our successes had unfortunately inspired us with a contempt for our foes."[1] The *New York Times* correspondent also noted this lack of security and thought it strange to move a column of troops through the enemy's country without flankers and with only an advance guard of cavalry to give warning.[2]

There were several possible explanations for the speed of the movement but absolutely no excuse for the lack of security. The correspondent who had noted the lack of flank security also noted in his account that on the day before, no one, including General Seymour, supposed that an advance would be made for a few days. This was evidenced by the activities of the men and officers in constructing shelters and other conveniences to provide additional comfort, something that certainly would not have been done if an immediate move was expected. "Sometime during the night General Seymour received information of the enemy's whereabouts and plans which led him to believe that by pushing rapidly forward his column, he would be able to defeat the enemy's designs and secure important military advantages. Whatever that information may have been, the events of Saturday would indicate it was by no means reliable, or that General Seymour acted upon it with too much haste."[3] Several other writers who were present on the expedition agree that General Seymour expected to meet the enemy forces at Lake City; one believed that Seymour was looking to an encounter at the Suwannee River.[4] General Seymour, in a report written after the battle, stated that he expected to meet an enemy force of between four and five thousand at or near Lake City and then push his mounted force on to destroy the railroad bridge over the Suwannee.[5]

Lieutenant Eddy, Third Rhode Island Artillery, from a bed aboard the hospital ship *Cosmopolitan* two days after the Olustee battle, wrote, "On Saturday morning, the twentieth, at seven o'clock, we started once more for a place called Lake City, thirty-six miles distant, which, if we had succeeded in occupying, we should have stopped supplies being sent to the Western armies of the enemy."[6] Lt. M. B. Grant, on the Southern side, said that the Federal troops were advancing so rapidly because they believed the Confederate forces were no larger than what had been met by Colonel Henry's force the week previous near Lake City.[7] Other than Seymour's statement in his report of the size of the enemy force he expected to meet at Lake City, there is unfortunately no record of what Seymour knew of the Confederate buildup that had been taking place during the previous week. At Sanderson, General Seymour received word that he would meet enemy forces in strength east of Lake City. One correspondent wrote, "Here [Sanderson] the most positive statements were made as to the large force which awaited the Unionists not more than ten miles beyond." Another noted that General Seymour seemed fixed on the idea of fighting a battle on the twenty-first near Lake City, despite warnings from native Floridians that Finegan and Gardner had collected a larger army than his. "All these statements seemed to make no impression on his mind."[8]

While eating lunch about 2:00 P.M. at the house of a Mrs. Canova in Sanderson, a place the general and his staff had visited on the previous advance, Captain Dana recalled that Mrs. Canova was "very saucy and said, 'You will come back faster than you go' which we took to be a brag."[9] A Union medical officer present believed General Seymour discounted the information as dubious regarding strength and position because the rebels were not thought capable of concentrating that quickly. He therefore, apparently, chose to disregard it as unreliable.[10] The opening shots of the battle were heard during the meal.

Colonel Hawley's brigade, in a formation of four columns of regiments abreast, centered on the Lake City road, had departed Barber's Ford at 7:00 A.M., following shortly behind Henry's mounted brigade. Hamilton's battery was on the road with the Seventh New Hampshire and the Seventh Connecticut to the right of the road and the Eighth U.S. Colored Troops to its left. This order was followed for about five miles until

just before Sanderson, when the Seventh Connecticut was ordered by Colonel Hawley into the road to keep one-half mile in
advance of the rest of the brigade. Colonel Hawley later reported that "2 or 3 miles beyond Sanderson we came upon
Colonel Henry's command, apparently arranged for a bivouac."[11] Considering that Henry's unit was the only security
deployed, this action seems strange. The *New York Times* correspondent reported that at the point where the two Union
units met, Henry's command had been halted by a party of five
mounted rebels who were stationed behind an old deserted
mill, a little to the left of the wood. At this location, the
road, which was south of the railroad, crossed the railroad
to the northern side to avoid a swamp. The time was noted as
2:00 P.M.[12]

Henry's brigade had been facing scattered, mounted resistance on their approach march since an hour after departing
Barber's Ford. At 1:00 P.M. a halt had been called to allow the
infantry to come up. While the brigade rested, Company D of
the First Massachusetts Independent Cavalry, Henry's brigade,
was advanced about one-half mile to a point where the highway crossed the railroad. The picket line was laid out, and the
men posted. One of its members saw only one rebel cavalryman in sight, and he was "at a safe distance, on the railroad
track." Two hours later, the same rebel cavalryman remained
there for General Seymour to see. There was, however, a growing realization that the enemy were present in great force. One
Union trooper remembered counting over one hundred enemy
infantrymen as they jumped across the railroad. Soon the
Southerners opened fire upon the Union skirmishers. The
trooper reported that Corporal Dennet from his unit came in
from the extreme right, on the highway, and "minutely described how he had seen not less than three regiments march
by a commanding officer whom all the regimental officers sa-
luted. One can see a long distance through those forests of big
pines, entirely free from undergrowth."[13] The report was disregarded by General Seymour, who continued his two lead
regiments moving forward in a skirmish-line formation.

On the morning of February 20, the Confederate forces

were located in the vicinity of the entrenchments that were being constructed under Lieutenant Grant's supervision at Olustee. Upon receiving a report that the Union forces were advancing from the east, Col. Caraway Smith, commanding the Confederate cavalry brigade, was ordered to advance and meet them to determine their position and number.[14] One of the cavalry units that had just arrived had been in Gainesville on the day before the battle. Writing some years after the war, Lawrence Jackson of the Second Florida Cavalry recalled that they had left Gainesville that night for Olustee, camping for the night some thirty-five miles from their destination. After resuming their ride in the morning, they were still some fifteen or sixteen miles from Olustee when they heard the sound of cannon. At that point the unit was ordered to strike a gallop. Just prior to arrival, the unit's commanding officer, Lt. A. H. McCormick, halted the unit, and according to Jackson:

> He rode down to about the middle of the regiment and faced us; he pulled off his hat, raised himself as high as he could in his stirrups and spoke loudly and distinctly, saying, "Comrades and soldiers of the 2nd Florida cavalry, we are going into this fight to win. Although we are fighting five or six to one, we will die but never surrender. General Seamore's [sic] army is made up largely of negroes from Georgia and South Carolina, who come here to steal, pillage, run over the state and murder, kill, and rape our wives, daughters, and sweethearts. Let's teach them a lesson. I shall not take any negro prisoners in this fight."[15]

Taking all of the cavalry available, 250 men of the Fourth Georgia under Col. Duncan L. Clinch and 202 men of the Second Florida under Lieutenant Colonel McCormick, Colonel Smith moved forward and made contact with the Union forces "about four miles from our encampment, occupying in force the second crossing of the railroad from Olustee."[16] Smith immediately reported this position to General Finegan and then directed Colonel Clinch to advance skirmishers from his unit to attack the enemy's pickets.

At ten o'clock that morning, Col. George P. Harrison of the Thirty-second Georgia, commanding the Confederate Second

Brigade, was in the entrenchments near Olustee Station. At about noon, he was instructed by General Finegan to send forward the Sixty-fourth Georgia under Col. J. W. Evans and two companies (H and E) of the Thirty-second Georgia under Captain Mobley to meet the enemy, then reported three miles to the front, to engage them lightly and fall back, drawing them on to the main Confederate defensive position.[17] Shortly after noon, Colonel Colquitt received a written order from General Finegan to take the Sixth and Twenty-eighth Georgia regiments, the Sixth Florida Battalion, and a section of two guns from Gamble's Florida battery and to proceed to the front to drive the enemy's cavalry from the railroad, which they were reported to be tearing up at a point some distance below Olustee. Colonel Colquitt was just about to start forward from Olustee when he received another order, directing Colonel Harrison to send to him the Thirty-second Georgia and First Georgia regulars. The Chatham Artillery (Capt. John F. Wheaton) and the Twenty-third Georgia were ordered to the front at the same time. Colonel Colquitt moved forward with the first group of units, giving orders for the others to follow on as soon as they could be formed.[18]

After moving forward, Colonel Colquitt came upon the Sixty-fourth Georgia formed into a square to the rear of the point where the wagon road crossed the railroad. The Confederate cavalry forward of that point was retiring in a column on each side of the road, closely pursued by Union cavalry. Colonel Colquitt ordered Colonel Evans immediately to reform the Sixty-fourth in line of battle on the left of the road. A section of Gamble's battery was moved up to take a position at the crossing, and Colonel Neal was instructed to form his Nineteenth Georgia immediately on the right of the guns. The Sixth and Twenty-eighth Georgia were then formed on the left of the Sixty-fourth, and a staff officer dispatched to direct the cavalry to form on the flanks. Accordingly, Colonel Smith took his Second Florida to the right flank, and Colonel Clinch, the Fourth Georgia to the left.[19]

Confederate general Samuel Jones, in his account of the battle, points out that the regimental commander of the Sixty-fourth Georgia, a new regiment that had never been in action before, supposing that only mounted forces were advancing against him, had formed a square to resist cavalry.[20] Colonel Colquitt arrived just in time to save the square from being ripped open by Union artillery, and his initial, timely deployment of forces in line of battle while under fire gave the Confederate forces a superiority of firepower that was the key to their success. In his report of the battle, General Finegan stated that the movement of Colonel Colquitt forward with his brigade "was predicated on the information that the enemy had only three regiments of infantry, with some cavalry and artillery."[21] Like his Union counterpart, General Finegan had done little to scout his opponent and was ignorant about the size, composition, and weapons of the force he was facing.

Capt. Winston Stephens, Second Florida Cavalry, was with the mounted force that made contact with the advancing Union troops. After engaging the oncoming skirmishers, Stephen's unit fell back, firing until they reached the position held by the Sixty-fourth. He then took up flank security of the Confederate right with "sometimes Col. McCormick commanding and sometimes I was in command."[22]

Lt. Drury Rambo, Company A of the Milton Light Artillery, was ordered at 1:00 P.M. to move his thirty-pounder Parrott gun, which had been mounted on a railroad flatcar, down the railroad until he should receive orders. He immediately ordered the gun detachment of thirteen privates and a gunner aboard and, a locomotive having been furnished, proceeded down the railroad line. As directed, he reported his presence to Colonel Colquitt.[23]

Meanwhile, Colonel Colquitt was ordered to take command of the forces which had preceded him, including the cavalry, Sixty-fourth Georgia, and the two companies of the Thirty-second Georgia. Colonel Harrison with the remainder of the Second brigade of the Confederate forces minus the First Florida battalion and the Sixth Georgia (Colquitt's brigade) was ordered forward from the entrenchments about 1:30 P.M. for the purpose of supporting Colonel Colquitt. With these troop movements, it is obvious that General Finegan had changed his original plans to have the Union forces drawn onto the defensive works being prepared at Olustee; he had instead decided to move the bulk of his units forward to make contact with the enemy. With a limited knowledge of the disposition of the Union forces or the exact nature of the ground where the contact was taking place, this was a rather risky course of action. Furthermore, although the major part of his forces were forward and, from the growing sound of battle, engaged in combact, General Finegan stayed in the vicinity of the entrenchments at Olustee until the battle was about over.

The area in which the battle was about to take place was firm, level, even ground covered by pine and relatively free from undergrowth, with good visibility through the trees. The shape of the battlefield was roughly circular, with a diameter north of the railroad of about two-thirds of a mile from north to south. (See map 6.) To the north and west, it was bordered by a continuous, dense swampy bay; to the east and south were small isolated bays. In the northern sector there was an old cleared field where later the fighting would be very severe. Except for the pond and swampy areas, the ground was readily passable. Cover was afforded individuals by the scattered pine trees, but little was available for groups. The scattered pine trees, however, would render artillery somewhat less effective. Concealment was also limited, although forces could be maneuvered without detection at a distance.

The railroad crossed the southeastern sector of the battlefield in a general northeast to southwesterly direction, curving toward due west as it approached the western extremity of the area. The road from Sanderson to Olustee entered the area north of the railroad, crossed the field diagonally to the southwest, and then crossed the railroad to the south. The initial positions of the meeting forces were the Sixty-fourth Georgia, forming at the crossing of the railroad and road, and the advance elements of Henry's mounted brigade, at the place where the road branches as it enters the tract from the east. In distance, the site of the battle was located about three miles east of Olustee and six miles west of Sanderson. When the head of the Union column reached the battle area at 2 P.M., the men

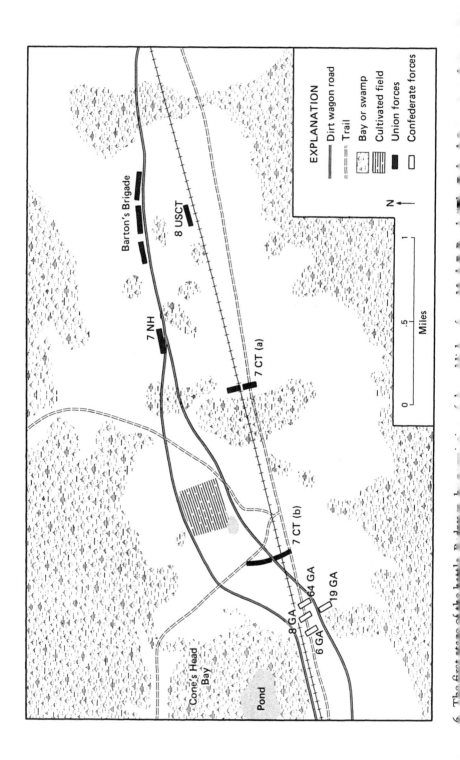

6. The first stage of the battle. Badaura hannen i i i i i lli i lli i lli i

had neither rested nor eaten since they had left Barber's some seven hours earlier and had covered sixteen tedious miles over a road that was at times loose sand, boggy turf, or covered knee-deep in water.[24]

At the junction of the Union forces belonging to Henry's and Hawley's brigades, General Seymour ordered the Seventh Connecticut to send two companies forward as skirmishers. The first two companies, under Capt. C. C. Mills and Lt. Jeremiah Townsend, moved up and deployed on the left of the railroad, with the Second Company as a reserve for the left of the line. Another company of the Seventh Connecticut moved forward to the right of the railroad, and the remainder of the regiment followed within supporting distance. Milton M. Woodford of the Seventh Connecticut was part of the advancing Union skirmish line. In a letter to his wife he described how the single line, stretching one-half mile with the men five paces apart, moved forward. "As we advanced, the enemy retired, keeping just in sight. Whenever we could get near enough to stand any chance of doing execution we would blaze away at them and they returned the fire in a way that showed that they were good marksmen, for their shots came plenty near enough, although none of us were hit."[25]

While the Confederate forces were deploying, the skirmishers from the Seventh Connecticut advanced. Although the unit was much reduced in numbers, the seven-shot repeating Spencer rifles gave it a collective firepower superior to units much larger in size. Sergeant Clement of the Independent Battalion was among the mounted Union troopers in contact with the retreating Confederate cavalry. His unit pursued cautiously at this point, until ordered by General Seymour to wheel to the left and halt in order that a probing shot from a Union cannon be fired down the road. There was no response to this shot, and the Confederate cavalry was no longer in sight because of a slight rise in the road. Samuel Elder's horse battery fired another shot and this time got a response that killed one of his horses.[26] Two companies of the Fortieth Massachusetts were ordered to the left with a view toward outflanking the Confederates but came upon a heavy line of skirmishers and were forced to withdraw to their original position.[27]

After the enemy guns had responded to Elder's reconnaissance by fire, the Seventh Connecticut was ordered forward by General Seymour to try to secure the enemy's battery. The remainder of the regiment, Third and Fourth companies, which had been in reserve, were brought up on the double upon the right of the railroad to join the line of skirmishers. Capt. B. F. Skinner, commanding the Seventh Connecticut, believed at this point the Confederates were making a flank movement to mass their advance on the Union right. What he probably saw was Colonel Colquitt extending his regiments on the left of the Confederate line. Captain Skinner pushed the line forward as rapidly as possible, paying particular attention to the enemy's guns on the left of the Union line and to the right of the railroad. After moving up two or three hundred yards, he found the enemy drawn up in a line and in a position to support their battery. He believed the enemy here showed a front of five regiments, flanked on the right and left by cavalry which made occasional demonstrations against the Union flanks but were easily turned back in disorder. Captain Skinner's men, after firing a few moments, pushed forward, thinking support was close. This advance forced the enemy back about two hundred yards in some confusion, but firing as they went. "Here I discovered the enemy was intrenched and delivered well-directed volleys of musketry."[28]

At this point Captain Skinner found his ammunition was almost expended and that he had pushed so far into the enemy's center that his line had formed a semicircle and he was taking fire from three sides. He decided to withdraw before being swallowed up, a movement he executed rapidly. The other elements of the Seventh Connecticut did little better. Captain Mills, with First Company as skirmishers and Second Company under Lieutenant Townsend in reserve, started to run into stiffening resistance and was soon almost entirely checked with his left flank now in a swamp and subjected to an intense fire from the Confederate right flank. Mills advanced his right flank a few rods to where the ground was more open and passable and ordered his men to lie down while maintaining a lively fire. In this position, his ammunition was soon exhausted, and he too withdrew his unit under pressure from an advancing enemy.[29]

Confederate captain John Wheaton, commander of the Chatham Artillery, reported that he received orders at noon to move one section of his battery to the front in company with the Sixth Georgia and the First Georgia Regulars. They had advanced about two miles when an artillery round from the Union forces (Elder's reconnaissance by fire) passed over the heads of his battery and killed a private from the Thirty-second Georgia, which was behind them. James M. Dancy later wrote that the shell exploded in the midst of where General [sic] Harrison and his staff were assembled, striking his brother, Robert F. Dancy, in the side with "a piece of shell as big as fist," knocking him off his horse and killing him instantly.[30]

At this time a courier from Colonel Colquitt arrived at the Chatham Artillery with orders for Capt. John Wheaton to move his battery out of the road and for him to report in person to the colonel. Upon doing so, Captain Wheaton was directed to post his guns one hundred yards to the right of Gamble's battery. Wheaton noted that while there was some firing of artillery and small arms from the Union side, it had not yet become general. Gamble's battery was in the rear of the infantry, with his left on the dirt road that crossed the railroad some fifty yards to the front. Wheaton's orders were to dress his battery on Gamble's and and to open fire as soon as his unit came into battery on the advancing enemy, which could now be seen about a thousand yards distant.[31]

Maj. George Gratten, Colquitt's adjutant, observed the effectiveness of the firepower being generated by the Spencer repeating rifles of the advancing, understrength Seventh Connecticut. The Sixty-fourth Georgia and Gamble's battery took the brunt of the fire, which caused considerable confusion and excitement among the inexperienced troops. The Sixty-fourth quickly lost all of its field officers and was on the point of breaking but for the coolness of the veteran Twenty-eighth Georgia on its flank, which helped restore control and ease the crisis.[32]

Colonel Colquitt, finding that the enemy were in strength,

sent a staff officer back to General Finegan to request reinforcements. The Union forces opened up with a battery of six guns,
and the rifle fire from both sides became brisk. The Sixth
Florida battalion, under Maj. P. B. Bird, came up at this time
and deployed while under fire to the right of the Nineteenth
Georgia in what would become a key position.

The first stage of the battle saw the two forces coming together in what is termed a "meeting engagement," with neither side anticipating a battle of the scope that Olustee was to
take. Neither side had preselected or made a detailed examination of the battlefield, and both sides commenced sending
units forward as they arrived on the scene, with little information about their opponent upon which to base plans or schemes
of maneuver. Both commanders were at fault in the matter of
security; General Seymour in his advance through enemy-held
country, and General Finegan for his failures to maintain better
contact with an enemy force of size in his proximity and to
select the location of the engagement. At this stage, it was anyone's victory, as both sides were close to evenly matched and
the ground offered neither side an advantage.

The Second Stage

The battle was initiated with no prior planning; the primary
idea for the Union forces seemed to be to attack whatever was
offering resistance in front of them. As this resistance solidified, General Seymour, a regular army artilleryman, massed
his artillery, placing Hamilton's and Langdon's batteries
alongside Elder's battery, which was in the center of the line
and well forward in the Napoleonic style, supported by the infantry from Hawley's brigade on either side. His intention was
to engage the enemy in front with the artillery, supported by a
regiment on either flank, while maneuvering a brigade to attack the left of the extending Confederate line.[33] The concept
involved good Napoleonic tactics, valid before the introduction
of conoidal bullets and rifled weapons. The application of such
tactics would prove disastrous for the Union forces. The sec-

ond stage of the battle, for the Union side, was characterized by the movements of the Seventh New Hampshire and the Eighth U.S. Colored Troops to take position on the right and left sides of the artillery, respectively, and somewhat forward of the guns. Elder's horse battery was already on the field, and when Hamilton's battery came up, it was deployed to the left of Elder's, with Langdon's battery later placed to the left of Hamilton's position, completing the massing of the Union artillery. (See map 7.)

As the Seventh Connecticut withdrew, dividing right and left to unmask the Seventh New Hampshire, General Seymour ordered up the remaining regiments of Hawley's brigade, which had been only a few minutes behind Henry's command as it was following the Confederate skirmishers. Colonel Hawley had been advancing with the Eighth U.S. Colored Troops and the Seventh New Hampshire abreast. He directed the Eighth U.S. Colored Troops, which had been moving along the railroad on the left, to leave the railroad, changing direction to the right, and move nearer to the highway. Leaving the Eighth to go in on the left of a pond or swamp which was near some Federal artillery, Colonel Hawley took the Seventh New Hampshire and moved to the right, sending for directions. He then met the skirmishers from the Seventh Connecticut who were falling back and, at what would prove to be a critical point in the battle, "distinctly ordered the Seventh New Hampshire to deploy on the eighth company, which would have brought the left of the line near the pond." The order was apparently misunderstood, for a portion of the regiment executed the wrong movement. Colonel Hawley, his staff officers, and Colonel Abbott, the regimental commander, attempted to correct the deployment in vain. All semblance of organization was lost in a few moments, except for about one company which faced the enemy and opened fire. The remainder constantly drifted back, suffering from the fire which "a few moments' decision would have checked, if not suppressed."[34]

The confusion in deployment of the Seventh New Hampshire was directly attributable to the conflicting orders given to it. Writing later in a unit history, a member of the

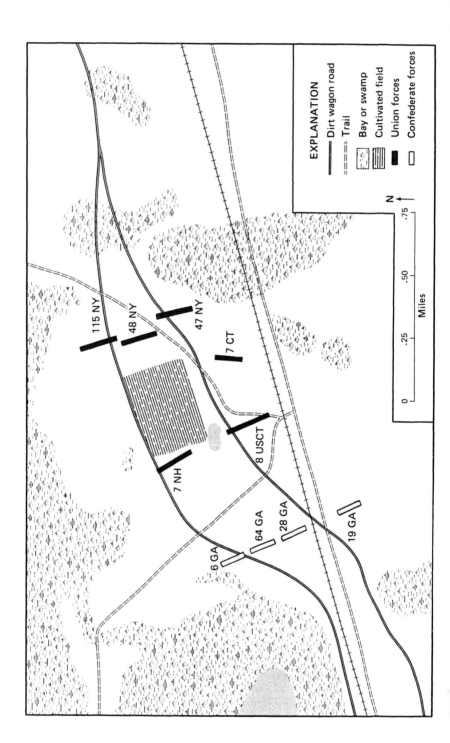

EXPLANATION

Dirt wagon road
Trail
Bay or swamp
Cultivated field
Union forces
Confederate forces

N

0   .25   .50   .75

Miles

115 NY

48 NY

47 NY

7 CT

7 NH

8 USCT

6 GA

64 GA

28 GA

19 GA

Seventh New Hampshire believed that Colonel Hawley had er-
roneously given the order to deploy on the Fifth Company,
which was the color company. Colonel Abbott repeated the
command. Hawley, realizing his command was wrong, now ordered deployment on the Tenth Company while the troops
were already trying to comply with the first order. The result
was mass confusion as units became mixed and bunched up in
disorder. The tragedy was that the unit was being subjected to
intense artillery and small-arms fire at the time it was most
vulnerable. The presence of artillery on the left would have
permitted a deployment only on the Tenth Company.

In the meantime the ground was becoming thickly dotted
with the bodies of the fallen. The men faced to the front and
did what execution was possible under the circumstances, although the whole left wing was armed with those same old
defective Springfields received in the ordered exchange for
their Spencer repeaters with some of the mounted troops but a
few days before.[35]

Sgt. Otis A. Merrill, writing home within the week after the
battle, confirmed the issuance of incorrect orders by commanders. He believed that the fault lay with Colonel Hawley,
as the brigade had marched for over a hundred yards under his
direction before the order was given to form a line of battle.
The sergeant reported that he stopped where the company
stood when the men began to start falling back until "the bullets came faster from the rear than from the front." The Tenth
Company of the Seventh New Hampshire was the only one
that stood fast and formed on the line. It fell back only when
the other companies had already fallen back, leaving it without
any support. The small-arms fire seemed to be doing most of
the damage at this time, as it was noted that the Confederate
artillery fire was too high to have an effect on the infantry line
on the right. Sergeant Merrill strongly believed that being
armed with defective weapons contributed to the breaking of
the Seventh New Hampshire.[36] One correspondent touched on
this point and gave it as the principal reason for the breaking of
the left wing of the Seventh New Hampshire.[37]

Colonel Abbott, commanding the Seventh New Hampshire,

stated in his report that he attempted to try to bring the unit back into column and restore order, but the men faltered while under fire. Confusion ensued, and in what amounted to a break, all but one hundred men who held their positions fell back to the rear. Most of the officers of the Seventh New Hampshire went back with their men, trying to rally them. One of Colonel Hawley's staff officers, Lieutenant Van Keuren, with the aid of a cavalry officer and his company, was able to stop some of the retreating soldiers; Colonel Abbott was able to stop others with cavalry help. In all, some two hundred men were thus gathered on the right of the field, where they remained firing until ordered to retreat. Colonel Abbott received no further orders from his brigade commander, Colonel Hawley, until the close of the battle.[38]

Sergeant Merrill recalled a remarkable display of courage and fortitude that took place during the confusion by Herman Maynard, better known as "Shaker," of Company C, of the Seventh New Hampshire.

> "Shaker's" arm was broken and badly shattered, and he sat behind a tree and shouted to the men to "Rally around the flag!" One of the men, whose finger had been shot away, was mourning over his misfortune in the hearing of "Shaker," who laughed at him and told him to look at his (Shaker's) arm. The next morning I went to the hospital at Barbour's Plantation to see some of the men, and there found "Shaker" with his arm in a sling, while with the well arm he was assisting to care for others, and cheerfully said, "Glad it was no worse."[39]

Another example of heroism was demonstrated by color-bearer Sgt. Thomas H. Simington of Company B, who "obeyed every word or signal, and sometimes faced the enemy alone."[40]

A truism taught all novice military leaders is "Order, counterorder, disorder." In the opening stages of the battle of Olustee, the Union forces were deprived of the effective services of a proven, veteran regiment. While later criticism would tarnish, undeservedly, the reputation of the Seventh New Hampshire, the blame more properly would lie with the general who ordered half of the unit to exchange their Spencer

repeaters for largely unserviceable weapons and with their regimental and brigade commanders for issuing conflicting orders
at a critical time. Had that unit been properly deployed and
able to use their full firepower, there might have been a different conclusion to the battle. Certainly the presence of three
hundred new recruits at this time was of no assistance.

The artillery that Colonel Hawley had noticed when the
Eighth U.S. Colored Troops was going forward to the left of a
pond was Hamilton's battery of the Third U.S. Artillery. Upon
the general engagement of the pickets, Colonel Henry had gone
forward to reconnoiter the Confederate position. Returning, he
informed Captain Hamilton, in General Seymour's presence,
that by positioning two sections of artillery at a spot he would
designate, it would be possible to enfilade the enemy's line.
The two sections were then advanced but, upon coming into
battery, were subjected to a brisk fire from a more extended
line of infantry than had been first observed. Captain Hamilton
noted that his battery was about 250 yards from the right of the
Confederate infantry, which was extended by an oblique line of
cavalry leading off to their right as far as he could see toward
the woods. Realizing it was a poor position, Hamilton was further handicapped by the deployment of the Eighth U.S. Colored Troops, which filled the intervals of his pieces, limiting
their ability to fire. At the same time, Hamilton felt that if he
limbered up and withdrew to a more advantageous position,
the inexperienced troops would run before the second line
came up to support.[41]

Captain Hamilton's battery came under intense fire from the
Confederate right, which wounded many of his gunners and
himself. Captain Langdon's battery took position on his left,
but at this time, Captain Hamilton directed Lt. John R. Myrick
to "get off the pieces" and reported to General Seymour who
sent him off the battlefield. Captain Hamilton recalled that his
own men did well, but the group of men attached to his battery
from the *Enfants Perdus* (Lost Children) behaved badly under
fire.[42] The *Enfants Perdus* were men from "Independent" battalions who had been a source of trouble in the Department of
the South. For this expedition, they had been divided up among

several of the veteran units to fill the ranks left vacant by the men home on leave. During this battle they proved to be a problem also to the other units to which they were assigned.

Lieutenant Eddy of Hamilton's battery, writing two days after the battle from the hospital steamer *Cosmopolitan* in Port Royal harbor, noted that the battery had gone in with eighty-two men, fifty horses, four guns, and four officers. In twenty minutes' time they lost forty-five men, forty horses, two guns, and all four officers.[43]

The Eighth U.S. Colored Troops had little in the way of advance warning of the impending battle. In a letter written to his sister, Lt. Oliver Wilcox Norton recalls marching some twelve miles that morning before reaching Sanderson, where the Eighth was halted. A few shots were heard, but the assumption was that the Union cavalry had met some pickets, since the main enemy forces were supposed to be at Lake City, still some twelve miles distant. After resuming the march, Norton was startled by the firing of artillery but supposed it was Elder's horse battery, which was with the advance guard. With an increase of firing, it began to be realized that a "brush" might be about to take place. After leaving the railroad along which the unit had been advancing, and when within about one thousand yards of the enemy, an aide came dashing through the woods to the unit and the order to "double-quick march" was given. The Eighth U.S. Colored Troops turned into the woods and ran in the direction of the firing for about half a mile until they reached the batteries north of the railroad and on the left of the Union line. General Seymour directed Col. Charles W. Fribley to "put your regiment in" and then left. With knapsacks on and weapons unloaded, the unit ran forward about one-half mile to within two hundred yards of the enemy and attempted to form a line and load their weapons while under severe fire from the Confederate right. In their initial engagement, the men at first were stunned, bewildered, and did not know what to do. They curled to the ground, and as men fell around them they seemed terribly scared, but gradually they recovered their senses and commenced firing. "And here was the great trouble—they could not use their arms to advantage. We have had very little practice in firing, and though they could stand and be killed, they could not kill a concealed enemy fast enough to satisfy my feelings."[44]

Writing to his father a few days later, Norton commented on the unit's preparation for its bloody baptism of fire. He noted that the regiment had been drilled too much for dress parade and too little for the field. "They could march well, but not shoot rapidly or with effect. Colonel Fribley had applied time and time again for permission to practice his regiment in target firing, and been always refused."[45]

Colonel Hawley, commanding the brigade to which the Eighth was attached, claimed the unit had reported to him only some two or three days before the battle, and he was unaware until afterward that they had never had a day's practice in loading and firing. He commented, "Old troops finding themselves so greatly overmatched, would have run a little and re-formed—with or without orders. The black men stood to be killed or wounded—losing more than 300 out of 550."[46] The regimental surgeon of the Eighth U.S. Colored Troops paid tribute to the courage of the men of his unit.

> Here they stood for two hours and a half, under one of the most terrible fires I ever witnessed; and here, on the field of Olustee, was decided whether the colored man had the courage to stand without shelter, and risk the dangers of the battlefield; and when I tell you that they stood with a fire in front, on their flank, and in their rear, for two hours and a half, without flinching, and when I tell you the number of dead and wounded, I have no doubt as to the verdict of every man who has gratitude for the defenders of his country, white or black.[47]

Colonel Fribley ordered the Eighth to fall back slowly, which the men did, firing as they retired. The colonel then fell mortally wounded, and command devolved upon Major Burritt, who received two wounds and left the field, leaving the regiment in the vicinity of Hamilton's guns. Capt. R. C. Bailey, commander of the company on the extreme right of the regiment, now took over as its commander. Although the unit was later criticized for its performance, one correspondent wrote that, considering that this was the first time the regiment had been under fire, it behaved remarkably well. He labeled as false the reports that it got into confusion and ran from the field. Noting the congestion and the limited maneuver area, the correspondent reflected on the limited options open to the Eighth. "To retreat at that time was impossible, for the road was filled with troops coming up, and the wood on either side would not admit of passage on the flank."[48]

When the fire became general, Surgeon Adolph Majer, on General Seymour's staff, began looking for a convenient ambulance depot. First riding to the right toward a couple of log houses, which were the only ones within miles, he found them too exposed. He spotted a cluster of pine trees two hundred yards to the rear of the Union left and directed that the twelve ambulances be drawn up in line and the surgeons prepare their instruments and equipment for use. As the roar of the battle escalated, the men began arriving, some walking, some on litters, and others in open ambulance wagons "first in single drops, then trickling, after a while in a steady stream, increasing from a single row to a double and treble, and finally into a mass."[49] Within less than an hour of the commencement of the battle, stray cannon shot breaking off parts of the pine trees forced the relocation of the ambulance depot one mile farther to the rear.

For the Confederate forces, the second stage of the battle involved less movement in the critical areas. The positions of the Twenty-eighth and Nineteenth Georgia on the right of the line, with the Nineteenth Georgia overlapping the Union left flank, enabled these units to pour a devastating fire in on the Union left as it was deploying. The Second Florida Cavalry, on the right flank and occasionally fighting dismounted, added something; how much it added would be the subject of an inquiry after the battle. The Sixty-fourth Georgia and the two companies of the Thirty-second Georgia that had initially occupied the position at the crossing of the road and the railroad track were shifted to the left of the Twenty-eighth Georgia and to the north of the railroad. The Sixth Georgia was sent still farther to the left to avoid what appeared to be a flanking movement being made by the Union troops. It was more probably the de-

ployment of the Seventh New Hampshire. Upon the completion of these troop deployments, Colonel Colquitt ordered the
Confederate line to advance. As he probed the strength of the
Union line, he sent back to General Finegan for reinforcements.

When this stage of the battle ended, the two advanced Union
regiments, the Seventh New Hampshire and the Eighth U.S.
Colored Troops, were shattered, taking heavy casualties from a
sustained musketry fire from four Confederate regiments plus
two companies of the Thirty-second, on line, and supported by
a section of artillery. The right of the Confederate line overlapped the left of the Union line where a green regiment (the
Eighth U.S. Colored Troops) was subjected to fire from two
regiments supported by cavalry occasionally fighting dismounted. The Union artillery was in an exposed position too
far forward, with its firing severely restricted by the presence of
friendly troops. As the infantry support dissolved, the exposed
artillerymen and their horses were being rapidly decimated by
accurate, small-arms fire.

The Third Stage

Colonel Barton's New York brigade, with Langdon's battery
attached, had been second in the column of brigades that composed the main body of the Union forces departing Barber's.
The initial formation of the brigade was in column of regiments, with Captain Langdon's battery, Battery M, First U.S.
Artillery, at about the middle of the brigade. The battery consisted of four light twelve-pounder brass guns and, with Lt.
Henry H. Metcalf's section of two guns from Captain James's
Third Rhode Island Volunteer Artillery, the brigade contained a
total of six guns. As the brigade approached Olustee, the firing
that could be heard was increasing in intensity. Colonel Barton
halted briefly and deployed one regiment on the right and two
on the left. When they again continued, the brigade moved forward in three columns, the regiments by the flank, and the
battery in a column of pieces.

An hour went by, during which the brigade halted a number

of times without covering much distance, the sound of the firing occurring with fewer intervals between the shots until it became almost a continuous sound of musketry. An aide now galloped to Captain Langdon, who brought orders to "come at once." He was shortly followed by a second aide whose message was to "come up as quickly as possible."[50] Captain Langdon moved up to where Captain Hamilton was standing with General Seymour and, after a short while, was sent over to the left, where help was needed. While moving to that location, he was overtaken by an aide who told him to send one section of guns to the right. Without stopping, Captain Langdon detached Lt. Tully McCrea's section of two guns and continued on with the four guns he had left.

Captain Langdon took position about 100 to 150 yards to the left rear of Elder's battery, which appeared to be on the extreme left of the line. Not being able to see the enemy, he fired a few rounds at a line of smoke in front of him but, dissatisfied with lack of results, limbered up and moved farther to the left, where he started to receive intensive rifle fire. As he was about to return fire, one of his caissons passed in front of his guns, masking their fire and preventing them from firing at the Confederate line. The drivers of the caisson, under fire from the nearby Confederate line, took off, leaving the caisson and horses entangled in some trees. Lt. Henry Metcalf's section of two guns from Company C, Third Rhode Island Artillery, suddenly limbered up and left for the rear, under orders (Captain Langdon later found out) from Capt. Samuel S. Elder, who thought they were in a dangerous position. Metcalf's section had been on the extreme left of the Union position, engaging the approaching Southern cavalrymen with three-and-one-half-and four-second shells, mixed with an occasional round of canister, until the Confederates were within fifty yards of his guns. Then Captain Elder ordered him to pull back, which he did, sending one of his guns back to the rear to act as reserve with the caissons, as all of his horses were killed or disabled.

Captain Langdon felt that his position was now becoming untenable and decided to move his remaining two guns. As he was limbering up, one of his limbers got caught in a tree and cost him time and casualties before he could correct the situation. He was able to fire at a group of advancing cavalry toward his left rear, with help from Metcalf's guns now farther to the rear, forcing the cavalry back. Seeing a sudden advance of the Confederate line toward the Union center, Langdon abandoned his attempts to pull back and instead directed the fire of his two guns to the right and obliquely across the front of the Union troops.

The battle intensified, and Captain Langdon soon found himself down to seven men. He requested more men from General Seymour, who was standing nearby, but was told none was available. The Union line now started to fall back, and Langdon noticed Lieutenant McCrea being carried off wounded after losing one of his guns. He recalled seeing very little of the infantry that was supposed to be protecting his position from the front or on the left except for small groups of from two to ten men huddling in and around his caissons, some firing through or over his battery. One individual stood out in his memory. A large, powerful man with a blue regimental flag took position to the left of Langdon's guns, in the position vacated by Metcalf. The color-bearer "stood there manfully and bravely to the last, and with but 2 or 3 companions, sometimes entirely alone; what became of him I am unable to say."[51]

Capt. John Keely of the Nineteenth Georgia was part of the Confederate line that was pressing on the Union center. He recalled that his unit had a good start and were hard to stop, when a battery was wheeled into position by the enemy and opened on them with grape and canister shot, doing much damage. The Nineteenth Georgia was halted, dressed, and ordered to charge this battery, which it did, killing the horses, defeating its infantry supports, and capturing the guns. While doing this, five of Captain Keely's company were killed and wounded while successively they grasped the flag as it fell from its previous bearer.[52]

Captain Langdon reported that he lost eleven men killed on the field and twenty-three wounded; he also lost twenty-eight horses killed (principally at the guns), eleven horses wounded, three of his four guns, two caissons, and two limbers.[53] Captain Hamilton was Seymour's chief artillery officer, whose job included advising General Seymour (also a career artilleryman) as to the disposition of the artillery. Hamilton later claimed that he had been too busy acting on the line of infantry as a general staff officer at the time and, if free to do so, would not have directed Langdon's battery into the position it took. He felt the sacrifice of the five pieces of artillery was the price of saving the Union left and keeping "a simple defeat or beating back" from becoming a rout.[54]

As the Sixth Florida battalion and the Twenty-third Georgia arrived on the field, Colonel Colquitt quickly fed them into the Confederate line of battle. The Twenty-third Georgia went in on the left of the Sixty-fourth Georgia; the Sixth Florida battalion, assigned to the right flank, further overlapped the Union left, adding to the Confederate firepower directed at that part of the Union line. (See map 8.) One section of Captain Wheaton's Chatham Artillery had initially been to the right of Gamble's battery on the extreme right of the Confederate line. When the firing had become general, the Chatham Artillery, following orders, fired and prepared to follow the infantry as it advanced. Captain Wheaton, however, looking to his left, noticed that Gamble's battery had ceased firing and was the scene of great confusion. Some of the horses had become unmanageable and were running down the road at full speed and without their drivers. The trail of Gamble's twelve-pounder howitzer had been crushed during the recoil action of the gun, but the crew continued firing until the broken end of the trail was so deeply embedded into the earth as to make the gun unserviceable. Wheaton was ordered to move to a position directly in front of Gamble's battery, keeping his battery as close to the center of the Confederate line as possible, and move to the front as the infantry advanced.[55]

Lt. Drury Rambo, Milton Light Artillery, was still standing by with his thirty-pounder Parrott gun mounted on the railroad flatcar awaiting orders from Colonel Colquitt. From his position, he judged that because of the thick pines that intervened, any firing of his gun might do as much damage to his own troops as those of the enemy. He did receive orders some two

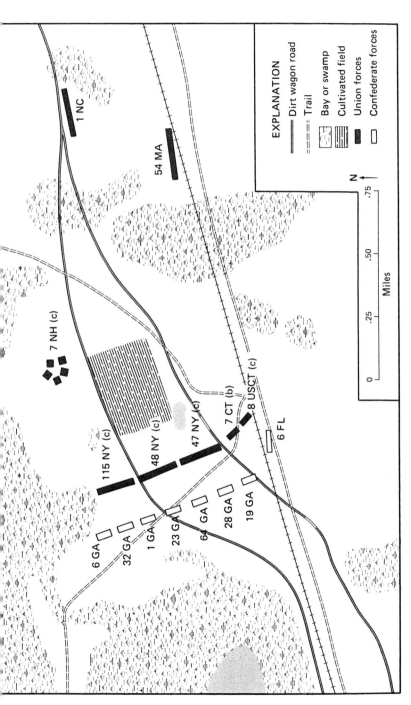

8. The third stage of the battle. Redrawn, by permission of the publisher, from Boyd, "Federal Campaign," p. 3.

EXPLANATION

——— Dirt wagon road
===== Trail
Bay or swamp
Cultivated field
Union forces
Confederate forces

N

0   .25   .50   .75

Miles

1 NC

54 MA

7 NH (c)

115 NY (c)

48 NY (c)

47 NY (c)

7 CT (b)

8 USCT (c)

6 FL

6 GA

32 GA

1 GA

23 GA

64 GA

28 GA

19 GA

hours later to throw a few shells among the Union troops, which he did. In the process of firing, his gun became damaged when five spokes of the right wheel broke from the recoil.[56] Surprisingly, after the battle a number of reports mentioned the railroad gun, greatly exaggerating its actual participation.

Col. George P. Harrison was already moving up to the front with the Second Brigade from the entrenchments at Olustee when he received Colonel Colquitt's message requesting that he move up quickly. He brought with him the remainder of the Thirty-second Georgia, the First Georgia Regulars, Bonaud's battalion, and one section of Guerard's light battery, arriving soon at the place at which the road crossed the railroad tracks. Colonel Harrison was given command of the left of the Confederate line and assigned a position on the left between the Twenty-third and Sixth Georgia regiments, the Sixth Georgia being moved to the extreme left. The Chatham Artillery was ordered to the center of the line, and the section of Guerard's battery moved to the extreme right flank with orders not to fire unless the enemy advanced.[57] Shortly after having taken position, Colonel Harrison was informed by Colonel Colquitt that he was in the correct position. The Confederate forces now started to advance.

Col. William B. Barton brought his brigade onto the field *en echelon* in three parallel lines, with the Forty-seventh New York on the left, the Forty-eighth New York in the center, and the 115th New York on the extreme right flank. The Forty-eighth was split, a part of the regiment to the right of Hamilton's battery, and another part of the regiment to the left.[58] The brigade occupied the same ground recently vacated by the Seventh New Hampshire in its retreat and was soon subjected to the same concentrated fire. The 115th New York swept forward in line "in the face of a galling fire, through reeds higher than our heads, over logs and fences, until the hateful columns of southern grey were plainly visible." The unit halted and, as one of its members later described the scene, the battle was now a continuous roar on both sides, lasting for the next three long hours with no lull. "The leaden messengers of death hailed down in increasing torrents. Grape and canister swept by with hideous music, and shell after shell tore through our ranks and burst amid heaps of our wounded heroes."[59]

The 115th New York lost 7 officers and 289 men killed, wounded, or missing. The correspondent from the *New York Tribune* corroborated the carnage, describing the rapid and furious cannonade and concentric fire. The cannon shots generally crashed among the trees and brought down branches upon the wounded in the rear, adding injuries upon the helpless men and their attendant surgeons. The enemy's sharpshooters on the opposite side of the railroad, in the treetops or the long grass, poured in bullets upon the bleeding fugitives and succeeded in making it necessary to remove the wounded eight miles away to Sanderson. The stream of disabled men naturally took the railroad track as the easiest path from the battlefield, and many were killed in their flight.[60]

A wounded member of the 115th New York, on the extreme right flank, recalled that in his movement to the rear upon being wounded, he came across a surgeon with about twenty wounded lying around him, engaged in the bloody work of amputation.

> Just then a cruel shell burst in their midst, and sent the mangled remains of several of them flying in all directions.
> I turned away from the sickening sight with horror.
> I next approached the quarter of our own surgeon, and found him surrounded by fifty wounded, his arms crimsoned with blood, and himself engaged in cutting out balls. With the stream of wounded men from different regiments, I hurried on towards Sanderson.[61]

The New York brigade's commander, Colonel Barton, noted that the fire his unit was receiving was both direct on the front and oblique on the flanks, both artillery and musketry, and rapid, accurate, and well sustained. From the intensity of the fire being received, Barton believed that he was outnumbered and recalled that the enemy was taking good advantage of cover.[62] In the few hours the brigade was engaged, Colonel Barton lost a total of 811 men killed, wounded, and missing. Both the writer from the 115th New York and the one from the

Forty-eighth New York agreed that the Union artillery was placed too far forward (one said Hamilton's battery was within 150 yards of the Confederate position), allowing the rebel sharpshooters to pick off the artillerymen with fatal precision.[63]

Colonel Hawley stated that after he tried in vain to help rally the Seventh New Hampshire, he moved to the rear and found there the officers and men of the Seventh Connecticut along with the unit's colors and buglers. Once the New York brigade was committed, Colonel Hawley moved the Seventh Connecticut a little to the left and rear of that brigade's left and sent for the reserve ammunition to replenish the Seventh's supply, which was almost exhausted. After being resupplied, the Seventh Connecticut moved forward to fill a gap that had opened as the regiments on either side of them moved forward. The Confederate lines now appeared some six hundred yards distant and a little to the left. The Seventh Connecticut took them under fire with the sights of their Spencer rifles set at six hundred yards, which appeared to check the enemy advance. The Seventh Connecticut remained in this position until recalled to cover the retreat.[64]

Capt. Romanzo C. Bailey, now in command of the shattered Eighth U.S. Colored Troops, while trying to get control of that unit, noticed what he believed to be at least a regiment moving down the railroad to attack his left flank. With his regiment's ammunition almost exhausted, he took the responsibility of attempting to withdraw the regiment from the field, moving by the right flank, passing to the rear of the Fifty-fourth Massachusetts now coming on to the field. The Eighth remained to the rear until the retreat commenced.[65] In the process of retreating, the Eighth U.S. Colored Troops lost its national colors.

Lt. Elijah Lewis of the Eighth reported that in the retrograde movement, the Eighth did not move directly to the rear, but obliquely to the right, passing near where the colors were. Noticing a flag on the ground, he picked it up and discovered it was the national colors. At that time, one of the artillery battery officers rode up to him and said, "Don't leave the battery;

bring your flag and rally the men around it."[66] Lieutenant Lewis carried the colors up to the gun, where he was told by Lt. Oliver Norton, also of the Eighth, to give the flag to one of the men and help form some sort of line. Lt. Andrew F. Ely also came up to help collect the men of the Eighth. One man observed that "the guns had been jammed up so indiscriminately, and so close to the enemy's lines, that the gunners were shot down as fast as they made their appearance."[67]

Suddenly, the horses attached to the limber of one of the guns bolted and ran through the group of the Eighth that the officers were trying to rally. Lieutenant Lewis gave the colors to one of the men and grabbed the bridle of the near leader and, with the help of some of his men, stopped the horses. This diversion apparently ended the efforts to rally the men, and what was left of the unit continued to fall back. Not until sometime later was it realized that the colors had been left to be captured along with Hamilton's guns.[68] The regimental colors had already cost the lives of three of the Eighth's colorbearers. Sergeant Taylor of Company D, who carried the regiment's battle flag, had his right hand nearly shot off but hung on to the colors with his left and brought it out with him.[69]

Surgeon A. P. Aeichhold, of the Eighth U.S. Colored Troops, found his hands full with the wounded. About a dozen Confederate cavalrymen fired a volley into where the wounded were being treated along the railroad, knowing it was a hospital, and were about to charge when the Fifty-fourth arrived and drove them off. Sensing defeat, Aeichhold sent as many of the wounded as he could toward Barber's and then dispatched a crowded ambulance. He was forced to leave a few of the wounded behind, where they probably fell into the hands of the enemy. "It could not be helped; I had but one ambulance to a regiment, and the railroad was useless because we have no locomotive."[70]

The third stage of the battle saw the arrival of the remainder of the Confederate troops from the entrenchments, who were then moved into the extending Confederate line. One unit, the Sixth Florida battalion, was placed on the right flank, which proved to be a key position because its fire reinforced that of the Nineteenth and Twenty-eighth Georgia regiments on the Union left, contributing to the crumbling of that portion of the line. The other units were placed on the Confederate left, where it appeared a flanking movement was taking place by the Union forces. In actuality, it was the abortive deployment of the Seventh New Hampshire followed by its withdrawal and subsequent replacement by Colonel Barton's New York brigade. The Confederate troops on this flank also overlapped the Union flank, with the result that a concentric fire was being concentrated on the Union position. As a number of correspondents have noted, the Confederate artillery was not effective, but the musketry fire was producing heavy casualties. At the conclusion of this stage of the battle, both forces were facing each other in an extended line, and the battle had become general. The Confederate forces were attempting to move forward, while the Union forces were resisting stubbornly.

The Fourth Stage

Confederate major George C. Gratten, Colonel Colquitt's adjutant general, recalled that after the Confederate line had been formed with all of the regiments on line, the commanders of the cavalry were ordered to press upon the Union flanks while the infantry charged them in front. He noted, "Col. Smith dismounted his men and moved them out as skirmishers, but being badly armed and poorly drilled, they failed to attack with effect."[71] Colonel Caraway claimed that on two occasions he discovered the enemy attempting to cross the railroad on the right of the Confederate line and directed Lieutenant Colonel McCormick to dismount his troops and drive them back, which was done.[72] Capt. Winston Stephens, Second Florida Cavalry, felt exhilarated by the action.

> The enemy pressed us quite hard but our artillery and infantry opened up and the boys yelled and went to work as men can only work who are in earnest. Then the scene was grand and exciting

. . . I felt like I could wade through my weight in wildcats. The 2d Cav. was dismounted to fight on foot and I think we did good work. We went in with a wild yell and the Yanks and negroes give way, then we would remount and follow up and we continued to do that until the fight ended.[73]

Maj. G. W. Scott's Fifth Florida Cavalry Battalion was not brought onto the field until late in the afternoon because the men and horses were worn out from hard riding during the previous twenty-four hours. When they arrived, they joined Lieutenant Colonel McCormick on the right. Col. Duncan L. Clinch attempted a movement on horse but got bogged down in a marsh and accomplished little. The colonel was wounded in the leg early in the action, and Captain Brown took over command of the Fourth Georgia Cavalry.[74]

General Finegan now sent a written order to Colonel Colquitt assigning him to the command of all troops present at the front; he also sent forward all the troops that remained in the entrenchments at Olustee except for two guns of Gamble's battery and a small battalion. General Finegan advised Colonel Colquitt that if hard-pressed, he was to fall back to Olustee Station. Major Gratten observed that Colonel Colquitt was well aware of the dangers that such a retrograde movement would entail under the existing situation and "reposing every confidence in his troops who were fighting with a steadiness never excelled—ordered a general charge."[75]

After bringing his right section into battery at the center of the Confederate position, Captain Wheaton of the Chatham Artillery found that these two guns were the only Confederate artillery then in action against the Union's sixteen guns. He sent back to Colonel Colquitt to request another section be sent up, which was approved. The Federal artillery batteries were only five hundred yards away, and Colonel Colquitt directed Captain Wheaton to direct his fire against one of them in support of the Nineteenth and Twenty-eighth Georgia, who were moving forward to take it. (See map 9.) Lieutenant Rowe of Company E of the Twenty-eighth was later commended for planting his unit's colors over the two guns on the Federal left which were captured as that part of the line appeared to be giving way; the center and the right, however, were standing firm.[76] The Chatham Artillery's fire was then shifted to another part of the line, and the infantry moving forward seized three more of the Federal guns. The fighting was particularly intense on the left of the Confederate line where the Southerners faced the New York brigade. Capt. Henry Cannon and about 150 men of the First Georgia Regulars occupied a defensive position on the portion of the line that consisted of a depression filled with logs to the front. Captain Cannon refused to take cover with his men, remaining standing with his sword drawn, calling on the men to be steady. Lt. John Porter Fort urged him to take cover, but the captain was almost immediately hit. "He staggered backward saying, 'I am a dead man.' With my left arm under him I lowered him to the ground. He died at once."[77]

The Chatham Artillery moved forward to support the advancing infantry but were halted by the arrival of Union reinforcements and soon found themselves hard-pressed and running out of ammunition. Fortunately, the left section of the Chatham Artillery came up when the right section had expended all of their shells except canister, which had proved ineffective in the woods. The Chatham Artillery was now located at the very front of the Confederate line, directing their fire against whatever portions of the Federal line appeared to be giving the most trouble.[78]

At about 2:30 P.M., Colonel Montgomery's black brigade was resting at the road crossing. Small-arms fire had been heard in the distance, joined after a while with the sound of cannon. "'That's home-made thunder,' said one man. 'I don't mind the thunder if the lightning don't strike me!' was the response. Another remarked, 'I want to go home.' 'You'll stay forever, maybe!' was the reply."[79]

An orderly galloped up to the Fifty-fourth Massachusetts calling for the commanding officer, Col. Edward N. Hallowell, who was given an order to advance rapidly. In short order, the regiment was moving forward at the double-quick toward the sound of battle. As the troops hurried on, many started to

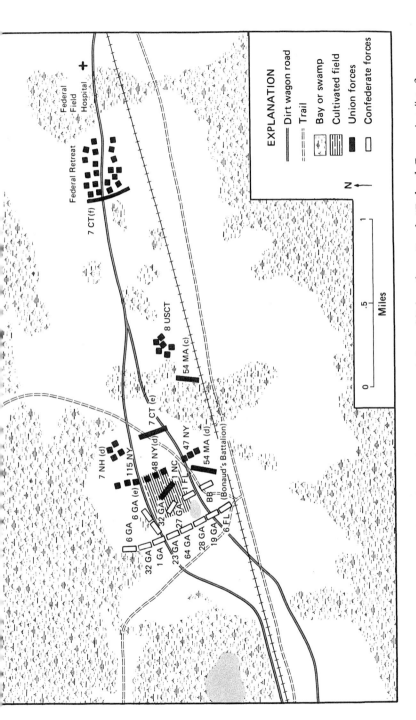

9. The fourth stage of the battle. Redrawn, by permission of the publisher, from Boyd, "Federal Campaign," p. 3.

lighten their loads by dropping haversacks, blankets, and knapsacks. At the railroad crossing, they were met by an aide from
General Seymour bringing the order to move forward into battle. Nearing the battlefield, amid the escalating sound of cannon shots and musketry, they came upon a dispiriting scene of
hundreds of wounded and stragglers. Lieutenant Emilio recalled hearing all sorts of discouraging shouts as the regiments
moved up such as, "We're badly whipped!" "You'll all get
killed." They pressed on, passing part of a disabled battery also
going to the rear, and, led on by Sergeant Cezar of Company D,
found breath to shout their battle cry, "Three cheers for Massachusetts and seven dollars a month!"[80]

The Fifty-fourth Massachusetts, minus the two companies
left back for security at Barber's, which gave it a strength of 13
officers and 497 men, arrived on the battlefield in company
with the First North Carolina about 4:00 P.M. The Fifty-fourth
went into the left of the line; the First North Carolina moved
forward on the right of the Union line, forming an angle of
about 120 degrees with the line of the Fifty-fourth Massachusetts. Colonel Barton's battered New York brigade retired
as the black brigade came up. The center of the line now was
the Seventh Connecticut, which had moved forward a short
distance, lay down, and with sights set at four hundred yards,
were firing their Spencer rifles at the enemy, who was "fairly in
view."[81]

A soldier with the Forty-eighth New York later recalled their
arrival as an incident that was well remembered. At a time
when most felt the day was lost, the two fresh regiments
moved up between the Forty-seventh and Forty-eighth New
York regiments on the double-quick into the battle, cheered by
those shattered regiments. Their arrival staggered the enemy
for a moment and prevented an effective pursuit.[82]

Lt. Col. William N. Reed, commanding the First North Carolina in the absence of Col. James C. Beecher, headed the regiment with sword in hand as they attacked the Confederate
position, initially driving them back. The Southerners rallied
shortly, however, and poured in a destructive fire on the fresh
Northern troops, killing Major Boyle and wounding the reg-

imental adjutant, William C. Manning, who had previously been wounded at Malvern Hill. Manning insisted on remaining until struck a second time. Colonel Reed, upon learning of the fact, embraced him, and implored him to leave the field. "The next moment the two friends were stretched side by side; the colonel had received his own death-wound. But the two colored regiments had stood in the gap, and saved the army!"[83]

A tribute to the First North Carolina was made by yet another observer of their performance that day. At this stage, he believed that the First North Carolina and the Fifty-Fourth Massachusetts held the left of the Union line, aided by artillery, and even pressed the enemy backward. The battle waged furiously all along the line, and the slaughter was terrible, yet each man seemed determined to do his whole duty.

> No regiment went into action more gallantly, or did better execution than the First North-Carolina (colored) troops. Their white comrades generally take pleasure in awarding them this honor. Men were dropping constantly all along the line, but the living fought all the more bravely. These freedmen evidently preferred falling on the field of battle to falling into the hands of their barbarous foes. This regiment was not in action over two hours and a half and yet its loss in officers and enlisted men was nearly as heavy as that of any other regiment.[84]

Lt. John R. Myrick, Battery E, Third U.S. Artillery, found himself left in command of the four artillery pieces belonging to his battery after Capt. John Hamilton and Lieutenants Eddy and Dodge were wounded and had left the field. Captain Hamilton's last instructions had been to get the pieces off, which Lieutenant Myrick tried to do. The location of the battery at this time was to the left and in advance of where Captain Elder's battery (now pulled back) had been. Lieutenant Myrick got two pieces to the rear but could not get off the remaining two pieces because the Confederate rifle fire killed or disabled the horses and men engaged in the effort. Lieutenant Myrick took the two guns he did manage to get off to the rear and joined Elder's battery and the remaining section of Lt. David Irwin's from Light Company E, Third U.S. Artillery, which was on Elder's left. Lieutenant Myrick continued firing on line with Elder's battery until nearly dark, when a wound forced him to turn his section over to Lieutenant Irwin and go to the rear.[85]

An officer of the Fifty-fourth Massachusetts believed the fault for the loss of guns rested with the artillerymen themselves. Writing to his father on March 7, 1864, about the loss of guns by Hamilton's and Langdon's batteries, Lt. C. M. Duren cited the loss of the guns by the regular artillery units as disgraceful. He mentioned that the artillerymen claimed that they were not being supported and their men and horses were all shot, "but I saw the Limbers and the Caissons—*fully horsed* and men enough to drive them leaving the field without their *guns*. Shameful!"[86] What Lieutenant Duren might have seen were the *Enfants Perdus*, who were assigned to the artillery but deserted their units during the battle.

A soldier in the Forty-eighth New York had an experience that stayed fresh in his mind a long time. Sgt. Henry Lang had been taken prisoner at Olustee; writing some twenty years after the battle from Budapest, Hungary, he recalled finding himself alone among the guns abandoned by Battery M, firing away at the Southerners with the sixty rounds he had in his pocket. As the enemy approached, moving from tree to tree, he found his canteen, haversack, and even the skirts of his blouse shot away as his ammunition was running out. After firing his fifty-seventh round, his leg was smashed by an incoming bullet. A friendly hand assisted him to a tree and then fled to escape capture by the oncoming Confederate line.

The first Southerners to arrive came rushing to the tree where he was and asked him if he was the man who had been firing from among the guns. Telling them he was, they all exclaimed, "Bully boy!" One asked him how many Union troops were present, and he told them about fifteen thousand. They then spoke about the Union regiments that had made such a devilish noise with their sharpshooters. Flushed with victory, the Confederate soldiers left him and moved about three hundred yards farther and called a halt.

Sergeant Lang grew fainter and fainter and yet, with an iron determination, raised himself from faintness, cut open his trousers, and, with the only handkerchief found about him and the help of a stick, succeeded in stopping the bleeding of his wound. Taking out his pipe and finding just enough tobacco, he began to smoke to keep away faintness and kill the fear that grew apace with the darkness spreading over the battlefield. While so doing, he could hear the groans of the dying and wounded and the blasphemous language of some marauding soldiers who were ill-treating wounded Negroes.

Two young Confederate soldiers now came up and, by holding a lighted match to his face, recognized him as one of the Forty-eighth Regiment. They inquired about their home in Savannah, which they had not seen during the war; they were sons of merchants of that city. Sergeant Lang could give them very little information, except what had been heard from the city through runaway soldiers at Fort Pulaski. At last one of them said to the other, "I would like to make the Yank a fire; look how he is shivering! He will not stand the frost tonight." So they kindled a blazing fire, which helped revive Lang's benumbed limbs. One of them unbuckled his blanket, covered Sergeant Lang with it, and brought him some water. "Then bidding me 'good-bye,' they left me—not, however, till the younger of them had given me a plug of good tobacco! May these Savannah boys be blessed even from Hungary, and across the ocean may this blessing reach them."[87]

The movement forward by the Confederate line drove the Federal forces from the position they had occupied at the beginning of the battle, with the loss of three twelve-pounder Napoleon guns from Langdon's battery and two ten-pounder Parrott rifles from Hamilton's battery, along with the Eighth U.S. Colored Troop's national colors. The two companies of the Thirty-second Georgia (H and E) that had been part of the first Confederate forces on the battlefield were credited with capturing Langdon's three guns, while the Nineteenth and Twenty-eighth Georgia regiments, reinforced by the Sixth Florida Battalion, overran Hamilton's battery. "We walked over many a wooly head as we drove them back," wrote Henry Shackleford, regimental musician, of the Nineteenth Georgia.

"How our boys did walk into the niggers, they would beg and pray but it did no good."[88]

As the Confederate line moved forward in the charge, it was somewhat broken, and as it was being reformed, realization came that the ammunition was almost exhausted. Along Colonel Harrison's left portion of the line, it was being whispered that the ammunition was running out, particularly in the Sixth and Thirty-second Georgia regiments, and no ordnance train was in sight. Colonel Harrison reported this fact to Colonel Colquitt, who urged that the ground be held, as ammunition would be up shortly. The units coming down from Georgia had been unable to bring their ammunition wagons to Florida. The ordnance office back at Olustee had been instructed to send ammunition down by train in the event there was any action, but the cars had not yet come down to where the battle was taking place. Colonel Colquitt's adjutant, Major Gratten, believed the situation had become critical. A line of skirmishers was sent forward supplied with ammunition taken from the dead Union soldiers lying in the area overrun by the Southerners. A section of artillery from Guerard's battery under Lt. W. Robert Gignilliat moved up to the left of the Chatham Artillery, reinforcing its fires. This was a fortunate move because the Chatham Artillery had again expended its solid shot and shells and was able to keep firing using ammunition from the chests of the newly arrived section.[89]

Colonel Harrison took direct action to alleviate the ammunition shortage on his portion of the line. He dismounted, turned his horse over to a member of his staff, and sent the remainder of his staff and couriers to convey ammunition from a train of railway cars one-half mile distant back to the battlefield. The staff officers brought up cartridges in haversacks, pockets, caps, or anything into which they could be crammed.[90] Making several desperate trips, they were able to ensure that a rapid and effective fire by the left of the Confederate line was maintained. Lt. Col. C. F. Hopkins's First Florida Battalion had come up with Gignilliat's section from the entrenchments. The First Florida was ordered to the support of the Sixty-fourth Georgia, whose ammunition was nearly all exhausted.

Gen. Samuel Jones, commenting on the difficulty of trying to hold a line while under heavy fire which could not be returned, pointed out the heroic actions of one staff officer, Lt. Hugh H. Colquitt. To keep the Union troops from thinking the line had broken, the lieutenant galloped up and down in front of the troops waving a battle flag and exhorting the men to stand fast where they could be seen.[91]

The Twenty-seventh Georgia and Maj. A. Bonaud's battalion also arrived at this time, and Colonel Colquitt moved these units quickly into position near the center and a little in advance of the line to hold the enemy in check until the other commands could be supplied with cartridges. Colquitt ordered the Chatham Artillery to fall back a little, but Capt. John Wheaton pleaded to be allowed to stay where he was, believing he could hold on another five minutes until the ordnance wagons came up. The colonel replied that he was afraid that the pieces would be lost. Captain Wheaton answered that if he were allowed, he would take the risk, that he could rely upon his men. The colonel acceded to his request but warned Wheaton to be sure and save the guns.[92]

Capt. John Keely of the Nineteenth Georgia recalled that his unit's ammunition was expended by 3:00 P.M. and that the enemy were in the act of advancing. In a desperate condition, the men fixed bayonets and advanced steadily to meet their charge. It was a fearful moment, with every nerve and muscle strained to its fullest tension, "when, to our joy, new supplies of cartridges came to us and we grabbed them more eagerly than hungry men ever grabbed loaves of bread, and now, in a minute, we were again masters of the field, for on our next volley the enemy fled precipitately."[93]

Captain Wheaton felt that one incident in particular involving his battery was significant. A solid shot from one of his cannon cut down a large tree, which fell directly into the midst of the Union forces. He felt that the Union line never recovered from the confusion that resulted and cited a conversation held after the war with a Union officer who believed that the fall of the tree at that time decided the fate of the left of the line.[94] While the falling of the tree may have had some effect, none of the writers on the Union side chose to mention it. The arrival of the ammunition cars from the rear alleviated the crisis the shortage of ammunition had created and gave the Confederate troops new life.

When the Fifty-fourth Massachusetts came onto the field, General Seymour believed that the Confederates were about to flank the Union left. The Fifty-fourth was assigned the task of checking this movement while a new line could be formed in the rear. Col. Edward N. Hallowell moved his unit by the flank into the woods on the left of the road and, formed by file into line, immediately opened fire. Lt. Luis Emilio, in a grove of pine trees on level ground, was able to see through the open forest some four hundred yards to where the Confederate lines were formed, with two guns (Wheaton's) well advanced but without much support. As it deployed, the regiment was being subjected to musketry fire described as "steady but not severe with a flanking fire of shell from the artillery on the unit's left front."[95]

Colonel Hallowell directed the regiment while standing on a stump behind the center of the line. Reacting to the pressure of the fire being received from the overlapping Confederate right, he ordered the two left-flank companies to pull back at an angle that would give a better front and protection from that quarter. Lieutenant Emilio described a growing impatience among members of the Fifty-fourth with the passive type of action they were experiencing. One eager trooper would dash forward beyond the line of battle, fire his piece, dash back to reload, and then dash out again to fire. It was shortly noticed that he fell, shot through the head. Lieutenant Homans, known as an impetuous and brave officer, seeing the exposed position of the two pieces of the Chatham Artillery, sprang in front of his line and shouting, "Now is a good opportunity; we'll try and take those guns!" started to lead his men in a charge but had to be ordered back into line. At another time, one of the regimental sergeants was observed carrying the national flag, moving forward followed by the men around him. They had gone some 150 paces before word from Colonel Hallowell caught up with them, ordering them back, lest the regiment follow them without support into a dangerous situation.[96]

The companies at the center of the Fifty-fourth Massachusetts were receiving an intensive musketry fire from the front and flank. Sharpshooters were seen in the trees but were soon brought down. Increasingly, however, the regiment's casualties were mounting. The regiment had been firing very rapidly; many of the men, by jarring their pieces on the ground, sent the loads home without using the ramrods. It was observed that the musketry fire of the Southerners was more effective than that of their artillery, whose shells were being fired too high, passing over into the trees to the rear of the Fifty-fourth. From the heavy gun on the railroad car came reports which dominated all other battle sounds.[97] This may have been the time that Lieutenant Rambo actually fired the few shells he did from his gun mounted on the flatcar.

It would appear, then, that at the critical stage in which the Confederate charge ground to a halt because of ammunition shortages, the Union forces were committed to a defensive posture in order to permit some units to withdraw and others to form a line farther to the rear. After the Confederate forces were resupplied with ammunition, Colonel Colquitt sent instructions to Colonel Harrison to move the Sixth and Thirty-second Georgia regiments around on the right flank of the Union forces. The Sixth Florida battalion had previously been turned so as to flank the Union left. The result was a concave-shaped Confederate line that further overlapped the Union line and was able to concentrate its full firepower upon that line from the front and both flanks. The First North Carolina lost 10 officers and 220 men were killed, wounded, or missing as a result of the enfilading fire from the Confederate left.

The entire Confederate line, led by the Twenty-seventh Georgia Regiment in the middle, now moved forward, driving almost all of the Union forces from their positions. The Fifty-fourth stood alone, occupying the blocking position it had originally taken when coming onto the field. Lieutenant Emilio could think of no reason why the Fifty-fourth was left thus exposed or why no measures were taken for its safe withdrawal. "It would seem either that the position of the regiment was forgotten, or its sacrifice considered necessary."[98]

While he was with the Seventh Connecticut in the center of

the line, Colonel Hawley received word that General Seymour wanted him to fall back, as it was believed that the enemy "were only feinting on our right, and were preparing to flank us in force." Capt. B. F. Skinner held his position until he believed the forces on either side of him had withdrawn and then took the Seventh Connecticut back a short distance, faced the Confederate line for a while, and then moved by the right of companies to the rear some distance to form a new line. At this position, Colonel Hawley had the Seventh Connecticut come into line on the left of a light battery (he did not know which one), with a cavalry unit on his right. Colonel Hawley recalled that the firing here was chiefly by artillery.[99]

Although the Seventh New Hampshire received a lot of criticism for its performance on this day, it did have its moment of glory. As the Seventh was leaving the field, Capt. James M. Chase proposed that all the men that could be gathered up act as a rear guard. Nearly a hundred soldiers were collected, the line dressed, and advanced back over the field toward the Southern lines. A Confederate skirmish line was soon encountered, and Captain Chase was wounded in the foot. Noticing a heavy line of battle following the skirmish line, the Seventh again retreated, firing as they went, for over one-half mile, until overtaking the main body of the regiment.[100]

Meanwhile, forward, Lieutenant Emilio noted at 5:30 P.M. that darkness seemed to come early amid the pine trees. The Fifty-fourth had taken serious casualties, and from the sound of the battle that came from the right rear, it became obvious that the rest of the Union forces had fallen back. Ammunition was running low (Colonel Hallowell later estimated the 480 men of the unit had fired some twenty thousand cartridges), and when more had been brought up, it proved to be of the wrong caliber. Col. James Montgomery, the black brigade's commander, was with the Fifty-fourth and wanted the unit to disperse, with every man trying to make it back to safety on his own. In the absence of Colonel Hallowell, who had become separated from the main portion of the regiment, Lieutenant Colonel Hooper took charge of the Fifty-fourth and ordered Color Sergeant Wilkins to stand fast. Getting help from officers and cooperative men that were nearby, he shouted, "Rally!" and a line was formed. To bring the unit under control, Hooper had it fix bayonets and then exercised the assembled troops under the manual of arms while under fire.[101]

A regimental staff officer who had ridden to the right returned and reported that the Confederates were following closely but without order. The regiment threw the useless ammunition into mud holes and gave nine loud cheers in the hope of deceiving the Confederates into believing they were receiving reinforcements. Then, in line of battle, the Fifty-fourth faced to the rear and marched off the field, stopping to fire every two or three hundred yards. After moving back some distance through the woods, they sighted the left flank of a unit armed with the Spencer rifles. This group retired, as did another group they approached. Eventually they caught up with Seymour's main body of troops, where the regimental commander, Colonel Hallowell, found it and resumed command. The regiment formed a new line on the right of the dirt road until dark, when it was given orders by Col. William B. Barton to march back to Barber's. The regiment lost eighty-six men killed, wounded, and missing.[102]

Lt. Henry Metcalf's section of Company C, Third Rhode Island Artillery, Elder's horse battery, and the Seventh Connecticut composed a rear guard. A member of Metcalf's battery remembered that at this time most of the army was in disorder, with everyone apparently looking out for himself. As the Southerners advanced in line of battle, the battery crossed an open field to the narrow road leading to the field where one gun loaded with double canister was placed. As the Confederate troops came within one hundred yards of the gun it was fired, "mowing them down like grass, this checking their whole army." While perhaps exaggerated in the claim that it was the "act that checked the advance of the rebel army and saved hundreds of men from being killed or captured," it might have added in some measure to the healthy respect the pursuing Confederates had for the Yankee firepower it had been facing for the better part of four hours.[103]

The fourth stage of the battle saw the Confederate forces advance, with the right of their line driving in the Union left, which crumbled and fled, leaving five pieces of artillery. As this was happening, Montgomery's black brigade was committed, with the First North Carolina on the right, the Fifty-fourth Massachusetts on the left, and a resupplied Seventh Connecticut occupying a position between them. The movement forward of the Confederate line was checked by its rapidly growing shortage of ammunition. As this occurred, Confederate reinforcements arrived from the entrenchments at Olustee. The First Florida was ordered to support the Sixty-fourth Georgia on the left, and Bonaud's battalion and the Twenty-seventh Georgia were moved to the center and in front of the Confederate line along with whatever skirmishers from the other units could be furnished with spare cartridges or those recovered from the Union dead. Desperate measures, such as Colonel Harrison's use of his staff to bring up ammunition as fast they could in whatever they could carry, resulted in some units being able to resume enough firing to keep the problem hidden from the Union side. A fresh section of artillery arrived in time to share some of its ammunition with the Chatham Artillery, which was in an exposed position in front of the Confederate line.

While the Confederate side was in this precarious position, the Union forces were in a defensive posture, apparently unaware of the Confederate predicament. The Union units in the forward positions perceived themselves as charged with a blocking mission of checking a Confederate advance while a new line was being formed. In the process, they were taking heavy casualties from an enemy line that overlapped them and was in a position to enfilade both their flanks. Several efforts by more offensive-minded soldiers were quickly suppressed. On the Union side, there appears to have been almost complete loss of control by General Seymour and some of his brigade commanders as individual units or parts of units were operating on their own, as best they could. Colonel Colquitt, by turning his right and left flanking units inward, formed a somewhat concave line that overlapped and enfiladed both Union flanks, causing tremendous casualties. The Confederate line now moved forward, aided by the cross fire of the flanking units, forcing the bulk of the Union forces backward. The Fifty-fourth Massachusetts, left behind, delayed the Confederate advance and then moved to the rear in an orderly manner, keeping its discipline while taking casualties. A line composed of the Seventh Connecticut, Henry's cavalry, and Elder's battery along with part of Company C, Third Rhode Island Heavy Artillery, screened the retreating Union forces, leaving the field to the oncoming Confederates.

6

Lost Opportunities

The Retreat and Pursuit

In the reports of the battle made by the commanding officers of both sides, there is general agreement on the conduct of the battle but disagreement on the retreat and pursuit. General Finegan's report claimed that the Union lines had broken and reformed several times before giving way entirely, with the pursuit continuing for some three miles from the battlefield. Finegan stated that he had directed Colquitt to continue the pursuit, intending to occupy Sanderson that night, but withdrew the order in deference to Colquitt's suggestion because of the fatigue of the troops, the absence of rations, the disadvantage of a pursuit in the dark, and a report (later proven false) of an advanced cavalry picket that the enemy had halted for the night. Finegan also stated that he gave repeated orders to Colonel Smith commanding the cavalry to "press the enemy on his flanks and continue the pursuit" but that Smith did not carry out these orders.[1]

Both Southern brigade commanders, Harrison and Colquitt, reported that the Federal forces retreated slowly at first under the pressure of the Confederate advance and then more rapidly and in growing confusion. The pursuit was maintained for several miles but stopped with the onset of darkness and, according to Harrison, by Colquitt's command. Both colonels agreed that orders had been given to the cavalry to pursue closely and to "seize every opportunity to strike a blow."[2] Confederate lieutenant M. B. Grant reported that the infantry pursued the retreating Union forces some two miles to the branch in the road, where they were halted by darkness, but the cavalry "did not pursue them beyond a few miles, which is to be regretted, as it is probable that in the disorganized and demoralized condition of the enemy we might have captured a large proportion of their troops, if not destroyed their army."[3]

Colonel Colquitt's adjutant noted that at the beginning of what was believed to be the Union rout, Colonel Colquitt had ordered the Confederate cavalry to the front in pursuit, but they went no farther than the point where the infantry halted. The officer leading the cavalry returned and reported that he had gotten close enough to see that the Federal troops had halted, stacked arms, and gone into camp, appearing to be in good order. General Finegan arrived on the battlefield at about that time and assumed command. According to Major Gratten, General Finegan directed Colonel Colquitt to leave one regiment in front to serve as an advance guard and to move the rest of the troops back to Olustee Station. The pursuit was not resumed until late the next day or the morning subsequent. "Nothing but our inaction and the inefficiency of the cavalry saved the entire Federal army from capture."[4]

Col. Caraway Smith, commanding the Confederate cavalry brigade, later received much criticism for failing to capitalize by a more vigorous pursuit on what was seen as the rout of the enemy. He reported that the onset of darkness, the inability to distinguish his own lines, the nature of the terrain favoring ambush, and the discovery of a large body of Union cavalry on the opposite side of a swamp caused him to become cautious until the situation was more developed. He claimed that, when he received the order to move forward, he received another advising him he was taking fire from his own forces. When possible, according to Smith, the cavalry did follow the enemy, gathering some 150 prisoners in the effort.[5]

On the basis of the above report, General Beauregard later subjected Colonel Smith to an investigation because of certain "inconsistencies" in his report and activities. Specifically:

1. Finegan's report (above quoted) stated that repeated orders were given to Smith by Finegan to continue in the pursuit, which apparently were not followed.

2. Colonel Colquitt's report stated that instructions were given to the cavalry to close upon the enemy and seize every opportunity to strike a favorable blow.

3. Colonel Smith's report did not show that the cavalry made any positive attack after the fight started.

4. No identification was made of the person who gave the information that Smith was under fire from his own men and to beware of an ambush. Furthermore, Colonel Smith could not make out his own lines but could "discover a large body of enemy cavalry across a swamp."

5. General Beauregard thought it curious that in the entire engagement, none of the 202 men of the Second Florida Cavalry were injured, and only 1 officer and 3 men of the entire cavalry brigade were casualties.

6. Finally, General Beauregard noted that General Finegan's report claimed that Finegan had received information from a cavalry picket (later proven false) that the enemy had halted for the night and taken a position.[6]

In a letter to his wife the day after the battle, Capt. Winston Stephens of the Second Florida Cavalry wrote, "Then we were thrown to the front and we got during the night some 200 Yanks that were wounded and not able to keep up with the main body."[7] However, in another letter to his wife written almost a week later, he claimed, "If we had only pressed them after the fight, we could have captured the whole army. I heard that Genl. [sic] Colquitt wanted to follow them but Genl. Finegan opposed." For whatever reason, the pursuit was not conducted aggressively and was terminated within a short distance of the actual battlefield. Writing many years after the battle, trooper Lawrence Jackson, also of the Second Florida, had an interesting observation. He claimed that late in the evening they found the enemy falling back, and it now remained for the cavalry to catch those who were fleeing for their lives. However, as the Confederate cavalry started to pursue, they found themselves handicapped in the dark because of telegraph wire stretched between the trees on both sides of the road.[8]

Jackson and his comrades probably ran into communication wire that had been put up during the battle and not with the objective of hindering the pursuit. Nevertheless, it might have contributed to a reluctance to pursue by horse at night.

The Union reports, on the other hand, stressed a relatively orderly withdrawal. Colonel Barton of the New York brigade reported that at about six or seven o'clock, the Union forces retired in order by alternate battalions screened by a rear guard composed of the Seventh Connecticut, Elder's battery, and Henry's mounted troops. After a sufficient gap between the opposing forces was opened, the Union troops were moved in brigades on parallel lines ready to deploy in case of attack.[9]

Colonel Hawley, writing sometime later in reviewing an account of the battle written by Gen. Samuel Jones, C.S.A., commented on Jones's statement that the Union forces at first yielded ground slowly and then gradually, in what became a confused flight. "This must have been borrowed from some of the wild reports made by the enemy immediately after the battle. Our last formation in line of battle (just referred to) was a few hundred yards in rear of the center of the field. It was fast growing dark in the pine woods. Not a yell nor a shot pursued us that long night."[10] This account is corroborated by the *New York Times* correspondent, who wrote two days after the battle, "The retreat was conducted leisurely and orderly. There was no confusion, no panic, nothing that indicated hurry."[11] Union army surgeon Adolph Majer reported that after he received an order to bring the wounded as far to the rear as possible, he used everything, including ambulances, caissons, army wagons, litters, single horses, carts, and every conceivable mode of carrying, in order to bring out as many of the wounded as possible. "There was no depression of spirits manifested and the morale of the command expressed the brave determination in the words, 'We will give it back to them.'"[12]

While passing through Sanderson, Majer sent telegrams to both Barber's and Jacksonville, alerting medical personnel there of the large number of wounded and requesting help and preparation for their arrival. While doing the best he could with the limited transportation available, Majer could not save all the wounded. Majer reported leaving some 40 wounded at the ambulance depot near the battlefield under the charge of Asst. Surgeon C. A. Devendorf, Forty-eighth New York Volunteers, and 23 badly wounded at Sanderson. Two companies of cavalry were dismounted, and their horses were used to save about 80 men. "We now had to take care of and forward by cars and wagons some 860 wounded."[13]

Seymour's signal officer, Captain Dana, was tasked with collecting all the wounded that could walk and starting them toward Barber's. Henry's mounted force was to assist by providing horses and men to lead them for those wounded who could not walk. Captain Dana reported that at a cotton house near the track, he found the floor covered with wounded, many of whom had died. It finally took three cavalry companies to mount them all. Even then it proved difficult to get the wounded started rearward. "They had to be awakened and scared into going by telling them the rebels would bayonet every wounded man they found."[14]

Sgt. A. J. Clement of the First Massachusetts Independent Cavalry, part of Colonel Henry's command acting as rear guard, stated that his company stayed over two hours on the edge of the field before slowly following the retreating Union forces. He recalled that "it was fearful work to keep the men attentive," as they did not "care a damn" for anything, believing they were sure to be gobbled up anyway. "But not a shot did they fire, nor did we discover that they followed us that night."[15]

Emilio, with the Fifty-fourth Massachusetts, described the road from the battlefield toward Sanderson as choked with a flowing torrent of soldiers on foot, wounded and unwounded, vehicles of every description laden with wrecks of men, while amid the horde rode others, many of whom roughly forced their jaded animals through the crowd. Within this mass of the shattered and beaten were seen generous and self-sacrificing men helping along disabled comrades and some shaking forms with bandaged heads or limbs, still carrying their trusty muskets. Along the sides of the road exhausted or bleeding men

were lying, unable to proceed, resigned, or thoughtless of inevitable captivity.[16]

A graphic description of the contrast in moods between the
men in their approach march that morning and their retreat
that night was penned by a member of the Forty-eighth New
York. He wrote of the march that clear and beautiful morning,
which had been through swamps and along sandy roads
through pine forests fragrant with the resinous odors of the
trees, with the troops buoyed by the anticipation of meeting
the enemy in open battle, where they hoped to achieve a victory. "But the march back through the night, with many of
their comrades killed and wounded and left upon the field, and
others desperately struggling along on the retreat, was a sad
disappointment to their hopes."[17]

Clark, with the 115th New York, had one of the worst eve-
nings of his life. He found himself as part of a stream of men
from different regiments hurrying back toward Sanderson.
Some men lay down along the road and declared that they
could go no farther, others were fast bleeding to death, and
some fell down exhausted to die. He reached Sanderson after
traveling what he believed to be nine miles and with others
who felt they could go no farther went into a hotel and lay
down on the floor. A surgeon soon came in and said that unless
they made all possible haste toward Barber's, they would all be
captured, as the rebels were close by. Concluding that it would
be better to die walking or even crawling toward freedom than
to starve to death in a rebel dungeon, the group of wounded
moved off toward Barber's.

A company of the Fortieth Massachusetts Mounted Infantry
came along and generally dismounted, helping thirty of the
men on their horses, saving most of the party from capture.
The animal Clark rode carried him for a mile with great difficulty and then lay down in the mud to die. Clark started on
again by foot and was shortly approached by a mounted officer
who, after inquiring his name, rank, and regiment, assisted in
getting the wounded man to mount his horse, which Clark
rode another two miles, before he was again forced to walk.

Eventually, Barber's was reached about three o'clock in the morning, where Clark, nearly dead, found the remnant of his regiment asleep. "I sat down on a cracker box to warm myself by a camp fire, when I fainted away and pitched into it headlong."[18]

Lieutenant Colonel Hall, New York Engineers, in his capacity as provost marshal, galloped back and forth on the line of retreat trying to establish order and rallying stragglers. Upon his arrival in Sanderson about 9:00 P.M., he found that Captain Bridgman of the Fifty-fourth Massachusetts had been doing the same, collecting some one thousand men. While some of this group were wounded, ranging from slight to very serious, others were just men who had helped wounded comrades to the rear and had not returned.[19]

Maj. John Appleton of the Fifty-fourth Massachusetts was finally relieved of security duty at Barber's by the arrival of Col. Alfred S. Hartwell with six companies of the Fifty-fifth Massachusetts. Along with twenty-five men from the Eighth U.S. Colored Troops who had also come up, Major Appleton hurried forward with his two companies to rejoin the regiment. Although firing from the battle had been heard as far away as Barber's, his first warning of the defeat came when he met a surgeon some ten miles west of Barber's. Moving on quickly, Major Appleton halted within one mile of Sanderson and deployed his men to restore order. As Lieutenant Emilio recalled, "The sight of his compact little force was encouraging; and the unwounded, when approached, readily placed themselves in line until some six hundred men were collected."[20] Major Appleton soon received orders to escort the logistic train to Barber's, and did so, arriving at 2:00 A.M. on the twenty-first.

After reaching Sanderson, Colonel Hawley put Colonel Abbott's reorganized Seventh New Hampshire and Captain Bailey's Eighth U.S. Colored Troops in line north of the town to block any attack by the enemy from that quarter. After the stragglers and wounded had left Sanderson, in response to General Seymour's orders, Colonel Hawley used his blocking force to guard the logistic train, "marching those two regiments by the flank and by the side of the wagons and ambulances to

Baldwin, where we bivouacked on the ground we left eighteen hours before, having marched about 32 miles, and having been about three hours in a battle."[21]

The Fifty-fourth halted at Sanderson until the place was cleared of wounded and vehicles and fires set to whatever might be of value to the Confederates. Then, with the Seventh Connecticut deployed in rear of the infantry and Henry's mounted men covering all, the army retired to Barber's, destroying bridges and the railroad as they proceeded. Emilio remembered seeing the welcome bivouac fires of the Fifty-fifth at Barber's, which was reached about 2:00 A.M. "Then the regiment, worn out with the enervating events of the day, and the march of thirty-two miles since the preceding morning, went to rest on the ground previously occupied."[22] For some the rest was brief, as the two companies who had been with Major Appleton at Barber's were now ordered to picket duty across the St. Marys River, one in a blockhouse, and the other on line. They were joined by pickets from the Fifty-fifth, as an attack was expected.

Capt. B. F. Skinner arrived at Barber's with the Seventh Connecticut at about 3:00 A.M. after having been in the rear guard deployed as skirmishers most of the eighteen miles from the battlefield. They, too, reoccupied the same ground they had bivouacked on the morning before, after having marched a distance of thirty-six miles over what Skinner described as "bad ground; many swamps, ditches, pickets, and fences intervened to obstruct my march."[23] Captain Dana also reached Barber's at 3:00 A.M. and noted an immense accumulation of rations which the staff officers had collected in a pile and set fire to.[24] Sgt. A. J. Clement, with the mounted force, wrote that his unit reached Barber's about daybreak and "there got out of our saddles for the first time in twenty-four hours, and fed our horses."[25]

In the morning, the casualties were loaded as well as possible aboard the railcars that had brought out supplies to Barber's. One of the wounded remembered that there were only four cars for the hundreds of wounded and considered himself fortunate to get on one. The cars were terribly crowded, with as many as seventy being on a small platform, and several had to hang together to keep from falling off. Drawn very slowly by mules, it took the whole of Sunday until midnight that night to reach Jacksonville. "Some of the poor fellows suffered badly. They had nothing to eat or drink, were so crowded that they could not sleep, and no chance to change their cramped and painful positions."[26] Those wounded who were not as fortunate were placed on whatever ambulances, wagons, or vehicles were available and started toward Baldwin. Remaining behind with those wounded that were unable to travel or had been left on the battlefield were several surgeons who volunteered to do so. They were joined by Mr. Day of the Sanitary Commission and the Reverend Mr. Taylor of the Christian Commission, who had come out from Jacksonville. When the news of the battle was received, he immediately loaded a car with medical and sanitary stores and left for the front. Mr. Day had twice already been a prisoner by staying behind with the wounded.[27]

Colonel Hawley's command, which now included the Seventh Connecticut, Seventh New Hampshire, Eighth U.S. Colored Troops, and the Fifty-fourth Massachusetts, departed Barber's at 9:00 A.M. in three parallel columns, following the wagon train. Also under Hawley's command was Colonel Montgomery's brigade with Companies A and E of the Fifty-fourth Massachusetts attached, which followed next, formed in line of battle, covering the other infantry. At the very rear was Henry's light brigade. About a half mile out from Barber's, the Seventh Connecticut was again detached to serve as rear guard with the light brigade.[28] Sergeant Clement's Company D of the Massachusetts Independent Cavalry was the last Union unit to go through the ford as they left Barber's following the rest of the army eastward.[29] One correspondent noted that the road "from Barber's to Baldwin was strewn with guns, knapsacks, and blankets."[30]

Upon reaching Baldwin, everything of military value was burned or destroyed, including 183,000 rounds of Enfield and two boxes of Spencer ammunition, which were thrown in a water-filled ditch beside the track. The burning of a warehouse filled with immense barrels of crude turpentine was particularly memorable. "I think the comrades of our regiment will remember what a dense, black smoke-cloud the resin and cotton made, so black, even, that we could not see the sun, although the day was fine and clear."[31]

The Fifty-fourth arrived in Baldwin about 4:00 P.M. after passing through Darby's, where an immense pile of barrels of turpentine was also being burned. What they saw was the destruction of the property of a man named Darby by the orders of General Seymour. It was believed that Darby had sought and obtained protection from the Union forces and then had gone over to the Confederates with information.[32] The Fifty-fourth was not permitted to pick up their clothing and personal effects that had been left at Baldwin, and these were destroyed with the other stores. The regiment rejoined its A and E companies and continued on with Hawley's brigade, leaving Baldwin at 7:00 A.M. on the twenty-second.

After having marched only about four miles, General Seymour sent orders to Col. E. N. Hallowell to march his regiment back to Ten-Mile Station to tow forward the railroad train, as the locomotive had broken down. The foot-weary men retraced their steps, and "the thought of cars laden with the wounded nerved them to the task." Ropes were fastened to the engine and the cars, which were then dragged by pure muscle power as far as Camp Finegan, where horses were finally provided for the rest of the trip. In his regimental history, Lieutenant Emilio quotes Dr. Marsh of the Sanitary Commission, who was present.

> Through eagerness to escape the supposed pursuing enemy, too great pressure of steam was employed and the flue collapsed; and here the immortal Fifty-fourth (colored) did what ought to insure it higher praise than to hold the field in the face of a victorious foe,—with ropes it seized the engine (now useless) and dragged it with its doomed freight for many miles. . . . They knew their fate if captured; their humanity triumphed. Does history record a nobler deed?[33]

Upon arriving at Baldwin with the rear guard, Captain Skinner received permission from Colonel Barton to recall his men from their position as skirmishers with the rear guard and allow them to reclaim their knapsacks, which had been left there under guard. In this, they were more fortunate than the Fifty-fourth Massachusetts. General Seymour had detailed the Seventh Connecticut to remain in Baldwin overnight, and it was there when Colonel Henry's mounted brigade came in. Captain Dana had been sent into Jacksonville to get the chief quartermaster to send out every horse there with any kind of a harness. The cars arrived about 3:00 A.M. Captain Skinner was tasked by Colonel Henry to provide a detail to load the cars, which was done. When the train left, Captain Skinner was also directed to send off half of his command with it. The remainder of the Seventh Connecticut was employed scattering turpentine and rosin around the railroad building in preparation for burning it down. Captain Dana later claimed that the horses finally arrived "just in time to pull the train over the crest of the hill as the rebels came into view."[34]

Skinner's men finished their preparations for burning Baldwin and were en route to Jacksonville by way of the railroad when, between Baldwin and Ten-Mile Station, they found three cars which had left Baldwin that morning. Captain Mills, with a portion of the command that volunteered, pushed the cars about three miles.[35] Sergeant Clement, with Henry's mounted brigade, arrived at Baldwin on the afternoon of the twenty-first and found there huge quantities of Union supplies in addition to stores of cotton and resin. His unit stayed there that night and the next. On the second night, the town was fired as the troops departed to the sound of exploding Spencer cartridges on their way to Camp Finegan, which was reached by morning, after destroying every bridge at the many little "runs."[36]

Captain Skinner picked up the rest of his command at Ten-Mile Station and, after a short rest, continued on to Jacksonville, arriving about seven o'clock after a march of some twenty miles. Here, he was ordered by General Seymour to encamp in front of the redoubt. In the morning, General Seymour ordered the Seventh Connecticut to occupy a position about six hundred yards forward and to the right across a railroad, where it stayed for a day or two. The unit was finally relieved to rejoin Hawley's brigade on King's Road at Six-Mile Creek. Not until the unit was in the entrenched lines at Jacksonville on the twenty-fifth were its members able to catch up on their sleep.[37] This five-day period has to be one of the high points in this unit's history. Whether as point or rear guard, they were constantly positioned where the commanding general expected trouble, and their performance under the most stressful conditions were consistently outstanding.

Colonel Hawley's brigade moved from Baldwin to McGirt's Creek, where they bivouacked for the night. The logistic train and Barton's command passed through, and Colonel Montgomery took the First North Carolina on to Camp Finegan. The Seventh New Hampshire stopped at Camp Finegan on the way back to Jacksonville for a welcome respite. Here they found the stores which had been captured at the time of the Union advance, consisting of bacon or smoked sides, tobacco, sugar, and clothing, which were dealt out indiscriminately to all the troops. What was not used or taken by the men was destroyed. After resting here for a short while, the Seventh New Hampshire again started on the march, reaching a place on King's Road about six miles out of Jacksonville that night, where they went into camp temporarily and were at once ordered on picket duty.[38]

The Fifty-fourth also stopped for a short while at Camp Finegan, where the men were able to get something to eat. The unit left Camp Finegan at 4:00 P.M. on the twenty-second and arrived in Jacksonville some four hours later, going into camp on the same ground they had originally occupied at the start of the expedition, but in a much different condition. Nearly half of the regiment was without shoes and, having dropped their blankets and knapsacks when they went into combat, also without rations or shelter. After a march of twenty-two miles that day, "with crippled feet and weary limbs they cast themselves on the bare ground for rest." The adjutant general of Massachusetts reported that "the Fifty-fourth marched 120 miles in 102 hours, yet the roll-call showed no stragglers."[39]

By the evening of February 22, most of Seymour's infantry

was either back in Jacksonville or in the vicinity. Henry's mounted brigade was at Cedar Run, and reinforcements in the form of Brig. Gen. Israel Vogdes with Generals Foster's and Ames's brigades were en route. In the three days preceding the arrival of the defeated Union forces from Olustee, all the troops in Jacksonville, including the newly arrived Twenty-fourth Massachusetts and the Fourth New Hampshire, were at work strengthening the defenses. As the various units arrived, they joined in the work.

Immediately after the battle, the Confederate forces at Olustee were involved in taking possession of the battlefield and all it held. Captain Wheaton's battery was ordered to collect the Union artillery that was left on the field, taking back three of the five captured pieces to their bivouac at Olustee Station. Some of the men of the battery were engaged all night and the day following gathering ammunition and artillery stores from the battlefield and taking care of the wounded.[40] For some of the men involved in cleaning up the battlefield, there were rewards. Shackleford, of the Nineteenth Georgia, recalled, "How we did enjoy captured coffee, hams, bread, and everything else." He also noted that the men of his regiment picked up oilcloth blankets, knapsacks, "and a number of gold and silver watches."[41] In a letter to his wife composed the day after the battle, Winston Stephens of the Second Florida Cavalry wrote:

> We had one of the hottest contested battles of the war on yesterday, commencing about 2 o'clock P.M. and ending half past 5 P.M. and during the whole time there was not a moment's cessation in the fire. Men never fought better than our men did, and God seemed to shield them from destruction as the loss on our side is comparatively light. . . . I passed over the field this morning and the dead Yankees and negroes are strewn thick all over the field. . . . I am now writing this with a Yankee pen, Yankee ink and on Yankee paper. . . . I got several things of value, a blanket, tent, 2 oil cloth haversacks full of provisions and 2 flannel shirts, 1 pr. drawers, 1 pr. gamulletts, 3 canteens and I have got a fine sword from one of my men that got it on the field.[42]

It would appear that the Confederate troops spent the crucial hours and days following the battle in cleaning up the battlefield rather than in pursuit. One report by General Finegan stated the Federal forces in retreating left 418 wounded on the field, near 400 Union dead were buried, and about 200 prisoners were captured.[43] Another report by General Finegan, this one written from Sanderson on February 23, three days after the battle, blamed part of the slowness of the pursuit on the enemy's destruction of the railroad, which "delays my movements one day," and then went on to say that he had several hundred of the enemy's wounded which were still being removed from the battlefield the day before when he departed Ocean Pond.[44]

An article from the *Tallahassee Floridian* written shortly after the battle read: "Some 200 Yankee wounded have been brought to this city since the battle of Olustee, mostly foreigners and negroes; the foreigners were miserable looking fellows, not a bit too good to be put on an equality with the negroes; and in the hospital in every case, whites and negroes were laid side by side, in order to give the whites a taste of the equality they are fighting for."[45]

General Seymour, reporting to the Department of the South on March 2, 1864, stated that "reliable information" had been received from a railroad employee at Lake City that close to thirty railroad cars of wounded from Olustee had arrived in Lake City by the night of the twenty-first. The source also reported that the Union wounded had been taken to Tallahassee "so far as they could be moved safely; the remainder to Lake City, where the citizens generally showed them every kindness, cooking for them and paying them all the attention in their power."[46]

On February 23, Finegan reported to Beauregard from Sanderson that he had forwarded 150 prisoners (not wounded) to Major General Gilmer, among which were three Negroes, and asked for information as to what to do with the large number of enemy wounded, many of whom were Negroes. He also reported that he "will have more wounded than I first supposed. The list will reach between 600 and 700, 300 or 400 of whom will be fit for duty in a few weeks, being but flesh wounds."[47] Lieutenant Grant's report explained the large number of minor wounds incurred by the Confederate soldiers. While the infantry fire during the whole engagement had been continuous and effective, the artillery fire from both sides was entirely too high, judging from the marks on the trees, and did comparatively little damage. "Our men sheltered themselves behind the trees as was evident from the number who were wounded in the arms and hands, thus gaining considerable advantage over the enemy who used the trees to a lesser extent."[48]

Given a situation in which there were large numbers of wounded and dead to be taken care of, and weapons and supplies to be salvaged, General Finegan's pursuit of the retreating Union forces still was conducted, to say the least, in an overly cautious manner. Speculation can be made as to whether his concern for the repair of the railroad stemmed from military necessity or from his former position in constructing that railroad and his current position in partnership with former senator Yulee and others in ownership of the company. From his correspondence, it can be determined that by the twenty-third, the day after the Union infantry was safely back in Jacksonville, General Finegan was at Sanderson, only six miles from the battlefield.[49] Lieutenant Grant reported to his superior, "Upon the fourth day after the battle our forces advanced to Sanderson where you found us upon your arrival."[50]

Captain Dana, on General Seymour's staff, was sure that Finegan had gotten only as far as Baldwin by the twenty-fourth. He remembered being sent by General Seymour with a request to General Finegan to have the Union wounded paroled and returned so that they could get better care. The Union forces had not received all of their expected reinforcements by the twenty-third, and one object of the request was to learn how far away the Confederate forces were. Under a flag of truce and accompanied by six cavalrymen, Dana got as far as Baldwin, twenty-one miles from Jacksonville, before he made contact with sixteen mounted Confederate officers. After handing over his dispatches for General Finegan to the senior officer, Dana requested to know how long he would have to wait for an answer. "After some study over that, he named the time which showed me that the general was at Barber's and I already had all the information I needed." Captain Dana also learned that some of his efforts in the previous few days had been in vain. The heat from the burning depot and hotel in Baldwin had dried up the ditch into which Captain Dana's work detail had been dumping the Union cartridges, and the Confederates were able to salvage the bullets from the 183,000 rounds that had been thought destroyed.[51]

Through Captain Dana, General Seymour also requested of General Finegan information concerning Col. Charles W. Fribley of the Eighth U.S. Colored Troops, whose body had been left on the field, asking that his "grave may be so marked that at some future day his family may be able to remove his remains."[52] Writing on the twenty-fourth, General Finegan denied both requests, stating that the wounded had already been sent forward and that Colonel Fribley's body had not been identified.[53]

The matter of the overly cautious pursuit was of particular interest to General Beauregard, who felt that it had been handled poorly. Complicating the situation was the question of who was in command of the Confederate forces in Florida. Upon learning that the Union forces had landed in Florida, General Beauregard was unable to have Richmond send a relief for him to enable him to take personal charge in Florida. His next recourse was to send an officer experienced in field command to the scene. Unaware that Brig. Gen. William M. Gardner, who normally commanded Middle Florida (and who outranked Finegan), had returned to duty from sick leave and was available, General Beauregard ordered Gen. William B. Taliaferro to Florida. Upon learning General Gardner was available, Beauregard telegraphed him to tell him to take charge of the Confederate forces that were converging on the area. In the meantime, the battle of Olustee had been fought, and General Gardner found himself in the delicate position of notifying General Finegan that he, Gardner, was in command. In attempting to do so, without jeopardizing the continuation of the action that was initiated with the battle, General Gardner found himself and General Finegan at odds.

Upon being notified by General Beauregard that he was to take command until General Taliaferro arrived, General Gardner sent a letter to General Finegan from Tallahassee on February 22 which included a copy of his appointment by Beauregard. Gardner then tactfully suggested that Finegan stop offensive movements and prepare a strong defensive position on the west bank of the St. Marys River until reinforcements currently en route reach him. Finegan was instructed to picket the area thoroughly with cavalry, to monitor all enemy movements carefully, and to select a suitable fording place by which his troops could conduct a flanking attack. If the Union troops were on the western side of the river, Finegan was to act entirely on the defensive and to fall back to the entrenchments at Ocean Pond if threatened. Gardner closed with a request for acknowledgment of the receipt of his letter and asked to be kept informed of all movements.[54] General Finegan stated on the twenty-seventh that he had never received the above communication from General Gardner.[55]

General Gardner sent another message to General Finegan from Tallahassee dated February 23, in which he suggested that the moment for following up the victory at Olustee appeared to have been lost and that the enemy had "doubtless taken advantage of the interval since the battle of the 20th instant to reorganize his defeated forces" and receive reinforcements while strongly entrenching himself. Gardner again advised caution but now suggested Finegan cross the St. Marys with his main body of troops if he could determine that the enemy was not located in force between that river and Jacksonville and if he provided for a safe retreat. Finegan replied quite testily to Gardner on the twenty-fourth that it would give him great pleasure to turn over command to either Gardner, General Taliaferro, "or any other superior officer whom the commanding general may assign to the command whenever he shall arrive in this district and assume the responsibilities of the movements and supply of the troops." Until that time, however, General Finegan stated that in the interests of the service, he would continue in charge. He finished by stating that his advanced force was in Baldwin and that his whole force would be there later on the twenty-fourth.[56]

General Gardner did arrive and take charge on the twenty-sixth, but by that time, the Union position was too strong to attack. In response to an inquiry from General Beauregard in reference to a remark made by Finegan that implied that Gardner had halted the pursuit on the twenty-second, General Gardner provided the information that Finegan did not reach McGirt's Creek until the twenty-sixth. Fearing he would be held responsible for any disaster that occurred and believing that the opportunity to exploit the success of the twentieth had been lost, Gardner halted the army on the twenty-sixth until he could better assess the situation and because "of my utter want of confidence in the brigadier-commanding to handle an army on the field of battle, as manifested under my own eye at the battle of Olustee."[57]

In the meantime, in response to General Beauregard's continual efforts to get more experienced generals in his department, Maj. Gen. James Patton Anderson was assigned to take charge in Florida. Upon Anderson's arrival in Florida, he handled the problem of the friction between Generals Finegan and Gardner by restoring Finegan to command of East Florida (which amounted to a vindication of Finegan's actions) and restoring Gardner to command in Middle Florida. In view of the fact that the battle was conducted on the Confederate side without any evidence of planning and the pursuit of a "routed" Union army took the victors four days· longer than the vanquished to go the same distance, one wonders why General Finegan was so honored.

The retreat and pursuit after the Olustee battle, for all intents and purposes, ended when the Union troops were safely back in the entrenchments at Jacksonville by the night of February 22, 1864. The Union forces retreating from the battle were a mixture of orderliness and chaos. There was much more security on the retreat than there had been on the approach march, but within the retreating columns there was some breakdown of unit integrity, command, and control. A determined pursuit utilizing coordinated cavalry and infantry could have come closer to seizing those "fruits of victory" that General Beauregard believed to have slipped away. The wonder is that the Union forces were able to get back to Jacksonville in the strength and condition that they were in. The Confederate troops, save some cavalry units, were in much better physical condition at the battle, having had at least one day's rest; the Union troops were handicapped by their having marched sixteen hard miles before fighting. Although Confederate cavalry commander Col. Caraway Smith was made the Confederate scapegoat, General Finegan's failure as the commanding general to push the pursuit is inexcusable.

While in Baldwin on February 21, General Seymour sent a dispatch to Gen. J. W. Turner, Department of the South, informing him that "authentic information" on the Confederate force he had faced at Olustee placed their numbers at from ten to fifteen thousand. He believed that the defensive position that had been constructed at Baldwin was inadequate to face even half that force and therefore intended to set up a defensive position closer to Jacksonville.[58] Meanwhile, the Department of the South was taking steps to reinforce the Union troops in Jacksonville. The Tenth Connecticut, headquartered at St. Augustine, was alerted to move to Jacksonville and pulled back their two companies from Palatka. Col. J. L. Otis, the regimental commander, reported that he was prepared to assist in "everything possible with the means at my disposal," although he reposed little faith in the 16 musicians, 50 recruits, and 30 staff clerks that were part of his available 180-man force.[59] Gen. Adelbert Ames, Department of the South, was directed on February 22 to embark some 1,300 troops by 5:00 A.M. the following day "with all possible dispatch, sending them to report at Jacksonville as soon as the vessels can cross the bar after receiving troops."[60]

The remainder of General Ames's brigade and the major portion of Gen. Robert S. Foster's brigades were embarking on the twenty-third at Folly Island, South Carolina, with the objective of sailing at high water on the morning of the twenty-fourth, for Jacksonville. Captain Dana reported that both brigades arrived in Jacksonville on the evening of the twenty-fourth and the morning of the twenty-fifth, "luckily . . . for our pickets were driven in at noon and Gen. Ames was sent out to hold our line."[61] On the twenty-fifth, General Seymour reported that his defenses were "sufficiently advanced to insure, I believe, a successful defense" but that, although Ames's and Foster's brigades had arrived, he wished to retain Col. Louis Bell's Fourth New Hampshire a day or two longer in case of attack. He then gave his organization of the troops in the Jacksonville area as follows:

Brig. Gen. Israel Vogdes's Division
First: Brigadier General Foster's brigade with the Fourth New Hampshire and Twenty-fourth Massachusetts Volunteers, attached
Second: Colonel Tilghman, First North Carolina and Third U.S. Colored Troops
Third: Colonel Montgomery, Second and Third South Carolina Volunteers, and Langdon's Battery of the First U.S. Artillery

Brigadier General Ames's Division
First: Colonel Noble's Brigade
Second: Colonel Hawley's Brigade
Third: Col. M. S. Littlefield, Fifty-fourth and Fifty-fifth Massachusetts Volunteers, and Captain James's Battery, Third Rhode Island Artillery

Colonel Barton's Brigade, Colonel Henry's command, and Captain Hamilton's Artillery, unassigned.[62]

Colonel Hawley was directed on February 25 to keep at least a company of Henry's cavalry in front of him as a patrol, with the intention of giving early warning of any Confederate approach. In the same message, Colonel Hawley was informed that General Seymour did not plan to defend the positions currently occupied by the Union troops but to fall back on the positions being prepared at Jacksonville. Colonel Henry was specifically directed, if not in contact with the enemy, to push a reconnaissance force across Cedar Creek to determine where the enemy was. He was also requested to provide an escort for a Mr. Jackson to the front.[63]

Mr. Jackson was an aide-de-camp to the late Colonel Fribley of the Eighth U.S. Colored Troops and carried a request in a reply from General Seymour to General Finegan's message stating that Colonel Fribley's remains had not been identified. This request was for a renewed effort to identify the colonel's personal articles and to allow Mrs. Fribley, accompanied by the late colonel's adjutant, to pass through the lines, with the hope of obtaining more information.[64] General Finegan turned this request down, as he had the earlier one.[65] Later, General Gardner did allow several of Colonel Fribley's personal items to be forwarded to his widow but informed Seymour that, lest he be misunderstood, he had no sympathy for the fate of any officer commanding Negro troops, "but compassion for a widow in grief, had induced these efforts to recover her relics which she must naturally value."[66] A letter published in the *Savannah Daily Morning News*, March 30, 1864, was less compassionate.

> Such was the case with the redoubtable Col. Frieble [sic], of a negro regiment, in whose pocket was found a letter from his wife (query, white or black?) asking him to "confiscate" for her "a nice saddle when he reached Tallahassee."
>
> Yes! The black-hearted Frieble had a dog's burial. A leader of a horde of infuriated negroes, on a mission of murder, robbery and rape, ought he not have been left to rot on the plain, to the obscene birds to fatten on his vitals, and the great wolves to gnaw on his bones?

On the twenty-sixth General Seymour reported to his headquarters that all was relatively quiet, with the enemy's cavalry reported at McGirt's Creek. He stated that his defensive works were almost completed, although he needed more guns, and that the Fourth New Hampshire was to be sent back that night. His current assessment of the situation was that, while several places could be held along the St. Johns River, the current Confederate strength and ability to concentrate precluded any attempt to advance into the interior. He concluded his message with the statement that, since he expected General Gillmore shortly, he was planning no movements other than to concentrate on the construction of the defensive works.[67]

On February 28, General Seymour directed that a signal tower be constructed on the blockhouse on Yellow Bluff so that communication could be established with the coast. Accordingly, a 110-foot-high tower was so built. An 83-foot-tall station had already been built on a church steeple on the west side of town. Communications were now available from the advance lines to General Seymour's headquarters and from there to the navy at Mayport. On March 18, another tower high enough to see as far as Yellow Bluff as well as any vessels for a distance up or down the river was constructed on Bay Street.[68]

General Gillmore informed General Seymour on February 28 that the forces in Florida were to be reduced as soon as the position in Florida was secured.[69] This indication of the downgrading of the priority of the Florida expedition may have been in response to a letter sent to General Gillmore by General Halleck on February 26, but seemingly before the defeat at Olustee was known by Halleck. General Halleck referred to the letters he had been sent by Gillmore on February 13 and 16 saying, first, that Gillmore's request to come north was refused unless another officer was assigned to command in his place. Second, since the letters referenced had indicated that the expedition had accomplished its objectives in Florida, Gillmore was to report the numbers of men and batteries that might be freed for possible operations at other locations along the Atlantic or Gulf coast.[70]

On February 27, Seymour was directed to send back General Vogdes and to retain only three of the transports that had been used to bring in reinforcements. Concerning other matters, he was to send for the lumber still at Albertis's Mills (left there when the Ninety-seventh Pennsylvania returned to Fernandina), he was authorized to use the railroad iron stored on Amelia Island should he desire to complete the railroad from

Fernandina to Baldwin, and he was encouraged to build a field-work at Yellow Bluff to protect his communications on the river.[71]

General Seymour replied on February 28 to these suggestions. He believed that all that was necessary on Yellow Bluff would be a blockhouse, and he had two companies engaged in building one. There was no intention to complete the railroad to Baldwin, which was no longer in Union hands, and if rail connection should be desired later, it should be from Jacksonville to Baldwin, as that route was shorter. The lumber still at Albertis's Mills had been burned, but it was anticipated that another sawmill would be in operation within a couple of weeks. It was General Seymour's intention to occupy and fortify Palatka as soon as the defensive position at Jacksonville was completed; last, he believed he should mount another regiment, as the enemy was believed to have five times the number of his mounted force. "No activity can be anticipated or expected, offensively, while the disparity is so great."[72] He revealed a hardening defensive attitude on February 29 when he informed the navy forces supporting him that he no longer needed as large a force as was presently there.[73] On the same date, he directed General Foster to keep his troops constantly employed clearing up and preparing the ground on the opposite side of the stream "so as to increase the strength of Jacksonville as a military position."[74]

The Confederate troops in position on McGirt's Creek were meanwhile engaged in constructing an elaborate fortification of breastworks and stockade. Capt. Winston Stephens wrote:

> You will see by this that we are gradually closing upon the Yanks and their brother Negroes. . . . Our main force rests on the West side of the branch from your Uncle George's old place. . . . Their [the Federal troops] main force are entrenching on the east side of Cedar Creek about ¾ miles from [John] Prices. . . . I don't know Genl. Finegan's program, but I think if any Yankees sleep on the west side of Cedar Creek, it will be their last sleep. . . . I would not be surprised at anytime to be thrown into the midst of battle with all grandure and at the same time with all dangers.[75]

On March 1, Colonel Henry sent out a reconnaissance patrol from his mounted brigade's position in front of the Union forces at Jacksonville. Commanded by Maj. Atherton Stevens and composed of two companies and a platoon from the Independent Massachusetts Cavalry Battalion, one company from the Fortieth Massachusetts Mounted Infantry, and one gun from Elder's battery, its mission was to check out the enemy's position at Ten-Mile Station. They made contact around 10:00 A.M. with about one hundred Confederate cavalry with two guns about one mile east of Pickett's. After driving the Confederate pickets in, the Union force advanced about three miles beyond Cedar Creek, where they ran into a larger enemy force. Lt. M. Leahy, Battery B, First U.S. Artillery, was directed to put his gun into action. He opened with shell and case shot and then, as the larger Confederate force advanced, two rounds of canister at the head of their column, which was within five hundred yards and closing.[76] This fire may have caused the death of Capt. Winston Stephens, the one casualty suffered by the Confederate force.[77]

The Union troops began to pull back slowly, followed by the Confederate forces, until they reached their prepared positions at Cedar Creek, where they were reinforced by Colonel Henry with another piece of artillery and all but one squadron of the Fortieth Massachusetts. The Union forces held this position for about one-half hour under command of Colonel Henry, who had sent Major Stevens back to ready the Union position at Three-Mile Run.[78] The Confederate cavalry (estimated by Henry as a battalion) crossed Cedar Creek, flanking Henry on the right and forcing the Union forces again to retreat slowly, this time to their position at Three-Mile Run. The skirmish lasted from 10:00 A.M. until about 3:00 P.M. and covered some five miles of ground. Union casualties were one killed, four wounded, and five taken prisoners, and while the Union forces claimed they had inflicted as many as fifty casualties on the Confederates, the Confederates reported only the death of Captain Stephens.

A member of the Twenty-seventh Georgia reported that his unit, the Eleventh South Carolina, and a force of cavalry, while on a reconnaissance, ran into a Union force at Cedar Creek, supposedly out for the same purpose. "After a short engagement, the enemy were completely routed; and but for the failure of the cavalry to execute Colonel Charles Zachry's (Twenty-seventh Georgia) orders, the entire party would have been captured."[79]

On February 22, General Beauregard sent a letter to President Davis from Georgia in which he assessed the current military situation within his command. He called attention to the movement of Union troops from in front of Charleston, citing the Union's advantage in rapid transportation and the ability to concentrate, but took issue with the president's claim that Beauregard had sufficient forces to handle his mission. Beauregard claimed that what troops he had were spread from North Carolina to the Alabama border and that six thousand of those were artillerymen, who could not be withdrawn without permitting Union penetration of his lines before Charleston and Savannah.

> Over 6,000 are cavalry, 2,000 of which are in Florida; rest defending lines of communication between this and Savannah, and thence with Florida, so vital at this juncture; 3,000 are light and seige artillery, leaving about 15,000 infantry now in Florida or en route. Except barely enough for weakest possible supports and pickets for works on John's, Sullivan's, and James Islands and at Savannah, every man I can spare with hope of safety has been ordered to Florida and Savannah.[80]

Beauregard closed, saying that he hoped he would soon be in a position to be able to send General Johnston and the Army of the Tennessee at least eight thousand troops of all arms at an early date.[81]

The seventeen thousand men in or on the way to Florida were desperately needed elsewhere by the Confederacy at that time. Brig. Gen. H. W. Mercer, commanding the Confederate troops at Savannah, believed that the troops sent to Florida from Georgia had left his defenses vulnerable. In a February 27 letter to General Beauregard's headquarters, he reported that he was sending the Twenty-sixth Virginia that day to Florida, as directed, but that Savannah was now left without any adequate means of defense and was unable to resist a serious attack. The heavy withdrawal of troops to Florida left him only four regiments, two battalions, two batteries, and several companies for the defense of the city, most of which were stationed at fixed batteries from which they could not be withdrawn with safety.[82]

General Beauregard was finally able to get to Florida on March 2, arriving at Camp Milton after two days and nights of traveling with little rest. Since Maj. Gen. James Patton Anderson had not yet arrived to take command, General Beauregard did so and carefully reconnoitered the Confederate position and its surroundings. In a March 3 message to Gen. Sam Cooper, General Beauregard reported that the situation was quiet, with the enemy fortifying Jacksonville under cover of the Union gunboats. He estimated the Union forces at about twelve thousand and expecting more reinforcements, while his own forces, positioned in the rear of McGirt's Creek, numbered some seven thousand. Both the Confederate and the Union pickets were located some seven miles from Jacksonville. He closed with the statement, "The victory at Ocean Pond was complete, but pursuit, especially by cavalry, was unsatisfactory."[83] General Cooper's return endorsement stated that General Beauregard's estimate of enemy's forces was considered excessive and suggested that the Union forces should be "expelled from Florida by prompt and decided measures."[84]

While at Camp Milton, Beauregard reorganized the Confederate forces. He dissolved the temporary division commanded by General Taliaferro and had the units that had composed that division report instead directly to him; General Gardner was directed to report back to his command in Middle Florida. On March 6, Beauregard ordered the following:

1. Transfer of the Twenty-sixth Virginia from General Finegan's brigade to Colonel Harrison's brigade.
2. Transfer of the Fifty-ninth Virginia from General Finegan to Colonel Harrison.
3. Transfer of the First Georgia Regulars from General Finegan to Colonel Colquitt.

4. Capt. J. J. Dickison of the Second Florida Cavalry to take his company to Palatka.

5. The commanding officer of the Fourth Georgia Cavalry to render any assistance Dickison may require and to be prepared to support Dickison with his whole command, if necessary.

6. Brigadier General Gardner to reestablish the military posts from Clay Landing on the Suwannee to Tampa with the troops that had been furnished to General Finegan when the Federal forces had landed the previous month.[85]

Additionally, on the same day, transfer was effected from South Carolina to Florida of the following units which were already either in Florida or en route: the Eighteenth South Carolina Volunteers, Holcombe Legion, Fifth Regiment Georgia Cavalry, Villepigue's Battery, Thirty-second Georgia Volunteers, Twenty-sixth and Fifty-ninth Virginia volunteers, Twenty-third, Twenty-seventh, and Twenty-eighth Georgia volunteers (Colquitt's brigade), Eleventh South Carolina Volunteers, Wheaton's battery light artillery, and one company of the South Carolina siege train.[86]

Turning next to General Cooper's suggestion that he attack and expel the Union forces (and after receiving written estimates of the probability of doing so from each of his brigade commanders—all of whom replied in the strong negative), General Beauregard gave the opinion that the Union forces in Jacksonville could not be driven out "with our present means."[87] He went on to say that if the gap between Lawton and Live Oak had been filled by a rail line connecting those two points, as he had recommended over a year earlier, the reinforcements he was sending at the very moment he was being asked to send ten thousand men to General Johnston would have arrived in time to cooperate in the action at Ocean Pond, and the enemy would have been driven out of Florida. Because of no rail connection, two entire days were lost in the passage through the gap of a portion of the reinforcements. While the victory was complete, there were not enough good troops to pursue the enemy vigorously, and he had time to fall back to Jacksonville, where he had been extending his entrenchments and, aided by gunboats, making his position too strong to be taken by the Confederate forces available in the area. "If however, the Department be of the opinion that under such circumstances, and with the means at hand, another officer can expel the enemy from Florida by prompt and decided measures, I will be most happy to surrender the command to him." General Cooper referred this letter to General Bragg, who commented on March 23 in his return endorsement, "No action seems to be called for in the public interest."[88] In any event, no further suggestions to attack and expel the Union forces came from Richmond.

On March 8, General Beauregard made some more changes. He ordered Colonel Harrison to locate a regiment from his brigade on the Jacksonville road as near as practicable to Camp Finegan and within one mile of the rear of Colonel Anderson's Fifth Georgia Cavalry to act as support for the cavalry. Lt. Col. Charles C. Jones was directed to furnish both the cavalry and its infantry support with a section of guns. The name of the camp occupied by the army on McGirt's Creek was renamed Camp Milton; the Sixty-fourth Georgia was ordered to Colonel Harrison's brigade from General Finegan's, with the Twenty-sixth Virginia reporting back to General Finegan; and General Finegan was ordered to reoccupy the posts from Clay Landing on the Suwannee to Tampa.[89] General Finegan was being stripped of most of the troops he had commanded and sent back to a less important position. Even the camp that had been named for him now bore someone else's name.

What General Beauregard had in mind for Confederate operations in East Florida is perhaps best illustrated by the views that were expressed to Lt. Col. Alfred Roman in a letter written at Savannah, Georgia, on February 27 by Maj. Henry Bryan, assistant inspector general. The letter contained an endorsement by General Beauregard dated March 10, 1864, and the words "The views herein expressed meet with my entire approval."[90]

General Beauregard reviewed the situation of trying to defend a large area with a small force when the enemy had the initiative because of their naval forces. He discounted fortifications on the coast as impractical and stated that such fortifications in the interior would serve only as temporary checks because they could readily be bypassed. The solution was to allow the enemy to land where he chose but to concentrate rapidly an adequate force to attack him. The best method by which to concentrate would be to use railroads and, to do this effectively, the most important step was to have "a continuous line of railroad from East Florida to the points whence reenforcements may be drawn." Since the enemy also wanted to make use of the railroads, those portions within twenty miles of the coast must be removed. Additionally, to harass the enemy as he moved inland, a mounted regiment should be scattered in the area ready to assemble at a particular point if word came by a telegraph system which was to be established.[91] Beauregard elaborated on this plan of operations to General Cooper in his report on the action at Olustee, stating that, unless there was a considerable increase of his forces, amply supported with means for a regular siege of Jacksonville, Southern operations should be confined to the defensive, that is, preventing the penetration of the enemy into the interior, either on the line toward Lake City or into the lower part of the state. In regard to the lower part of the state, he had selected a position on the St. Johns a few miles above Jacksonville for a battery of one rifled thirty-two pounder, three rifled thirty pounders, one twenty pounder, one ten-pounder Parrott, and two eight-inch siege howitzers, by which, "with torpedoes in the river, it is expected transports at least can be obstructed from passing with troops beyond Jacksonville."[92]

General Beauregard showed a much better grasp of the evolving character of modern war than his adversaries. The strategy he wished to employ was based upon a defense of the interior, utilizing mobile forces that could be concentrated, by rail or horse or both, at threatened points. Both the initiative and the coast were conceded to the Union. A Confederate "choke point" was to be constructed on the St. Johns River above Jacksonville at Fleming Island to prevent Union gunboats and transports from getting into the interior by way of the river, and rails were to be removed near the coasts to prevent Union use of the railroads for the same purpose. In general terms, this was the same strategy proposed by General Lee when he commanded the department. It was now two years later, the battle of Olustee had demonstrated the wisdom of this approach, and yet Florida was no better prepared to employ it than they had been in 1862. There was still no rail connection with Georgia, internal transportation within the state was inadequate, there were few effective mobile cavalry forces, and former senator Yulee continued to frustrate efforts to make the strategy viable by his fight for the rail belonging to the Florida Railroad Company.

The Union forces, however, were not looking to penetrate the interior in the immediate future. After having been in Jacksonville for several days, Gillmore sent instructions to Seymour through his chief of staff General Turner from his headquarters at Hilton Head, South Carolina, informing him in no uncertain terms that he was only to secure his own position and not to risk another advance at the present time. General Seymour was further advised to protect his lines of communication, and it was suggested that he occasionally land troops below Jacksonville to prevent ambushes from guerrillas. A suggestion was made that infantry replace Colonel Henry's mounted pickets so that Colonel Henry could save his horses and do some recruiting.[93]

General Gillmore replied on March 10 to General Halleck's letter of February 26. In relation to the current situation, he stated that the unfortunate events at Olustee had frustrated his original plans and forced him to keep three times the number of troops in Florida he had planned to keep there. He justified the Federal presence in Florida by writing: "The value of Florida to the enemy has been overlooked by us to a great extent. I am convinced that they have drawn from the counties along the line of the Fernandina and Cedar Keys Railroad an average of 2,000 head of cattle per week during the last year."[94] General Gillmore closed his letter with suggestion that, after talking with Rear Admiral Dahlgren, he was now ready to resume operations against Charleston.[95] General Halleck's March 16 reply contained the following statement: "Until Lieutenant-General Grant returns from the West I presume no additional instructions will be given by the War Department in regard to military operations in your department."[96] There appeared to be little interest left in the Florida expedition in either Washington or Hilton Head.

Colonel Barton, reinforced by five companies of the Fifty-fifth Massachusetts and two sections of Capt. Martin James's battery, occupied Palatka on March 10 and, under the supervision of engineer Lt. Peter S. Michie, started to construct defensive works that could be held by a five-hundred-man garrison. General Gillmore's instructions were that no offensive operations were to take place until the town was so fortified "that the position can be held against great odds."[97] General Gillmore seemed to be still trying to salvage something out of his original plan to create an enclave marked by the line from Fernandina to Baldwin, Palatka, and St. Augustine.

General Beauregard was recalled to Savannah on March 20. Before leaving, he gave specific directions on the conduct of future operations in Florida to Gen. James Patton Anderson, now commanding the District of Florida. The current Confederate forces in the area were inadequate to drive the Federal forces out of Jacksonville, although an operation against Palatka might be done with some risk. The Confederate emplacements along McGirt's Creek were to be considered temporary until more secure ones were completed at Baldwin. Upon occupying the finished fortifications at Baldwin, General Anderson had the following courses of action to pursue:

> Should the enemy advance on you from Jacksonville, you should retire on Baldwin slowly drawing him after you. About one brigade will take position in the lines there, with some cavalry on the left; the other two brigades and main body of cavalry will take position on the right ready to take the enemy in flank and rear by advancing between the Little and Big Cypress Swamps, should he attack the lines in front. In the event of his again being defeated, he should be pursued vigorously by the cavalry on his flanks and the infantry in his rear. Should the enemy divide his

forces by re-enforcing strongly those already at Palatka, the proposed battery at Fleming's Island on the Saint John's should be constructed at once, and torpedoes put in the river so as to prevent its navigation. Should the enemy, after fortifying strongly Jacksonville and Palatka, leaving those two places with only a strong garrison in each, a battery should be put up at once near the mouth of Trout Creek, a few miles below Jacksonville, to cut off its communication with the mouth of the river; this will ensure the fall or evacuation of both places.[98]

Gen. Braxton Bragg's endorsement on these instructions was the terse comment, "The enemy's forces appear to me largely overestimated, and our own operations too defensive."[99]

After some initial sparring by the two forces in the weeks after Olustee, a general stalemate existed by the middle of March 1864, with the Union forces entrenched in Jacksonville and Palatka, and the Confederate forces entrenched at McGirt's Creek while constructing a strongpoint at Baldwin. The activity that had been generated by the Union landing at Jacksonville on February 7 had settled into a standoff. The Union forces were committed to a defense of Fernandina, Jacksonville, and St. Augustine, with occasional occupation of Palatka. From these areas, raids would be mounted into the interior to disrupt Confederate communications, recruit blacks, and seize or destroy supplies. The Confederate operations, primarily conducted by Capt. J. J. Dickison and his cavalry band, were guerrilla in nature, attacking, harassing, destroying, or capturing Union facilities and people.

In a number of letters written home from Jacksonville by Justus Silliman of the Seventeenth Connecticut while a headquarters clerk for General Vogdes, a good description is given of the effect of the Union raids.[100] Quite a few cattle, deserters, "professed Union men," and refugees poured into the Union enclave, as had been envisioned by General Gillmore in his original plan of operations. This flow accelerated as Southern fortunes deteriorated. Trade revived in the area with the arrival of more people from the North and from the interior. Esther Hill Hawks, whose husband was a surgeon with the Third U.S. Colored Troops, was in Jacksonville at this time and operating a free school. Her published diary confirms Silliman's description of the revival of activity in the Federally occupied and controlled areas during the year after Olustee.[101] Thought of severing Florida from the Confederacy was ended, and the Department of the South turned its attention back to matters elsewhere. William Watson Davis summed up what he felt the Federal expedition had accomplished.

> The immediate results of this expedition to Florida were about as follows: the capture, confiscation, stealing, or destruction of cotton, lumber, timber, turpentine, forage, live stock, food, clothing, and military supplies to the amount of more than $1,000,000; the recruitment of a few score negroes for the black regiments; the capture of a few score Confederate soldiers and eight cannon; the failure to reconstruct the state government on a basis of loyalty to the Union; the loss of about 2,000 men in a bloody battle; the hasty retreat of the invading army.[102]

Davis failed to appreciate fully the wider ripples that the Federal expedition sent forth.

7

Heroes, Goats, and Survivors

For the Union, on the basis of the percentage of casualties, the battle of Olustee was the third bloodiest of the entire war! Of the 5,115 Union soldiers involved, 1,355, or 26.5 percent, were casualties. Only the combined battles of the Wilderness and Spotsylvania in 1864 and the June 14, 1864, battle of Port Hudson had a higher casualty rate for Union forces.[1] This is all the more startling because both Union and Confederate forces at Olustee were approximately equal in strength and fought on a field that offered neither side any significant advantage. Since neither side had a preconceived plan of action, the reason for the high rate of Union casualties has to rest with the Union leadership.

General Finegan had the good fortune to have had Colonel Colquitt on the field of battle at the beginning of the action. Upon arrival at the initial Confederate position, Colonel Colquitt quickly formed a line of battle with the units he had, elongating that line with arriving units. The Confederate units deployed successively and were in position often just moments before the opposing Union forces started to deploy. The result was that the Confederates from the beginning were able to bring superior firepower to bear on the Union forces as they were being committed piecemeal. The extension of the Confederate lines to both flanks resulted in a concave line that overlapped the Union lines on both flanks and permitted a devastating, concentrated, converging, and enfilading small-arms fire to be directed at the Union forces.

Olustee Battlefield Monument. Courtesy of the Florida State Archives, Tallahassee.

There was little or no reserve for this extended line. Had the Federal forces been able to penetrate and punch through the Confederate line, things could have become very difficult for the Southerners, who had little support in their rear. The Confederate position might have been bypassed, had the Federal forces not blundered into the engagement so quickly and completely, but then the Union forces themselves would have been vulnerable to the danger of a flank attack by the Confederates.

The Confederate forces were inferior in artillery strength to the Union forces and compounded the problem by poor employment of what artillery they did have. Although the Southern forces had twelve guns, for a significant portion of the battle only one section of the Chatham Artillery (two guns) was in action. It was later located so far forward that it could have been captured (and almost was, had not some more adventurous members of the Fifty-fourth Massachusetts been stopped by their commander). The initial positioning of the Union artillery so far forward, despite the presence of experienced, regular army artillerymen, including General Seymour and Captains Hamilton, Langdon, and Elder (later Gen. U. S. Grant's chief of artillery), was a critical mistake. The guns and gunners were well within effective rifle range of the Confederate infantry, who created havoc by picking off the men and horses who serviced the Union guns.

General Seymour committed a basic error by using tactics that were made obsolete by technological advances. Subsequent attempts to protect the artillery by pushing forward infantry only increased the casualty rate. Although all sixteen of the Federal guns were put into action, they were much more of a liability than an asset because of their location, the nature of the battlefield, their employment, and, in some cases, the absence of veterans and the presence of troublemakers from other units who had been temporarily assigned. A number of observers present at the battle commented that the artillery for both sides was generally ineffective, judging by the marks reported to be on trees, which were entirely too high. The battle was essentially one of small arms, a characteristic of a style of warfare that did not change until the invention of the shrapnel shell.

Although both sides claimed to have employed their cavalry on the flanks, there is little evidence to show that anything positive was contributed by this arm before, during, or after the battle. By numbers, the cavalry and mounted forces made up some 20 percent of the troops on the field. Furthermore, some of the mounted units of the Fortieth Massachusetts had been armed recently with the seven-shot Spencer repeating rifles that had once belonged to members of the Seventh New Hampshire. The potential mobility and firepower of this unit were wasted. Failure on the part of both sides to use their cavalry effectively forced the engagement into a head-on, toe-to-toe battle of attrition.

Once the battle was joined, the initiative for both sides devolved upon the brigade and regimental commanders. In this, the Union was at a disadvantage. A Union officer later pointed out that a great deal of the misfortune was undoubtedly attributable to the fact that all the troops were unused to field service and that Seymour's brigade commanders were all inexperienced colonels. "In the meantime five general officers, four of whom had considerable experience in field operations, were lying idle on Folly Island."[2]

In his account of the battle, Henry F. Little of the Seventh New Hampshire pointed out a number of mistakes made by the Union leadership. He felt that any experienced field commander would, upon having his skirmishers develop enemy strength to the front, deploy several regiments into line as a precautionary measure rather than trying to do so while under fire and "almost upon the line to be assaulted."[3] Furthermore, there were other Union troops in the area that should have been moved up to supporting positions at Baldwin, Barber's, and Sanderson, with more effective use made by the railroad (one locomotive having just been put into service) as far as Sanderson. The Union units referred to were the Twenty-fourth Massachusetts, Fifty-fifth Massachusetts (at Barber's), Third U.S. Colored Troops, Fourth New Hampshire, Tenth Connecticut (St. Augustine), and Ninety-seventh Pennsylvania (Fernandina). These units, which were for the most part idle at the time, could have been better used by General Seymour to strengthen his raiding force, interdict the area, provide a handy reserve, or conduct supporting operations. While General Seymour may have been unaware that a locomotive had just become available, his logistic support problems might have been alleviated had he broken through the Confederate lines and taken the railroad equipment that was supporting the Confederate forces.

On the Southern side, Lieutenant Grant noted in his report, "So far as I was able to learn there was no preconceived plan of battle or combined movement of our troops after General Colquitt put them in position on the field."[4] Once the Confederate forces were directed into line and deployed by their regimental commanders, all other movements were relatively simple. One wonders what an experienced commander such as General Beauregard or Gen. James Patton Anderson might have done in coordinating the efforts of all of the Confederate infantry and artillery on the field.

The Union forces might have fared better if the units directly involved in the battle had been up to their normal capabilities. While at Hilton Head, half of the Seventh Connecticut had re-enlisted and gone home for a thirty-day leave.[5] The remaining men were reorganized into four companies and led by a captain. Had the Seventh been up to strength, the firepower from their Spencer rifles at the opening of the battle would have created difficulties for their opponents. The Seventh New Hampshire also had a number of veterans home on leave, replaced with over three hundred new recruits. With half of the regiment armed with largely unserviceable Springfields, their normal firepower was considerably reduced. To have then attempted to deploy them too close to the enemy's lines while under fire after their leaders had given them conflicting orders borders on the criminal. A crucial stage of the battle was the breaking of the Seventh New Hampshire, a setback which could have been prevented.

The Forty-eighth New York had been recovering at St. Augustine from the attack on Battery Wagner, where it had suffered severe casualties. While at St. Augustine, it had received replacements from a notorious independent battalion that had been broken up in the Department of the South.[6] Langdon's battery had also received some of these men as replacements.

The unit historians of both of these organizations pointed out the negative contributions made by these "rotten apples." The First North Carolina and the Fifty-fifth Massachusetts were understrength because of men being held back who had either been exposed to, or were suffering from, smallpox.[7] The Fifty-fourth Massachusetts went into battle minus a field grade officer and two companies assigned to security duty that could have been handled by other units. Light Battery C, Third Rhode Island, was a composite of men from the remaining sections of its parent unit because so many men had gone on leave.[8]

General Seymour's force included several new regiments that had never been under fire before. General Gillmore's original plan had been to take only seasoned troops and replace them on siege duty at Charleston and Savannah with the newly formed colored regiments. An experienced unit in place of the Eighth U.S. Colored Troops might have reacted differently. Finally, General Gillmore had initially wanted to take a larger mounted force on the expedition, but this was negated by higher authority. For a raiding force of this type, the larger mounted force would have provided the mobility, surprise, and shock that would probably have defeated General Finegan's forces at Lake City and accomplished, at that time, the destruction of the bridge at Columbus. Certainly, a strong mobile force operating out of the redoubts that General Gillmore had planned for Baldwin and Palatka would have posed a considerable threat to the scattered Confederate forces, providing the punch to make his defensive-offensive strategy work. The attempt to beef up the mounted force by providing them with the Seventh New Hampshire's Spencer rifles was an action that came back to haunt the Federal forces. Had the expedition included a stronger mounted force, the problem with the exchanged rifles might not have happened.

When the Seventh Connecticut's skirmishers made contact with the Confederate infantry, the Union artillery was massed too close to the Confederate line, where they were subjected to heavy, accurate small-arms fire. The infantry regiments were then committed to their support before being fully deployed and were subjected to the same fire. The Eighth U.S. Colored

Troops, a completely new and combat-inexperienced unit which had never even practiced firing their weapons, was one of the lead units in the Northern column approaching the battlefield, a questionable choice of position by the Federal commanders. Sent into action with weapons empty, to deploy and load their weapons while under fire, it was remarkable that they stayed where they were for an hour and a half. The brigade commander, Colonel Hawley, gave them an order to go into battle, without knowing anything about their training and experience, and then left the Eighth to go with the Seventh New Hampshire, having no further contact with the Eighth until the retreat.

Colonel Hawley subsequently lost contact with Colonel Abbott of the Seventh New Hampshire after that unit broke. Colonel Abbott stated previously that he received no further orders from Colonel Hawley until the retreat. Colonel Hawley, the commander of the lead Union brigade, lost control of his brigade, remaining with his former regiment (the understrength Seventh Connecticut) until the retreat. A more experienced brigade commander might have worked harder to reestablish control and reorganize his unit. When needed as a brigade commander, Hawley was playing regimental commander.

Colonel Barton's New York brigade performed creditably, but by this time the Confederate line had been established and overlapped the Union right flank. The brigade did all that could be done in just holding their portion of the line. The arrival of Colonel Montgomery's colored brigade initiated a defensive posture by the Union forces at a time when the Confederate line had about exhausted their ammunition, a situation of which the Union leadership was unaware. The enfilading fire by the Sixth Florida battalion on one side of the Union line and that of the Sixth and Thirty-second Georgia regiments on the other side were strong contributions to the Confederate victory. The success of the Confederate side has to be largely attributable to the rapid organization of their line by Colonel Colquitt, enabling the Southerners to bring up and deploy their entire force, bringing maximum firepower to bear on the Northern troops, who were being committed piecemeal. This success was aided by the constant pressure the Confederates kept on the Federal forces, giving the Northerners no breathing space in which to regroup. After brilliant execution on the battlefield, Southern fortunes declined with the start of the Northern retreat.

The Union forces were allowed to conduct a generally organized and controlled retreat, while the Confederate forces, who had done so well up to this point, lost a tremendous opportunity to exploit their success. The Union forces managed to keep an effective screen in place, behind which they brought off a large part of their force along with a large number of their wounded and some supplies. General Finegan, as the senior Confederate commander, bears the responsibility for this failure to pursue immediately and closely. He compounded this failure by not organizing an effective pursuit within the next few days. At the end of the battle, the Confederate troops were better organized and in better physical and psychological shape than the Union troops, who were handicapped by the presence of large numbers of wounded. General Beauregard had good reason to be upset over the conduct of the pursuit and the performance of the cavalry.

In his initial assignment of units to the expedition, General Gillmore limited the amount of medical supplies and ambulances to be brought, on the assumption that there would be minimum casualties. In view of what happened, this proved costly in terms of what could be done for and with casualties. The number of wounded who might have received saving treatment or at least been removed from the battlefield can only be speculated. General Gillmore's reputation with his troops suffered somewhat when it was learned that he was at a party when the first wounded from the battle arrived by ship at Hilton Head.[9]

The treatment of black prisoners is still an open area of inquiry. Lt. Col. A. H. McCormick of the Second Florida Cavalry made a speech to his men before the battle, claiming the blacks were there to rape and pillage and stating he would take no prisoners.[10] The wounded man left among the abandoned guns, Henry Lang from the Forty-eighth New York, claimed he heard "marauding soldiers who were ill-treating wounded negroes."[11] Henry Shackleford of the Nineteenth talked of walking over "many a wooley head" and how the begging of the Northern blacks did them no good.[12] William Penniman of the Fourth Georgia Cavalry was mystified as he rode over the field immediately after the battle to hear shots being fired "almost frequently enough to resemble the bark of skirmishers." The mystery was solved for him by a Confederate officer he met who informed him that his men were "Shooting niggers Sir. I have tried to make the boys desist but I can't control them." When Penniman suggested that he thought it a shame to kill wounded prisoners, the officer replied that one of the people doing it had a twenty-three-year-old wounded brother murdered by blacks at Fort Pillow and "had already killed nineteen and needed only four more to make matters even."[13] The sounds of firing continued.

James Jordan of the Twenty-seventh Georgia wrote his wife immediately after the battle about the bloody carnage that had taken place. He related that many Northern blacks were killed and wounded in the battle and said, "Our men killed some of them after they fell in our hands wounded."[14] Winston Stephens of the Second Florida wrote to his wife after the battle, "Tell the negroes if they could have seen how the [Northern] negroes are treated I think it would cure them of all desire to go."[15] Jacob Roach, a soldier from Georgia, witnessed this treatment and related (with original spelling), "I tell you our men slayed the Negrows & if it had not been for the officers their would not one of them been spaired."[16]

Southern whites were not the only ones maltreating the Northern blacks. Winston Stephens went on to tell his wife how one of the blacks in the Southern camp killed a captured Northern black who offered to shake hands with him.[17] Edwin Tuttle, who arrived later with the Twenty-sixth Virginia, wrote that black cooks from the Georgia regiments went around after the battle and "knocked many of the Wounded in the head with light wood knots."[18] The *Atlanta Intelligencer* published an account concerning a visit to the battlefield by a gentleman in company with his body servant. Seeing a good pair of boots on the feet of a black soldier lying on the ground, the body servant attempted to remove them. The wounded soldier commenced kicking and yelling to leave his boots alone, as he was not dead. The body servant replied, "Well, den, if you ain't dead, I'll deaden you" and killed the soldier with a lightwood knot, bearing off the coveted boots.[19]

William Penniman visited the battlefield the next day and observed:

> The results of the shooting of the previous night became all to [sic] apparent. Negroes, and plenty of them, whom I had seen lying all over the field wounded, and as far as I could see, many of them moving around from place to place, now . . . all dead. If a negro had a shot in the shin another was sure to be in the head.
>
> A very few prisoners were taken, and but a few at the prison pen. One ugly big black buck was interrogated as to how it happened that he came back to fight his old master, and upon his giving some insolent reply, his interrogater [sic] drew back his musket, and with the butt, gave him a blow that killed him instantly. A very few of the wounded were placed on the Surgeon's operating table—their legs fairly flew off, but whether they were at all seriously wounded I have always had my doubts.[20]

In September 1864, Brig. Gen. John P. Hatch wrote a letter to Maj. Gen. E. A. Hitchcock, commissioner for the exchange of prisoners, in which he stated that, soon after the battle of Olustee, a list of wounded and prisoners in the hands of the enemy was forwarded to the Union lines by the commander of the rebel army. What attracted attention immediately was the very small number of black prisoners.

> It is well known that most of the wounded colored men were murdered on the field. Those outrages were perpetrated, so far as I can ascertain, by the Georgia regulars and the Georgia Volunteers of Colquitt's brigade.
>
> As many of these troops are now in our hands as prisoners, an investigation of the circumstances might easily be made.

All accounts represent the Florida troops as not engaged in the murders.[21]

The list of wounded he cited may be corroborated by General Finegan's report that he had "forwarded 150 prisoners of which only three were negroes."[22] However, when Brig. Gen. J. W. Turner, General Gillmore's chief of staff, was being questioned by the Congressional Joint Committee on the Conduct of the War, which investigated the Federal expedition, he testified that he knew little about the treatment of the black prisoners. He stated that after questioning many Confederate deserters who had entered Union lines after Olustee, he believed that both white and black prisoners were receiving the same treatment and that no outrages had been committed upon them.[23] The blacks who were taken prisoner at Olustee and survived the killing and maltreatment on the battlefield were incarcerated at Andersonville. Their treatment at the hands of their Southern captors must have caused them to wonder if they had been indeed fortunate to have survived.

The nine days that intervened between the skirmish at Lake City and the start of the Federal raid toward the Suwannee River enabled the Confederate forces to build up a strength almost equal to the Union forces. Most of those Southern troops had to come by way of one railroad, which could have been seriously damaged or, at the very least, watched to give advance warning of what was being done by the Confederate side. While no commander in a battle has all the intelligence information he would like to have, it is a cardinal sin not to try to get all that can be obtained. General Seymour's failure to learn of the Confederate buildup in the nine days prior to Olustee and his failure to interdict the area of operations was compounded by a failure to provide adequate security while on the march in enemy-controlled territory.

General Seymour was an officer who experienced combat in three different wars. Yet he made his decision to move after over a week's inactivity in the middle of enemy-occupied territory with little knowledge of the strength or location of his opponent and with inadequate logistic support. Within a few short days he had completely reversed his assessment of the expedition and disregarded the advice he had sought from his immediate subordinates. Although informing General Gillmore that he would be on the move on or about February 17, he did not move until three days later, and all indications are that the move was the result of a quick decision. Whatever compelled General Seymour to override prudent military judgment and make his fateful decision will never be known. We can only speculate on his strange behavior the week prior to Olustee and the factors that contributed to that decision.

Looking at the larger picture, the demonstration by General Schimmelfennig on John's Island would have accomplished its purpose, had General Seymour not procrastinated. It did give the Federal troops in Florida an overwhelming numerical superiority for at least ten days. In view of what could be reasonably expected from such a diversionary effort, it was a success. The Federal expedition was given sufficient time to accomplish its objectives, had General Seymour continued his initial momentum.

Coordination between the Departments of the South and of the Gulf might have produced the type of combined operation that General Beauregard most feared when he inquired about a second landing at St. Marks. With most of the Confederate troops defending Florida concentrated at Olustee, a relatively small force from the Gulf would have had an easy time destroying the bridge General Seymour was after or creating havoc in the Confederate rear. Such coordination was General Gillmore's responsibility. If the operation had been proposed properly through the military chain of command, rather than as a seemingly political ploy, with suggestion from the planners, General Halleck might have widened the scope to include both departments.

Up until about the seventeenth of February, the Union strategy that Gillmore intended to use—occupying certain key defended points while pushing out raiding parties in different directions—was highly effective, as witnessed by the Gainesville and Callahan/King's Ferry raids. To meet the threat posed by the Federal expedition, General Beauregard was forced to

weaken the defenses around Savannah and Charleston by sending seventeen thousand troops to Florida to protect the vitally
needed shipments of commissary supplies. This came at a time
when his own Atlantic coast defenses were being serious de-
pleted by the expiration of enlistments of a significant part of
his own army.

To complete the squeeze, General Beauregard chose to delay
sending the ten thousand troops Richmond had requested for
the Army of the Tennessee, which was losing the vital areas of
East Tennessee and about to open the gates to Georgia to the
Union forces. In so doing, he tied up critically short transportation assets. The priority transportation of troops on those assets and the Federal activities in Florida must have been a
severe crimp in the supply of commissary products to both
Beauregard's and Johnston's armies. At the same time, Beauregard was fortunate that the Union leadership did not take
advantage of his weakened coastal defenses and run a substantial operation against Savannah, Charleston, the Branchville
railroad junction, or similar targets.

Union armies taking Knoxville and Chattanooga in the fall
of 1863 severed the major supply line from Atlanta to Richmond,
complicating the supply of Gen. Robert E. Lee's Army of
Northern Virginia. There was pressure for a spring offensive
among the Confederate leadership, but General Johnston in
Mississippi and later in North Georgia and General Bragg in
Tennessee both claimed supply, transportation, and manpower
shortages. General Lee's chief commissary reported on February 28 that the Army of Northern Virginia was down to two
days' bread and only a few days' meat.[24] The primary source of
the problem was deteriorating rail transportation. Nevertheless, the Federal expedition into Florida during the height of
the Confederate supply crisis in early 1864 disrupted for a
while shipment of commissary supplies from Florida and
added to that crisis.

While there was less recruitment of blacks for Union units
than had been hoped for, the psychological effect upon both
Southern whites and blacks of seeing free, armed, and effective
black Union soldiers in the Florida interior must have been

traumatic. The demonstration of professional military competency by units such as the First North Carolina and the Fifty-fourth Massachusetts under fire would erode the myth of the inferiority of the black soldier. Furthermore, what slaveholder could sleep peacefully, convinced his "loyal" slaves would not run off to the Union lines or do worse?

Even though the Confederates won at Olustee, Maj. George W. Scott, the Florida cavalryman, wrote a detailed letter to his wife telling her what to do and where to go in the interior to escape the Yankees.[25] He was expressing the fear that other incursions were to follow. Others may have felt the same. Certainly a lot of evidence exists of the widespread apathy for the war and Confederate cause that resulted in increasing numbers of deserters, refugees, and "professed Union men" entering the Union lines after the battle of Olustee.

The expedition did not achieve the restoration of Florida to the Union. President Lincoln was initially castigated by the press for sacrificing five thousand soldiers for three nominating votes. However, shortly after the Olustee defeat, the *New York Times* published an editorial entitled "The Real Military Importance of Florida," which stated, "We trust that, despite the ill-luck that has met the opening of the Florida campaign, the work may still be kept up, if its results [in severing Confederate supply lines] should promise to be really as important as surmised. The newspaper later published two more editorials defending the president; one acquitted him of any blame connected with the Olustee defeat and placed the blame on the military commanders involved.[26]

The Joint Committee on the Conduct of the War exonerated the president but strangely enough did not place any blame on the military commanders. Nor did General Gillmore follow up on what was a clear case of insubordination and disobedience of orders by General Seymour. President Lincoln had never intended the operation to be directed at restoration of Florida to the Union. There was some political gain though; a number of Floridians made expressions of loyalty to the Union and would later form the basis for a reconstruction government.

General Seymour's blundering in allowing his forces to be committed piecemeal and defeated in detail (something he had done before in the abortive attack on Battery Wagner) pretty well ended hopes for what could have been achieved. General Seymour was too limited in vision to have commanded the advance force of the Federal expedition. He was more concerned with the idea of preventing the Confederacy from removing rail iron from Florida than he was with the possibilities of what a Union force with the advantage of surprise and mobility could do over a large area that was a key source of subsistence supplies. His disregard for security while in the enemy's territory, his failure to develop reliable intelligence, his failure to appreciate the strengths and weaknesses of his own units, his inertia when his forces had the advantage, his too-rapid piecemeal commitment of his units into an unknown situation, and his contradictory statements and behavior within a short period of time were responsible for the failure of what was potentially a low-cost, significant Union victory.

General Gillmore shares the blame on a higher level for not thinking in larger terms, coordinating with other commands, or planning adequately and for his choice of subordinate leaders. Between Generals Seymour and Gillmore, a beautiful opportunity was lost to demonstrate the power of combined operations and provide a classic example of a new form of warfare by waging war on the enemy's resources but with minimum destruction. Gen. William T. Sherman would soon demonstrate successfully a more violent way of doing the same thing.

Surprisingly, General Seymour's military career managed to survive both Battery Wagner (listed as the sixth bloodiest defeat for the Union) and Olustee.[27] He was transferred to the Army of the Potomac, where he was captured at the Wilderness. After being exchanged, he commanded a division in the Shenandoah Valley, at the siege of Petersburg, and in the Appomattox campaign, being brevetted a major general in both the Regular Army and the Volunteers at the end of the war. He was promoted to the substantive rank of major in the Fifth Artillery in 1866, and he served in that position until he voluntarily retired in 1876. He then moved to Florence, Italy, where he died in 1891.[28]

On the Confederate side, General Finegan received a great

deal of credit for doing relatively little. One wonders how he was able to keep himself so busy so as not to appear on the battlefield until the Union forces were in full retreat. The failure to coordinate the efforts of the individual Confederate forces and immediately to pursue the defeated enemy rests on his shoulders. James A. Harley of Sparta, Georgia, wrote later of how Southern veterans of the battle revisiting Olustee were astounded to see the inscription on the monument there crediting Finegan as the "Hero of Olustee."[29] Colonel Colquitt, the real hero of Olustee, did an excellent job with the infantry but did not make enough use of the artillery and cavalry. General Seymour, given all his blunders, was fortunate in having General Finegan for an opponent.

As a postscript to the battle, Lt. T. E. Buckman reported the following ordnance and ordnance stores that were collected on the battlefield and along the line of Union retreat:

Napoleon gun	3
Ten-pounder Parrott gun	2
Small arms	1,600
Accouterment (sets)	400
Small-arm ammunition (rounds)	130,000[30]

The small arms were distributed among the Confederate infantry and cavalry, which, in the case of the Florida cavalry, was sorely needed. The artillery pieces were distributed among the Chatham, Gamble, and Guerard batteries. The Milton Light Artillery received nothing to replace what they had lost. For the other Florida units, at least, it was a much-needed and welcome supply.

8

A Final Look

The 1864 Federal expedition into Florida had the potential of being an early example of classic modern warfare. The objectives stated in the requests for permission to stage the expedition were a combination of political, military, economic, social, and psychological ones whose accomplishment, in terms of the zero-sum game, would have resulted in a significant Federal gain and proportionate Confederate loss. The Federal expedition failed to realize its full potential because its execution at critical points involved people with limited vision, abilities, and aggressiveness. The expedition was not a total failure; it did have successes, some more long range than immediate. An examination of its initial objectives and accomplishments might assist in reaching a better evaluation of the expedition.

The expedition did not obtain the numbers of black recruits for the colored regiments in the Department of the South that had been anticipated. The black units that participated did demonstrate by their presence and the publicizing of the Emancipation Proclamation that freedom was available to those still in slavery in the South. Unfortunately no information is available on how many blacks eventually left their Southern masters in Florida as a result of the expedition. The heroic behavior of the Fifty-fourth Massachusetts at Olustee, after their equally heroic performance at Battery Wagner, provided concrete proof of the courage and ability of the well-trained and well-led black soldier in combat. These attributes were demonstrated to a lesser degree by the Fifty-fifth Massachusetts and the First North Carolina. The unfortunate Eighth U.S. Colored Troops was a victim of circumstances beyond its control. Even under extreme conditions, its inexperienced and untrained members did not break and run but died in groups where they stood. Their misfortune was the result of the mistakes of others. While gaining few new black recruits, the expedition did have a positive effect on Federal efforts because of the presence of black troops and proof of their ability under fire.

Politically, the expedition had the potential of severing Florida from the Confederacy and restoring the state to the Union, as had already happened in Louisiana and was underway in other states. The defeat at Olustee, after the bitter experiences of the previous Union evacuations of Jacksonville, dampened efforts at restoration. Union occupation of an enclave marked by a line from Fernandina to Baldwin, Palatka, and St. Augustine, as originally intended by General Gillmore, might have achieved the stability and security that would have led to restoration via Lincoln's Ten Percent Plan. Restoring Florida to the Union, however, was not the major objective of the expedition, as others have inferred. Neither President Lincoln nor John Hay intended the expedition to be directed toward that purpose, and John Hay made this clear to General Gillmore before the expedition took place. The fact that restoration did not take place has contributed to the belief that the expedition was a total failure.

After the expedition, the continued presence of Federal forces in East Florida and their activities solidified Federal control over that area to the point where some success was made in recruiting members for a white Federal cavalry unit. The expedition did not sever Florida from the Confederacy; in effect, the state's geographic vulnerability and limited manpower resources that were exhausted by the end of 1862 had to a large degree already accomplished that. Politically, the power base of those who would be in charge during reconstruction was being consolidated by the continued presence of Federal troops in Florida, while the power base of those who had led the movement toward secession was being eroded. Progress toward the less obvious but longer-range goal of ensuring that Florida would willingly stay within a restored Union was also being made.

The disruption of the rail system in northern Florida was accomplished to a lesser degree than intended. The bridge over the Suwannee River was not destroyed; this could have been easily accomplished with either a little coordination of effort between the Federal Departments of the Gulf and of the South or better use by Generals Gillmore and Seymour of speed and more decisive action to capitalize on their initial advantage of surprise and superiority of forces. Federal efforts to prevent the removal of rails were aided by those of Southerner David L. Yulee, who successfully delayed by court action the removal of rail from the line of the Florida Railroad Company, which he controlled. Eventually, some of those rails were used in the connector line between Live Oak and Lawton that tied the Florida and Georgia rail systems together. This linkup took place in 1865, too late for effective use during the Civil War.[1]

The Federal retreat from Olustee to Jacksonville gave temporary control of the rail junction at Baldwin to the Confederate forces. Control of Baldwin was a key element in the Federal plans of General Gillmore. It could have been a perfect example of the execution of Gen. George B. McClellan's concept of the offensive-defensive strategy, whereby key points on the Confederate lines of communication were to be seized and defended, forcing the Confederates into making costly attacks in situations where the rifled gun had given the advantage to the defense. The Federal forces eventually raided Baldwin, destroying the Confederate fortifications there and forcing the Confederates to move their transportation activities farther westward. Even then, Federal raids from Jacksonville and from various places on the Gulf on the Florida rail system to destroy bridges and tear up track continued until the end of the war. Baldwin was no longer the key transportation center it had been before the Federal expedition, and Confederate efforts at moving people and materials were hampered by its loss. The already-limited rail system in Florida was able to continue in operation until the end of the war but was restricted to Middle Florida and subjected to periodic disruption.

In terms of availability of commissary supplies, Florida was considerably more valuable to the Confederacy in 1864 than she had been in 1861. Federal action had progressively reduced the areas from which the Confederacy could draw subsistence supplies, to the point where supplies from Florida were a major factor in the logistic support of both General Bragg's and General Beauregard's armies. The Federal expedition's objective of cutting off the shipment of commissary supplies from Florida may have been the most important of any of the stated objectives. The possibility of restoring Florida to the Union, however, forced the expedition to operate under strict restraints against the destruction of private property, forcing operating units to depend on a slow, inadequate supply system handicapped by inability to use the railroad for lack of locomotives. This kid-gloves policy was evidenced, in particular, during the Gainesville raid, where some two million dollars' worth of property was left untouched by the Federal forces. Although property was destroyed at Baldwin, Barber's, and Sanderson, this property was clearly identified as Confederate supplies. Later in the year, General Sherman would be less discriminatory and more effective in his ability to live off of the land while, through his destructive efforts, bringing the war home to the Confederacy.

The Federal efforts to cut off the source of commissary supplies had only a temporary effect. After Olustee, shipment of supplies resumed over modified transportation routes but in reduced amounts. Availability of those supplies created some controversy in Florida among Confederate commissary agents collecting the "tithe," impressment agents buying at an arbitrary figure, local officials purchasing food for the destitute in their area, and merchants trading for a profit.[2] Furthermore, the amount of supplies that were available to the Confederacy was reduced from earlier figures by a steadily decreasing productivity because of decreased agricultural acreage and manpower and raids by Federal armies and dissident elements within the state that confiscated, stole, or destroyed crops and storehouses. Additionally, unpatriotic citizens evaded taxes, increased amounts of the state's resources were needed for destitute members of soldiers' families, and Yankee carpetbaggers exploited the local situation. The deteriorating economic situation contributed to hoarding, resisting impressment, and profit making.

A large amount of the commissary supplies that were collected in Florida and the lower South and in the hands of Confederate commissary officials, however, rotted in storage facilities.[3] At this stage of the war, rail transportation was unable to get sufficient quantities to the Confederate armies, and Confederate logistic organization was deficient.[4] The Federal expedition did put a crimp in Confederate logistic efforts for a short period during the critical winter of 1863–64. Poor Confederate supply management, failing transportation, manpower shortages, and Sherman's advance through Georgia and South Carolina overshadowed the Federal efforts in Florida to hamstring the Confederate armies logistically. Still, in 1864, a situation existed wherein the Confederate armies were unable to stockpile supplies, and any disruption of the supply pipeline was a calamity. The Federal expedition did manage to contribute to Confederate supply problems by disrupting shipping and transportation facilities and destroying some stockpiled goods. After Olustee, the Federal raids that took place until the end of the war continued that effort.

Union troops in the Department of the South had been engaged for several years in relatively static siege operations. The Federal expedition gave large numbers of them an opportunity to go on the offensive and gain experience that would aid them, later when transferred north, while not jeopardizing the siege operations in Georgia and South Carolina. The reverse of this situation created severe problems for the Confederate side. To meet the threat in Florida, scarce manpower assets were stripped from the coastal defenses, leaving them vulnerable, and sent to a relatively unimportant location at a time when they were desperately needed with the Army of Tennessee.

The Federal forces occupying East Florida were handicapped

because so much of the area they controlled depended upon Federal support. This situation was created by current Federal regulations which allowed only Port Royal, South Carolina, to be an open port. If a port could be opened in Florida, the local economy could be revived (with some profit to the occupying forces), and the local residents would be less dependent upon the Federal government. This objective was not immediately achieved by the Federal expedition. However, the port of Fernandina was opened before the end of 1864, solving a number of problems for the Federal troops in Florida.

The collective objectives of the 1864 Federal expedition were legitimate, valid, and attainable. The potential of that expedition was great but was recognized more by Southern leaders such as General Beauregard and Governor Milton than by the Federal leaders who proposed, planned and executed it. Capitalizing upon Federal seapower for surprise and using what was considered at that time a minimum-size force, an optimum scenario for the Union might have seen the realization of the full potential of the Federal expedition. This would involve accomplishment of all objectives listed in the initial proposal, including the severance of Florida from the Confederacy; seizure of Savannah, Charleston, and the Branchville rail junction, or a combination of these, by a surprise landing of concentrated Union forces against a very weakened defense; diversion of manpower and transportation resources from critical areas to less critical ones; and finally, additional pressure applied to a rapidly deteriorating Confederate logistic effort—all this at a relatively low expenditure of Union manpower without jeopardizing the current Federal situation. In the Clausewitzian concept of the zero-sum game, the potential for Federal gain and Confederate loss contributing to final victory was great. The responsibility for this optimum scenario not being realized rests fully on the shoulders of the Union leadership.

In a total war where all elements are interrelated and nothing is won or lost or decided until final victory, the criterion for evaluating the 1864 Federal expedition in to Florida is its value in relation to that final victory. Despite the disaster for the Union forces at the battle of Olustee, it had a positive value. It would have had a greater one without that defeat for the Federals by demonstrating the efficiency and effectiveness of a highly mobile, water-based strategy, used to attack the enemy's resources, with the least possible negative effect on the civilian environment. Instead, the massive, plodding, toe-to-toe war of annihilation that brought success would be fixed on our experience, and the concept of combined operations would be discarded and forgotten until more contemporary wars.

Notes

Preface

1. Grady McWhiney and Perry D. Jamieson, *Attack and Die: Civil War Military Tactics and the Southern Heritage* (University: University of Alabama Press, 1982), p. 11.
2. Michael Howard and Peter Paret, eds., *Carl von Clausewitz: On War* (Princeton: Princeton University Press, 1976), p. 78.

1. The Jilted Bride: Florida's Early Years in the Confederacy

1. Yulee to Finegan, January 1, 1861, U.S. War Department, *The War of the Rebellion: A Compilation of the Official Records of the Union and Confederate Armies*, 128 vols. (Washington, D.C.: Government Printing Office, 1880–1901), ser. I, vol. I, pp. 442–43 (hereinafter cited as *ORA*, with all citations in series I, unless otherwise noted).
2. Yulee to Floyd, December 21, 1860, *ORA* I, pp. 348–49; Yulee and Mallory to Holt, January 7, 1861; Holt to Yulee and Mallory, January 9, 1861, pp. 350–51.
3. Perry to Duryea, January 5, 1861, *ORA* I, p. 332.
4. Powell to Maynadier, January 6, 1861, *ORA* I, pp. 332–33, 349; William Watson Davis, *The Civil War and Reconstruction in Florida* (New York: Columbia University Press, 1913), p. 72.
5. Douglas to Craig, January 7, 1861, *ORA* I, p. 333.
6. Meigs to Scott, November 1860, *ORA* LII, pt. 1, pp. 3–5.

7. Scott to Meigs, January 4, 1861; Scott to Tower, January 4, 1861, *ORA* I, pp. 350–51.

8. W. W. Davis, *Civil War,* p. 73.

9. Ibid., pp. 78–79.

10. *ORA* I, pp. 349–50. The ordnance at Fort McRee consisted of 125 "sea-coast and garrison" cannon, including 3 ten-inch and 12 eight-inch columbiads, 20 forty-two pounders, 24 thirty-two pounders, 64 twenty-four pounders, etc. Ordnance at Fort Barrancas consisted of 44 sea-coast and garrison cannon: 13 eight-inch columbiads and howitzers, 2 ten-inch mortars, 11 thirty-two pounders, 10 twenty-four pounders, 3 nineteen pounders, and 5 eighteen pounders. Barrancas Barracks had 4 six-inch field guns and 2 twelve-inch howitzers. See also W. W. Davis, *Civil War,* p. 83.

11. John Edwin Johns, *Florida during the Civil War* (Gainesville: University of Florida Press, 1963), pp. 32–33.

12. George C. Bittle, "Florida Prepares for War, 1860–1861," *Florida Historical Quarterly* 51 (October 1972): 144.

13. *ORA* IV:I, p. 333; W. W. Davis, *Civil War,* p. 89.

14. Johns, *Florida during the Civil War,* p. 35.

15. *ORA* IV:I, pp. 117–19, 211.

16. Fred L. Robertson, comp., *Soldiers of Florida in the Seminole Indian, Civil, and Spanish-American Wars* (Live Oak, Fla.: Democrat Book & Job Print, 1903).

17. *ORA* IV:I, pp. 211, 213.

18. *ORA* IV:I, pp. 222–23; Perry to Walker, April 19, 1861, p. 226; Walker to Perry, April 19, 1861; Perry to Walker, April 20, 1861, p. 227.

19. Perry to Walker, May 13, 1861, *ORA* LIII, pp. 165, 171; Perry to Walker, May 18, 1861, *ORA* IV:I, p. 333.

20. Walker to Perry, May 23, 1861, *ORA* IV:I, p. 352; Perry to Morton, Owens, and Ward, May 20, 1861, p. 174.

21. Perry to Walker, May 29, 1861, *ORA* IV:I, p. 361; Perry to Walker, June 1, 1861, *ORA* I, p. 469.

22. *ORA* IV:I, p. 412.

23. Robertson, *Soldiers of Florida,* cited in W. W. Davis, *Civil War,* p. 94.

24. *Journal of the Proceedings of the House of Representatives of the General Assembly of the State of Florida* (Tallahassee: Office of the *Floridian and Journal*), 11th sess., 1861, p. 81.

25. Milton to Davis, October 18, 1861, *ORA* IV:I, p. 290.

26. Rowland H. Rerick, *Memoirs of Florida, Embracing a General History of the Province, Territory, and State; and Special Chapters*

Devoted to Finances, Banking, the Bench, and the Bar, 2 vols. (Atlanta: Southern Historical Association, 1902) II, pp. 247, 300–301.

27. *ORA* IV:I, pp. 288, 291, 301–2, 315–17.

28. Benjamin to Trapier, October 22, 1861, *ORA* IV:I, pp. 292–93.

29. Benjamin to Dilworth, October 26, 1861, *ORA* IV:I, p. 296.

30. Benjamin to Milton, November 22, 1861, *ORA* IV:I, p. 328.

31. Milton to Davis, November 19, 1861, *ORA* IV:I, p. 325.

32. Milton to Davis, November 19, 1861, *ORA* IV:I, p. 325.

33. Benjamin to Milton, November 29, 1861, *ORA* IV:I, p. 334.

34. Milton to Davis, December 9, 1861, *ORA* IV:I, p. 342.

35. Ibid.

36. John F. Reiger, "Florida after Secession: Abandonment by the Confederacy and Its Consequences," *Florida Historical Quarterly* 50 (October 1972): 130; W. W. Davis, *Civil War*, p. 95.

37. Walker to Bragg, May 17, 1861, *ORA* I, p. 468.

38. *ORA* IV:I, p. 364.

39. Rerick, *Memoirs of Florida* I, p. 258.

40. *ORA* IV:I, p. 595.

41. *ORA* IV:I, p. 779; I:LII, pt. 2, pp. 12, 29; I, p. 408.

42. Walker to Perry, May 23, 1861, *ORA* IV:I, p. 352.

43. Johns, *Florida during the Civil War*, p. 37.

44. *ORA* XIV, p. 494.

45. Milton to Benjamin, October 29, 1861, *ORA* IV:I, p. 298.

46. Milton to Benjamin, October 31, 1861, *ORA* IV:I, pp. 308, 318–19.

47. Samuel R. Bright, Jr., "Confederate Coast Defenses" (Ph.D. diss., Duke University, 1961), p. 63.

48. *ORA* LIII, pp. 214, 248.

49. William C. Havard, "The Florida Executive Council, 1862," *Florida Historical Quarterly* 33 (July 1954): 80.

50. E. Merton Coulter, *The Confederate States of America*, vol. 7 of *A History of the South*, ed. Wendell Holmes Stephenson and E. Merton Coulter (Baton Rouge: Louisiana State University Press, 1950), p. 273; Rerick, *Memoirs of Florida* II, p. 180.

51. Francis B. C. Bradlee, *Blockade Running during the Civil War and the Effect of Land and Water Transportation on the Confederacy* (Salem, Mass.: Essex Institute, 1925), p. 207.

52. *ORA* IV:I, pp. 612, 778, 912.

53. *Journal of the House*, 12th sess., 1862, pp. 55–56.

54. Jerrell H. Shofner and William W. Rogers, "Confederate Railroad Construction: The Live Oak to Lawton Connector," *Florida Historical Quarterly* 43 (January 1965): 217, 227.

55. *Journal of the Proceedings of the Convention of the People of Florida Begun and Held at the Capitol in the City of Tallahassee on Thursday, January 3, 1861* (Tallahassee: Office of the *Floridian and Journal*, 1861), pp. 19, 42, 51–52, 63, 103–5.

56. Gilbert Sumter Guinn, "Coastal Defenses of the Confederate Atlantic Seaboard States, 1861–1862: A Study in Political and Military Mobilization" (Ph.D. diss., University of South Carolina, 1972), p. 111.

57. Ward to Walker, May 10, 1861, *ORA* I, pp. 466, 467.

58. *ORA* I, p. 468; IV:I, pp. 267, 276.

59. Grayson to Walker, September 13, 1861, *ORA* IV:I, p. 276.

60. *ORA* LIII, p. 301.

61. Guinn, "Coastal Defenses," pp. 114–15.

62. Milton to Mallory, October 2, 1861, *ORA* IV:I, p. 288.

63. Milton to Davis, October 18, 1861, *ORA* IV:I, p. 290.

64. Milton to Benjamin, October 24, 1861, *ORA* IV:I, p. 295.

65. Milton to Benjamin, October 28, 1861, *ORA* IV:I, pp. 298–99.

66. Milton to Davis, October 29, 1861, *ORA* IV:I, pp. 302, 300.

67. Milton to Brown, October 31, 1861, *ORA* IV:I, p. 304.

68. Trapier to Milton, November 1, 1861, *ORA* IV:I, p. 307.

69. Floyd to Milton, April 11, 1861, *ORA* LIII, pp. 233–34.

70. Grayson to Walker, September 13, 1861, *ORA* IV:I, p. 277.

71. *Official Records of the Union and Confederate Navies in the War of the Rebellion*, 30 vols. (Washington, D.C.: Government Printing Office, 1894–1927), ser. I, vol. XII, p. 600 (hereinafter cited as *ORN*, with all citations to series I).

72. *ORA* IV:I, p. 309.

73. Lee to Cooper, November 21, 1861, *ORA* IV:I, p. 327.

74. Lee to Dilworth, November 12, 1861, *ORA* LIII, p. 187.

75. Gill to Washington, November 27, 1861, *ORA* IV:I, p. 332.

76. Taylor to Lawton, December 18, 1861, *ORA* LIII, p. 201.

77. *ORA* IV:I, pp. 354–55.

78. Guinn, "Coastal Defenses," p. 132.

79. Lee to Gorgas, January 15, 1862, *ORA* VI, pp. 367–68.

80. Trapier to Cooper, January 23, 1862, *ORA* LIII, p. 215.

81. *Journal of the Convention of the People of Florida at a Called Session Begun and Held at the Capitol in the City of Tallahassee on Tuesday, January 14, 1862* (Tallahassee: Office of the *Floridian and Journal*, 1862); Guinn, "Coastal Defenses," p. 318.

82. Trapier to Davis, January 29, 1862, *ORA* LIII, pp. 216–17.

83. *Journal of the Convention of the People of Florida*, pp. 31–33, 103; Guinn, "Coastal Defenses," p. 319.

84. Taylor to Lee, February 14, 1862, *ORA* VI, pp. 380–81.

85. Benjamin to Lee, February 24, 1862, *ORA* VI, p. 398.

86. Milton to Benjamin, March 5, 1862, *ORA* VI, pp. 402–3.

87. *ORA* LIII, pp. 220–21.

88. Trapier to Washington, March 28, 1862, *ORA* VI, pp. 93–94.

89. Wright to Ely, April 13, 1862, *ORA* VI, pp. 124–25.

90. *ORA* I, p. 400.

91. Lee to Milton, April 8, 1862, *ORA* VI, p. 428.

92. Washington to Finegan, April 19, 1862, *ORA* XIV, p. 477.

93. Finegan to Cooper, September 29, 1862, *ORA* XIV, p. 614.

94. Cooper to Beauregard, October 7, 1862, *ORA* XIV, pp. 630, 665, 677, 684, 688, 689, 738.

95. Milton to Randolph, August 5, 1862, *ORA* LII, pt. 2, pp. 336–38.

96. *ORA* VI, pp. 426–27.

97. *ORA* IV:II, p. 649.

98. *ORA* LIII, p. 258.

2. Blockade and Raid:
The Middle Civil War Years in Florida

1. James R. Soley, *The Navy in the Civil War: The Blockade and the Cruisers* (New York: Scribner, 1883), pp. 44–45.

2. Soley, *Navy in the Civil War*, p. 36.

3. Ibid., p. 124.

4. Marcus W. Price, "Ships That Tested the Blockade of the Georgia and East Florida Ports, 1861–1865," *American Neptune* 15 (April 1955): 115; *ORN* XII, p. 232.

5. M. Price, "Ships That Tested the Blockade," p. 101.

6. Joe A. Akerman, Jr., *Florida Cowman: A History of Florida Cattle Raising* (Kissimmee: Florida Cattlemen's Association, 1976), p. 87.

7. Stanley L. Itkin, "Operations in the East Gulf Blockade of Florida, 1862–1865" (Master's thesis, Florida State University, 1962), p. 198.

8. Bern Anderson, *By Sea and by River: The Naval History of the Civil War* (New York: Knopf, 1962), p. 218.

9. M. Price, "Ships That Tested the Blockade," p. 97.

10. Ibid.

11. Trapier to Washington, January 20, 1862, *ORA* IV, pp. 75–76.

12. Trapier to Washington, January 31, 1862, *ORA* IV, pp. 76–77.

13. Wright to Pelouze, April 3, 1862, *ORA* IV, p. 129.

14. Wright to Pelouze, March 15, 1862, *ORA* IV, p. 100.

15. John D. Hayes, ed., *Samuel Francis DuPont: A Selection from His War Letters*, 3 vols. (Ithaca: Cornell University Press, 1969), I, p. 366.

16. *ORN* XII, p. 231.

17. M. Price, "Ships That Tested the Blockade," p. 120.

18. Hayes, *DuPont*, I, pp. 379–81.

19. M. Price, "Ships That Tested the Blockade," p. 119.

20. Hunter to Stanton, April 13, 1862, *ORA* VI, p. 263.

21. Wright to Ely, April 13, 1862, *ORA* VI, p. 125.

22. *ORA* VI, p. 251.

23. Hayes, *DuPont*, I, p. 374.

24. Ibid., II, p. 18.

25. Ibid., II, p. 69.

26. *ORA* VI, p. 217.

27. *ORA* IV, pp. 120–21, 127–43.

28. Saxton to Stanton, March 14, 1863, *ORA* XIV, p. 226.

29. Bryan to Jordan, March 26, 1863, *ORA* XIV, p. 845.

30. Saxton to Stanton, April 4, 1863, *ORA* III:III, pp. 116–17.

31. Thomas Wentworth Higginson, *Army Life in a Black Regiment* (1870; facsimile ed., Williamston, Mass.: Corner House Publishers, 1971), p. 128.

32. Beauregard to Gillmore, July 4, 1863, *ORA* XXVIII, pt. 2, pp. 11–13.

33. William J. Schellings, ed., "Blockade Duty on the Florida Coast, Excerpts from a Union Naval Officer's Diary," *Tequesta* 15 (1955): 71–72.

3. Renewed Interest in Florida

1. Benjamin Quarles, *The Negro in the Civil War* (Boston: Little, Brown, 1953), pp. 139–40; W. W. Davis, *Civil War*, p. 224.

2. Dudley T. Cornish, *The Sable Arm: Negro Troops in the Union Army, 1861–1865* (1956; facsimile ed., New York: Norton, 1966), p. 86.

3. Cornish, *Sable Arm*, p. 86.

4. Higginson, *Army Life*, pp. 76–77.

5. Cornish, *Sable Arm*, p. 138.

6. Finegan to Jordan, March 14, 1863, *ORA* XIV, p. 226.

7. *ORA* XIV, p. 423.

8. *ORA* XIV, p. 661.

9. Cornish, *Sable Arm*, p. 138.

10. Gillmore to Stanton, January 15, 1864, *ORA* XXXV, pt. 1, p. 278.

11. *ORA* XXXV, pt. 1, p. 279.

12. Gillmore to Stanton, December 14, 1863, *ORA* XXVIII, pt. 2, pp. 128–29.

13. Halleck to Gillmore, December 22, 1863, *ORA* XXVIII, pt. 2, p. 134.

14. Townsend to Gillmore, December 22, 1863, *ORA* XXVIII, pt. 2, p. 135.

15. *ORA* XXVIII, pt. 2, p. 135.

16. Milton to Davis, October 10, 1862, *ORA* LIII, pp. 260–61.

17. Table No. 41, Population of the United States by County, *Eighth Census of the United States: Population Schedules* (1860), pp. 248–49.

18. Houston to Walker, September 14, 1861, *ORA* IV:I, pp. 612–13.

19. Alfred Roman, *The Military Operations of General Beauregard in the War between the States* (Baton Rouge: Louisiana State University Press, 1955), p. 26.

20. *ORA* LIII, pp. 350–59.

21. Gov. John Milton to Secretary of War Seddon, July 20, 1863, John Milton Letterbook, 1861–63, Florida Historical Society Library, University of South Florida, Tampa, pp. 651–53.

22. Milton Letterbook, 1861–63, pp. 226–27.

23. Robert L. Clarke, "The Florida Railroad Company in the Civil War," *Journal of Southern History* 19 (May 1953): 180, 184, 188.

24. Ibid., p. 191.

25. Richard D. Goff, *Confederate Supply* (Durham: Duke University Press, 1969), p. 54.

26. Coulter, *Confederate States*, pp. 246–47.

27. Charles W. Ramsdell, "Confederate Government and the Railroads," *American Historical Review* 22 (July 1917): 806, 810.

28. Ruffin to Northrop, October 18, 1864, *ORA* IV:III, p. 738.

29. Goff, *Confederate Supply*, p. 196.

30. *ORN* XIII, p. 369.

31. Woodbury to Stone, December 23, 1863, *ORA* XXVI, pt. 1, p. 873.

32. *ORA* XXVI, pt. 1, pp. 873, 874.

33. Jackson to Cooper, August 12, 1864, *ORA* XXXV, pt. 2, p. 606.

34. "Memoranda of Comptroller," October 10, 1862, Milton Papers, Florida State Library, Tallahassee.

35. W. W. Davis, *Civil War*, p. 270.

36. Maj. A. G. Sumner to Maj. Pleasant W. White, December 31, 1863, Pleasant W. White Papers, Florida Historical Society Library, University of South Florida, Tampa.

37. John Milton Letterbook, November 27, 1863–March 21, 1865, Florida State Library, Tallahassee, vol. 7, ser. 32.

38. Akerman, *Florida Cowman*, p. 84.

39. Ibid., pp. 85, 88–90.

40. Maj. H. C. Guerin to Maj. Pleasant W. White, October 3, 1864, White Papers.

41. McClenaghan to Guerin, October 29, 1863, *ORA* XXVIII, pt. 2, pp. 459–62.

42. *ORA* XXVIII, pt. 2, p. 462.

43. *ORA* XXVIII, pt. 2, pp. 472–73.

44. Beauregard to Cooper, March 31, 1864, *ORA* XXXV, pt. 2, p. 394.

45. Anderson to Gardner, March 12, 1864, *ORA* XXXV, pt. 2, p. 351.

46. Ovid L. Futch, "Salmon P. Chase and Civil War Politics in Florida," *Florida Historical Quarterly* 32 (January 1954): 163.

47. Samuel Jones, "The Battle of Olustee, or Ocean Pond, Florida," in *Battles and Leaders of the Civil War*, ed. Robert U. Johnson and Clarence C. Buell, vol. 4 (New York: Yoseloff, 1888), p. 76.

48. George Winston Smith, "Carpetbag Imperialism in Florida, 1862–1868," *Florida Historical Quarterly* 27 (October 1948): 99–130; (January 1949): 259–99.

49. Futch, "Salmon P. Chase," pp. 169–70.

50. L. D. Stickney to Chase, December 11, 1863, in Salmon Portland Chase, *Inside Lincoln's Cabinet: The Civil War Diaries of Salmon P. Chase*, ed. David Herbert Donald. (New York: Longmans, Green, 1954), p. 190.

51. Tyler Dennett, *Lincoln and the Civil War in the Diaries and Letters of John Hay* (New York: Dodd, Mead, 1939), pp. 145–49.

52. Gillmore to Halleck, December 15, 1863, *ORA* XXVIII, pt. 2, p. 129.

53. Lincoln to Gillmore, January 13, 1864, *ORA* XXXV, pt. 1, p. 278.

54. Gillmore to Lincoln, January 21, 1864, Lincoln MSS, vols. 139, 140, Manuscripts Division, Library of Congress, U.S. Congress, Senate, *Senate Report*, 38th Cong., 1st sess., Report No. 47 (Washington, D.C.: Government Printing Office, 1864), p. 2, cited in Smith, "Carpetbag Imperialism," p. 281.

55. Carl Sandburg, *Abraham Lincoln: The War Years*, 4 vols. (New York: Harcourt, Brace, 1939), III, p. 6.

56. Gillmore to Halleck, January 31, 1864, *ORA* XXXV, pt. 1, p. 279.

57. W. W. Davis, *Civil War*, p. 273.

58. George Linton Hendricks, "Union Army Occupation of the Southern Seaboard, 1861–1865" (Ph.D. diss., Columbia University, 1954), p. 225.

59. George Linton Hendricks, "Union Army Occupation," p. 224.

4. Surprise and Success:
The Landing and Exploitation

1. Gillmore to Seymour, February 5, 1864, *ORA* XXXV, pt. 1, p. 280.

2. John Appleton Journal, February 5, 1864, John W. M. Appleton Papers, West Virginia University Library, Morgantown.

3. Gillmore to Seymour, February 5, 1864, *ORA* XXXV, pt. 1, pp. 280–81.

4. Beauregard to Cooper, March 25, 1864, *ORA* XXXV, pt. 1, p. 321.

5. Meriam to Dahlgren, February 11, 1864, *ORA* XXXV, pt. 1, p. 476.

6. George Bowerem, "From the Florida Expedition," *New York Tribune*, February 20, 1864, p. 1.

7. Meriam to Dahlgren, February 11, 1864, *ORA* XXXV, pt. 1, p. 476.

8. *New York Tribune*, February 20, 1864.

9. Luis F. Emilio, *History of the Fifty-fourth Regiment of Massachusetts Volunteer Infantry, 1863–1865* (Boston: Boston Book, 1891), p. 152.

10. Lester L. Swift, ed., "Capt. Dana in Florida: A Narrative of the Seymour Expedition," *Civil War History* 11 (September 1965): 246–47.

11. Emilio, *Fifty-fourth Massachusetts*, pp. 151–52.

12. *New York Times*, February 20, 1864.

13. Beauregard to Cooper, March 25, 1864, *ORA* XXXV, pt. 1, pp. 321–22.

14. Beauregard to Cooper, February 11, 1864, *ORA* XXXV, pt. 2, p. 110.

15. Beauregard to Gilmer, February 8, 1864, *ORA* XXXV, pt. 1, p. 579.

16. Beauregard to Gardner, February 8, 1864, *ORA* XXXV, pt. 1, p. 580.

17. Beauregard to Finegan, February 8, 1864, *ORA* XXXV, pt. 1, p. 579.

18. Beauregard to Cooper, February 9, 1864, *ORA* XXXV, pt. 1, p. 581.

19. Beauregard to Hill, February 9, 1864, *ORA* XXXV, pt. 1, p. 581.

20. Beauregard to Cobb, February 9, 1864, *ORA* XXXV, pt. 1, p. 581.

21. Beauregard to Seddon, February 9, 1864, *ORA* XXXV, pt. 1, p. 110.

22. *ORA* XXXV, pt. 1, pp. 557–58, 579.

23. Beauregard to Cooper, March 25, 1864, *ORA* XXXV, pt. 1, p. 321.

24. Gillmore to Halleck, February 9, 1864, *ORA* XXXV, pt. 1, p. 281.

25. Dahlgren to Gillmore, February 12, 1864, *ORA* XXXV, pt. 1, p. 475.

26. *ORA* XXXV, pt. 1, p. 475.

27. *New York Times*, February 20, 1864.

28. Ibid.

29. Benjamin W. Crowninshield, *A History of the First Regiment of Massachusetts Cavalry Volunteers* (New York: Houghton Mifflin, 1891), p. 260.

30. *New York Times*, February 20, 1864.

31. Finegan to Bryan, March 18, 1864, *ORA* XXXV, pt. 1, pp. 336–37.

32. Dunham to Thomas, March 18, 1864, *ORA* XXXV, pt. 1, pp. 346–47.

33. *ORA* XXXV, pt. 1, pp. 346–48.

34. James H. Clark, *The Iron Hearted Regiment: Being an Account of the Battles, Marches, and Gallant Deeds Performed by the 115th Regiment N.Y. Vols.* (Albany, N.Y.: Munsell, 1865), pp. 71–72.

35. Ibid.

36. *New York Times*, February 20, 1864.

37. Pleasant Woodson White to Col. L. B. Northrop, February 25, 1864, White Papers.

38. Seymour to Gillmore, February 9, 1864, *ORA* LIII, p. 99.

39. *ORA* XXXV, pt. 1, p. 35.

40. Isaiah Price, *History of the Ninety-seventh Regiment Pennsylvania Volunteer Infantry during the War of the Rebellion, 1861–1865, with Biographic Sketches of Its Field and Staff Officers and a Complete Record of Each Officer and Enlisted Man* (Philadelphia: Price, 1875), pp. 234–35.

41. Roman, *Beauregard*, p. 447.

42. Wendell D. Croom, *The War-History of Company "C" (Beauregard Volunteers), Sixth Georgia Regiment (Infantry), with a Graphic Account of Each Member* (Fort Valley, Ga.: Printed at the *Advertiser* Office, 1879), p. 22.

43. Gillmore to Abbott, February 9, 1864, *ORA* XXXV, pt. 1, p. 472.

44. *New York Times,* February 20, 1864.

45. Ibid.

46. Clark, *Iron Hearted Regiment,* pp. 75–76.

47. Winston Stephens to Octavia Stephens, February 11, 1864, Stephens Papers, P. K. Yonge Library of Florida History, University of Florida, Gainesville.

48. Finegan to Beauregard, February 13, 1864, *ORA* XXXV, pt. 1, p. 325.

49. *New York Times,* February 20, 1864.

50. *New York Tribune,* February 29, 1864.

51. *ORA* XXXV, pt. 1, pp. 594–95.

52. Ibid.

53. Smith to Waddy, February 10, 1864, *ORA* XXXV, pt. 1, pp. 582–83.

54. Gillmore to Seymour, February 10, 1864, *ORA* XXXV, pt. 1, p. 473.

55. Gillmore to Dahlgren, February 10, 1864, *ORA* XXXV, pt. 1, p. 472.

56. Gillmore to Seymour, February 10, 1864, *ORA* XXXV, pt. 1, pp. 473–74.

57. *New York Times,* February 20, 1864.

58. John Porter Fort, *A Memorial and Personal Reminiscences* (New York: Knickerbocker Press, 1918), p. 23.

59. *New York Times,* February 20, 1864.

60. Ibid.

61. Clark, *Iron Hearted Regiment,* pp. 77–78.

62. Finegan to Beauregard, February 13, 1864, *ORA* XXXV, pt. 1, p. 325.

63. Beauregard to Finegan, February 11, 1864, *ORA* XXXV, pt. 1, p. 600.

64. Seymour to Gillmore, February 11, 1864, *ORA* XXXV, pt. 1, pp. 281–82.

65. Swift, "Capt. Dana in Florida," p. 248.

66. Gillmore to Seymour, February 11, 1864, *ORA* XXXV, pt. 1, p. 282.

67. Seymour to Gillmore, February 11, 1864, *ORA* XXXV, pt. 1, p. 282.

68. Gillmore to Montgomery, February 11, 1864, *ORA* XXXV, pt. 1, p. 474.

69. Beauregard to Gilmer, February 11, 1864, *ORA* XXXV, pt. 1, p. 600.

70. Beauregard to Gardner, February 11, 1864, *ORA* XXXV, pt. 1, p. 600.

71. Asboth to Stone, March 8, 1864, *ORA* XXXV, pt 2, p. 12.

72. Woodbury to Stone, March 8, 1864, *ORA* XXXV, pt. 2, pp. 13–14.

73. Asboth to Stone, April 4, 1864, *ORA* XXXV, pt. 1, pp. 385–86.

74. Milton to Seddon, February 10, 1864, *ORA* XXXV, pt. 1, p. 594.

75. Beauregard to Cooper, February 11, 1864, *ORA* XXXV, pt. 1, p. 111.

76. Seymour to Gillmore, February 12, 1864, *ORA* XXXV, pt. 1, p. 283.

77. Gillmore to Seymour, February 12, 1864, *ORA* XXXV, pt. 1, p. 283.

78. Gillmore to Seymour, February 12, 1864, *ORA* LIII, p. 100.

79. Seymour to Gillmore, February 12, 1864, *ORA* LIII, p. 100.

80. Gillmore to Osborn, February 12, 1864, *ORA* XXXV, pt. 1, p. 479.

81. *ORA* XXXV, pt. 1, p. 35.

82. Seymour to Henry, February 13, 1864, *ORA* XXXV, pt. 1, p. 479.

83. Henry F. W. Little, *The Seventh Regiment New Hampshire Volunteers in the War of the Rebellion* (Concord, N.H.: Evans, 1896), pp. 218–19.

84. Gillmore to Halleck, February 13, 1864, *ORA* XXXV, pt. 1, p. 293.

85. Lawrence Jackson, "Memoirs of the Battle of Olustee, Fought in February 1864," in Edward C. Sanchez Papers, 1825–79, P. K. Yonge Library of Florida History, University of Florida, Gainesville.

86. *New York Tribune*, February 29, 1864.

87. Jackson, "Memoirs of the Battle of Olustee."

88. *New York Tribune*, February 29, 1864.

89. Seymour to Gillmore, February 17, 1864, *ORA* XXXV, pt. 1, p. 297.

90. Charles C. Jones, *Historical Sketch of the Chatham Artillery during the Confederate Struggle for Independence* (Albany, N.Y.: Munsell, 1867), pp. 174–75.

91. Clark, *Iron Hearted Regiment*, pp. 79–80.

92. Crowninshield, *First Regiment*, p. 262.

93. Clark, *Iron Hearted Regiment*, pp. 79–80.

94. I. Price, *History of the Ninety-seventh*, pp. 234–35.

95. *New South* (Hilton Head, S.C.), March 5, 1864, as cited in I. Price, *History of the Ninety-seventh*, p. 238.

96. *Fernandina Peninsula*, February 25, 1864, cited in I. Price, *History of the Ninety-seventh*, p. 238.

97. Terry to Smith, February 14, 1864, *ORA* XXXV pt. 1, pp. 480–81.

98. David R. Morgan, *Confederate Veteran* 26 (1918): 302.

99. Beauregard to Gilmer, February 14, 1864, *ORA* XXXV, pt. 1, p. 613.

100. Beauregard to Finegan, February 14, 1864, *ORA* XXXV, pt. 1, p. 613; Beauregard to Gardner, p. 613.

101. *ORA* XXXV, pt. 1, p. 481.

102. Frank E. Moore, ed., *The Rebellion Record: A Diary of American Events, with Documents, Narratives, Illustrative Incidents, Poetry, Etc.: With an Introductory Address by Edward Everett*, 11 vols. (New York: Putnam's Sons, 1861–68), VIII, p. 409.

103. *ORA* XXXV, pt. 1, p. 481.

104. Seymour to Gillmore, February 16, 1864, *ORA* LIII, p. 101.

105. Seymour to Gillmore, February 17, 1864, *ORA* XXXV, pt. 1, p. 284.

106. *ORA* XXXV, pt. 1, pp. 284–85.

107. U.S. Congress, Senate, Report No. 47, p. 9.

108. Joseph Hawley, comments on Samuel Jones, "Battle of Olustee," p. 79.

109. Seymour to Ira Harris, January 12, 1864, *ORA* LIII, pp. 95–98.

110. Ibid.

111. Ibid.

112. C. M. McClenaghan to H. C. Guerin, October 29, 1864, *ORA* XXXV, pt. 2, p. 461.

113. Gillmore to Halleck, January 31, 1864, *ORA* XXXV, pt. 1, p. 279.

114. Ezra J. Warner, *Generals in Blue: Lives of the Union Commanders* (Baton Rouge: Louisiana State University Press, 1959), pp. 176–77, 432–33.

115. Peter Burchard, *One Gallant Rush: Robert Gordon Shaw and His Brave Black Regiment* (Battleboro, Vt.: St. Martin's, 1965), pp. 133, 181.

116. T. Dennett, *Lincoln and the Civil War*, p. 164.

117. George F. Baltzell, Colonel, U.S.A., "The Battle of Olustee," *Florida Historical Quarterly* 9 (April 1931): 207.

118. Report of Lt. M. B. Grant, C.S. Engineers, April 27, 1864, *ORA* XXXV, pt. 1, pp. 338–39.

119. *ORA* XXXV, pt. 1, pp. 338–39.

120. C. C. Jones, *Historical Sketch of the Chatham Artillery,* pp. 178–79.

121. *ORA* XXXV, pt. 1, p. 542.

122. Ibid., p. 331.

123. Ibid., p. 288.

5. The Battle of Olustee

1. F. E. Moore, *Rebellion Record,* VIII, p. 409.

2. *New York Times,* March 1, 1864.

3. Ibid.

4. F. E. Moore, *Rebellion Record,* VIII, pp. 400, 405, 408.

5. Seymour to Gillmore, March 25, 1864, *ORA* XXXV, pt. 1, pp. 286–87.

6. *New York Times,* March 1, 1864.

7. Grant to Harris, April 27, 1864, *ORA* XXXV, pt. 1, p. 340.

8. F. E. Moore, *Rebellion Record,* VIII, pp. 411, 409.

9. Swift, "Capt. Dana in Florida," p. 249.

10. Majer to Swift, February 24, 1864, *ORA* XXXV, pt. 1, p. 299.

11. Skinner to Moore, February 25, 1864, *ORA* XXXV, pt. 1, p. 307; Hawley to Chadwick, February 26, 1864, p. 303.

12. *New York Times,* March 1, 1864.

13. Crowninshield, *First Regiment,* pp. 262–63.

14. Smith to Call, February 24, 1864, *ORA* XXXV, pt. 1, pp. 351–52.

15. Jackson, "Memoirs of the Battle of Olustee."

16. Smith to Call, February 24, 1864, *ORA* XXXV, pt. 1, pp. 351–52.

17. Harrison to Call, February 22, 1864, *ORA* XXXV, pt. 1, p. 349.

18. C. C. Jones, *Historical Sketch of the Chatham Artillery,* pp. 179–80.

19. Ibid., p. 180.

20. Samuel Jones, "Battle of Olustee," p. 79.

21. Finegan to Jordan, February 26, 1864, *ORA* XXXV, pt. 1, p. 332.

22. Winston Stephens to Octavia Stephens, February 21, 1864, Stephens Papers.

23. Rambo to Thomas, February 23, 1864, *ORA* XXXV, pt. 1, p. 348.

24. *New York Times,* March 1, 1864.

25. Milton M. Woodford, "A Connecticut Yankee Fights at Olustee: Letters from the Front," ed. Vaughn D. Bornet, *Florida Historical Quarterly* 27 (January 1949): 237–59.

26. Crowninshield, *First Regiment,* pp. 262–63.

27. *New York Times,* March 1, 1864.

28. Skinner to Moore, February 25, 1864, *ORA* XXXV, pt. 1, p. 308.

29. Ibid., pp. 308, 310.

30. James M. Dancy, "Reminiscences of the Civil War," *Florida Historical Quarterly* 37 (July 1958): 74.

31. C. C. Jones, *Historical Sketch of the Chatham Artillery,* pp. 184–85.

32. C. C. Jones, *Historical Sketch of the Chatham Artillery,* pp. 184–85.

33. Seymour to Turner, March 25, 1864, *ORA* XXXV, pt. 1, p. 288.

34. Hawley to Chadwick, February 26, 1864, *ORA* XXXV, pt. 1, pp. 303–4.

35. Little, *Seventh Regiment,* pp. 222–23.

36. Ibid.

37. F. E. Moore, *Rebellion Record,* VIII, p. 409.

38. Abbott to Hawley, February 27, 1864, *ORA* XXXV, pt. 1, p. 311.

39. Little, *Seventh Regiment,* p. 228.

40. Hawley to Chadwick, February 26, 1864, *ORA* XXXV, pt. 1, p. 304.

41. Hamilton to Chadwick, February 24, 1864, *ORA* LIII, p. 24.

42. Ibid., pp. 24–25.

43. F. E. Moore, *Rebellion Record,* VIII, p. 408.

44. Oliver Wilcox Norton, *Army Letters, 1861–1865, Being Extracts from Private Letters to Relatives and Friends from a Soldier in the Field during the Late Civil War, with an Appendix Containing Copies of Some Official Documents, Papers, and Addresses of Later Date* (Chicago: Deming, 1903), p. 198.

45. Ibid., p. 202.

46. Samuel Jones, "Battle of Olustee," p. 79.

47. Aeichhold to Davis, February 23, 1864, F. E. Moore, *Rebellion Record,* VIII, pp. 410, 416.

48. *New York Times,* March 1, 1864.

49. Majer to Swift, February 24, 1864, *ORA* XXXV, pt. 1, p. 299.

50. Langdon to Hall, March 25, 1864, *ORA* XXXV, pt. 1, pp. 316–18.

51. Ibid.

52. "Diary of Captain Keely," *Atlanta Constitution,* March 22, 1931.

53. Langdon to Hall, March 25, 1864, *ORA* XXXV, pt. 1, pp. 316–18.

54. Hamilton to Chadwick, February 22, 1864, *ORA* LIII, p. 25.

55. C. C. Jones, *Historical Sketch of the Chatham Artillery,* pp. 185–86.

56. Rambo to Thomas, February 23, 1864, *ORA* XXXV, pt. 1, p. 348.

57. Harrison to Call, February 22, 1864, *ORA* XXXV, pt. 1, p. 349.
58. F. E. Moore, *Rebellion Record,* VIII, pp. 410–11.
59. Clark, *Iron Hearted Regiment,* p. 85.
60. *New York Tribune,* March 1, 1864.
61. Clark, *Iron Hearted Regiment,* p. 85.
62. Barton to Chadwick, February 27, 1864, *ORA* XXXV, pt. 1, p. 302.
63. Abraham J. Palmer, *The History of the Forty-eighth Regiment New York Volunteers in the War for the Union, 1861–1865* (Brooklyn: Veterans Association of the Regiment, 1885), p. 130; Clark, *Iron Hearted Regiment,* p. 84.
64. Hawley to Chadwick, February 26, 1864, *ORA* XXXV, pt. 1, p. 304; Skinner to Moore, February 25, 1864, p. 308.
65. Bailey to Hall, March 10, 1864, *ORA* XXXV, pt. 1, pp. 312–13.
66. Lewis to Richardson, March 10, 1864, *ORA* XXXV, pt. 1, p. 313.
67. Aeichhold to Davis, February 23, 1864, F. E. Moore, *Rebellion Record,* VIII, p. 416.
68. Lewis to Richardson, March 10, 1864. *ORA* XXXV, pt. 1, p. 313.
69. Aeichhold to Davis, February 23, 1864, F. E. Moore, *Rebellion Record,* VIII, p. 416.
70. Ibid.
71. C. C. Jones, *Historical Sketch of the Chatham Artillery,* p. 181.
72. Smith to Call, February 22, 1864, *ORA* XXXV, pt. 1, pp. 352–53.
73. Winston Stephens to Octavia Stephens, February 21, 1864, Stephens Papers.
74. Smith to Call, February 22, 1864, *ORA* XXXV, pt. 1, pp. 352–53.
75. C. C. Jones, *Historical Sketch of the Chatham Artillery,* p. 182.
76. James Madison Folsom, *Heroes and Martyrs of Georgia: Georgia's Record in the Revolution of 1861* (Macon: Boykin, 1864), p. 57.
77. Fort, *Memorial,* p. 25.
78. C. C. Jones, *Historical Sketch of the Chatham Artillery,* p. 182.
79. Emilio, *Fifty-fourth Massachusetts,* p. 162.
80. Ibid., pp. 162–63.
81. Hawley to Chadwick, February 26, 1864, *ORA* XXXV, pt. 1, p. 305.
82. Palmer, *Forty-eighth Regiment,* p. 133.
83. *New York Tribune,* March 1, 1864.
84. F. E. Moore, *Rebellion Record,* VIII, p. 410.
85. Myrick to Langdon, February 24, 1864, *ORA* XXXV, pt. 1, p. 320.
86. Julien C. Yonge, ed., "The Occupation of Jacksonville, February

1864, and the Battle of Olustee: Letters of Lt. C. M. Duren, Fifty-fourth Massachusetts Regiment, U.S.A.," *Florida Historical Quarterly* 32 (April 1954): 277.

87. Palmer, *Forty-eighth Regiment,* p. 136.

88. Richard McMurry, "The Battle of Olustee," *Civil War Times* 16 (January 1978): 19–20.

89. C. C. Jones, *Historical Sketch of the Chatham Artillery,* p. 182.

90. Samuel Jones, "Battle of Olustee," p. 78.

91. Ibid.

92. C. C. Jones, *Historical Sketch of the Chatham Artillery,* pp. 187–88.

93. "Diary of Captain Keely."

94. C. C. Jones, *Historical Sketch of the Chatham Artillery,* pp. 187–88.

95. Emilio, *Fifty-fourth Massachusetts,* pp. 164–65.

96. Ibid., p. 166.

97. Ibid., p. 167.

98. Ibid., p. 168.

99. Hawley to Chadwick, February 26, 1864, *ORA* XXXV, pt. 1, p. 305.

100. Little, *Seventh Regiment,* p. 224.

101. Emilio, *Fifty-fourth Regiment,* pp. 168–69.

102. Hallowell to Hall, March 1, 1864, *ORA* XXXV, pt. 1, p. 315.

103. Patrick Egan, *The Florida Campaign with Light Battery C, Third Rhode Island Heavy Artillery* (Providence: n.p., 1905), p. 16.

6. Lost Opportunities: The Retreat and Pursuit

1. Finegan to Jordan, March 26, 1864, *ORA* XXXV, pt. 1, p. 332.

2. Colquitt to Call, February 26, 1864, *ORA* XXXV, pt. 1, pp. 344, 350; Harrison to Call, February 22, 1864, p. 350.

3. Grant to Harris, April 27, 1864, *ORA* XXXV, pt. 1, p. 341.

4. C. C. Jones, *Historical Sketch of the Chatham Artillery,* pp. 183–84.

5. Smith to Call, February 24, 1864, *ORA* XXXV, pt. 1, p. 353.

6. Bryan to Lay, March 7, 1864, *ORA* XXXV, pt. 1, pp. 353–56.

7. Winston Stephens to Octavia Stephens, February 21, 1864, Stephens Papers.

8. Jackson, "Memoirs of the Battle of Olustee."

9. Barton to Chadwick, February 27, 1864, *ORA* XXXV, pt. 1, p. 302.

10. Samuel Jones, "Battle of Olustee," p. 80.

11. *New York Times,* March 1, 1864.

12. Majer to Swift, February 24, 1864, *ORA* XXXV, pt. 1, p. 300.

13. Ibid.

14. Swift, "Capt. Dana in Florida," p. 251.

15. Crowninshield, *First Regiment,* p. 264.

16. Emilio, *Fifty-fourth Massachusetts,* p. 170.

17. Palmer, *Forty-eighth Regiment,* p. 135.

18. Clark, *Iron Hearted Regiment,* p. 89.

19. *New York Tribune,* March 1, 1864.

20. Emilio, *Fifty-fourth Massachusetts,* p. 171.

21. Hawley to Chadwick, February 26, 1864, *ORA* XXXV, pt. 1, p. 305.

22. Emilio, *Fifty-fourth Massachusetts,* pp. 170–72.

23. Hawley to Chadwick, February 26, 1864, *ORA* XXXV, pt. 1, p. 305; Skinner to Moore, February 25, 1864, *ORA* XXXV, pt. 1, p. 309.

24. Swift, "Capt. Dana in Florida," p. 251.

25. Crowninshield, *First Regiment,* p. 264.

26. Clark, *Iron Hearted Regiment,* pp. 89–90.

27. *New York Times,* March 1, 1864; *New York Tribune,* March 1, 1864.

28. Hawley to Chadwick, February 26, 1864, *ORA* XXXV, pt. 1, p. 305.

29. Crowninshield, *First Regiment,* p. 254.

30. *New York Times,* March 1, 1864.

31. Little, *Seventh Regiment,* pp. 228–29.

32. *New York Tribune,* March 1, 1864.

33. Emilio, *Fifty-fourth Massachusetts,* pp. 174–75.

34. Swift, "Capt. Dana in Florida," pp. 251–52.

35. Skinner to Moore, February 25, 1864, *ORA* XXXV, pt. 1, p. 309.

36. Crowninshield, *First Regiment,* p. 264.

37. Skinner to Moore, February 25, 1864, *ORA* XXXV, pt. 1, p. 309; Stephen Walkley, *History of the Seventh Connecticut Volunteer Infantry, Hawley's Brigade, Terry's Division, Tenth Army Corps, 1861–1865* (Hartford: n.p., 1905), p. 123.

38. Little, *Seventh Regiment,* p. 229.

39. Emilio, *Fifty-fourth Massachusetts,* p. 175.

40. C. C. Jones, *Historical Sketch of the Chatham Artillery,* p. 188.

41. As quoted in McMurry, "Battle of Olustee," pp. 20–21.

42. Winston Stephens to Octavia Stephens, February 21, 1864, Stephens Papers.

43. Finegan to Jordan, February 26, 1864, *ORA* XXXV, pt. 1, pp. 332–33.

44. *ORA* XXXV, pt. 1, p. 333.

45. Quoted in Clark, *Iron Hearted Regiment,* p. 92.

46. Seymour to Turner, March 2, 1864, *ORA* XXXV, pt. 2, p. 7.

47. Finegan to Jordan, February 23, 1864, *ORA* XXXV, pt. 1, p. 328.

48. Grant to Harris, April 27, 1864, *ORA* XXXV, pt. 1, p. 341.

49. Finegan to Jordan, February 26, 1864, *ORA* XXXV, pt. 1, p. 333.

50. Grant to Harris, April 27, 1864, *ORA* XXXV, pt. 1, p. 341.

51. Swift, "Capt. Dana in Florida," pp. 252–53.

52. Seymour to Finegan, February 23, 1864, *ORA* XXXV, pt. 1, pp. 329–30.

53. Finegan to Seymour, February 24, 1864, *ORA* XXXV, pt. 1, p. 330.

54. Gardner to Finegan, February 23, 1864, *ORA* XXXV, pt. 1, pp. 334–35.

55. *ORA* XXXV, pt. 1, p. 335.

56. Ibid., pp. 335–36.

57. Gardner to Beauregard, March 7, 1864, *ORA* XXXV, pt. 1, p. 334.

58. Seymour to Turner, February 21, 1864, *ORA* XXXV, pt. 1, p. 488.

59. Otis to Turner, February 27, 1864, *ORA* XXXV, pt. 1, p. 489.

60. Terry to Ames, February 22, 1864, *ORA* XXXV, pt. 1, pp. 488–89.

61. Swift, "Capt. Dana in Florida," p. 253; Seymour to Turner, February 25, 1864, *ORA* XXXV, pt. 1, p. 491.

62. Seymour to Turner, February 25, 1864, *ORA* XXXV, pt. 1, pp. 491–92.

63. Seymour to Hawley, February 25, 1864, *ORA* XXXV, pt. 1, p. 492.

64. Seymour to Finegan, February 25, 1864, *ORA* XXXV, pt. 1, p. 493.

65. Finegan to Seymour, February 26, 1864, *ORA* XXXV, pt. 1, p. 496.

66. *American Annual Cyclopedia and Register of Important Events for the Year 1864* (New York: Appleton, 1872), p. 51.

67. Seymour to Turner, February 26, 1864, *ORA* XXXV, pt. 1, p. 495.

68. Swift, "Capt. Dana in Florida," p. 253.

69. Gillmore to Seymour, February 28, 1864, *ORA* XXXV, pt. 1, p. 496.

70. Halleck to Gillmore, February 26, 1864, *ORA* XXXV, pt. 1, pp. 493–94.

71. Gillmore to Seymour, February 27, 1864, *ORA* XXXV, pt. 1, pp. 496–97.

72. Seymour to Turner, February 28, 1864, *ORA* XXXV, pt. 1, pp. 497–98.

73. Seymour to Balch, February 29, 1864, *ORA* XXXV, pt. 1, p. 499.

74. Seymour to Foster, February 29, 1864, *ORA* XXXV, pt. 1, p. 499.

75. Winston Stephens to Octavia Stephens, February 27, 1864, Stephens Papers.

76. Leahy to Elder, March 21, 1864, *ORA* XXXV, pt. 1, pp. 367–68.

77. Ellen Hodges Patterson, "The Stephens Family in East Florida: A Profile of Plantation Life along the St. Johns River, 1859–1864" (Master's thesis, University of Florida, 1979), p. 94.

78. Henry to Hall, March 26, 1864, *ORA* XXXV, pt. 1, p. 365.

79. Folsom, *Heroes and Martyrs of Georgia*, p. 68.

80. Beauregard to Davis, February 22, 1864, *ORA* XXXV, pt. 1, pp. 112–13.

81. *ORA* XXXV, pt. 1, pp. 112–13.

82. Mercer to Jordan, February 27, 1864, *ORA* XXXV, pt. 1, pp. 644–45.

83. Beauregard to Cooper, February 26, 1864, *ORA* XXXV, pt. 1, pp. 113–14.

84. *ORA* XXXV, pt. 1, pp. 113–14.

85. *ORA* XXXV, pt. 2, pp. 332–33.

86. Otay to Guerin, March 6, 1864, *ORA* XXXV, pt. 2, p. 333.

87. Beauregard to Cooper, with endorsements, March 6, 1864, *ORA* XXXV, pt. 2, pp. 334–38.

88. *ORA* XXXV, pt. 2, p. 334.

89. Special Order No. 1, March 7, 1864, *ORA* XXXV, pt. 2, p. 340.

90. Bryan to Roman, February 27, 1864, *ORA* XXXV, pt. 1, pp. 645–46.

91. *ORA* XXXV, pt. 1, pp. 645–46.

92. Beauregard to Cooper, March 25, 1864, *ORA* XXXV, pt. 1, pp. 323–24.

93. Turner to Seymour, March 7, 1864, *ORA* XXXV, pt. 2, p. 9.

94. Gillmore to Seymour, March 10, 1864, *ORA* XXXV, pt. 2, pp. 15–16.

95. *ORA* XXXV, pt. 2, pp. 15–16.

96. Halleck to Gillmore, March 16, 1864, *ORA* XXXV, pt. 2, p. 20.

97. Gillmore to Seymour, March 12, 1864, *ORA* XXXV, pt. 2, p. 15.

98. Beauregard to Anderson, March 20, 1864, *ORA* XXXV, pt. 2, pp. 366–67.

99. *ORA* XXXV, pt. 2, p. 368.

100. Edward Marcus, ed., *A New Canaan Private in the Civil War: Letters of Justus M. Silliman, Seventeenth Connecticut Volunteers* (New Canaan, Conn.: New Canaan Historical Society, 1984).

101. Gerald Schwartz, ed., *A Woman Doctor's Civil War: Esther Hill Hawks' Diary* (Columbia: University of South Carolina Press, 1984).

102. W. W. Davis, *Civil War*, p. 295.

7. Heroes, Goats, and Survivors

1. McWhiney and Jamieson, *Attack and Die*, p. 11.

2. John Chipman Gray and John Codman Ropes, *War Letters, 1862–1865* (Boston: Houghton Mifflin, 1927), p. 308.

3. Little, *Seventh Regiment*, pp. 226–27.

4. Grant to Harris, April 27, 1864, *ORA* XXXV, pt. 1, p. 341.

5. John Niven, *Connecticut for the Union: The Role of the State in the Civil War* (New Haven: Yale University Press, 1965), p. 180.

6. Palmer, *Forty-eighth Regiment*, p. 130.

7. Terry to Smith, February 14, 1864, *ORA* XXXV, pt. 1, pp. 480–81.

8. Egan, *Florida Campaign*, p. 6.

9. *Free South*, cited in Clark, *Iron Hearted Regiment*, pp. 93–94.

10. Jackson, "Memoirs of the Battle of Olustee."

11. Palmer, *Forty-eighth Regiment*, p. 136.

12. *Atlanta Intelligence*, March 2, 1864.

13. William Penniman Reminiscences, p. 60, William Penniman Papers, Southern Historical Collection, University of North Carolina, Chapel Hill.

14. James M. Jordan to wife, February 21, 1864, typescript in "Letters from Confederate Soldiers, 1861–1865," collected by the Georgia Division, United Daughters of the Confederacy, Georgia Department of Archives and History, Atlanta, vol. 2, p. 481.

15. Winston Stephens to Octavia Stephens, February 21, 1864, Edmund C. Lee, "Civil War Letters," copied by Historical Records Survey, State Archives Survey, 1937, Florida Room, Florida State Library, Tallahassee.

16. Edwin Tuttle to parents, March 7, 1864, Edwin Tuttle Papers, Robert W. Woodruff Library, Emory University, Atlanta.

17. Winston Stephens to Octavia Stephens, February 21, 1864, Lee, "Civil War Letters."

18. Edwin Tuttle to parents, March 7, 1864, Tuttle Papers.

19. *Atlanta Intelligencer*, March 19, 1864.

20. William Penniman Reminiscences, pp. 60–61, Penniman Papers.

21. Hatch to Hitchcock, September 25, 1864, *ORA* II:VII, p. 876.

22. Finegan to Jordan, February 23, 1864, *ORA* XXXV, pt. 1, p. 328.

23. *Supplemental Report of the Joint Committee on the Conduct of the War*, 2 vols. (Washington, D.C.: Government Printing Office, 1866).

24. Goff, *Confederate Supply*, p. 208.

25. Clifton Paisley, "How to Escape the Yankees: Major Scott's Letter to His Wife at Tallahassee, March 1864," *Florida Historical Quarterly* 50 (July 1971).

26. Richard A. Martin, "The *New York Times* Views Civil War Jacksonville," *Florida Historical Quarterly* 53 (April 1974): 425.

27. McWhiney and Jamieson, *Attack and Die*, p. 11.

28. Warner, *Generals in Blue*, pp. 432–33.

29. James A. Harley, *Confederate Veteran* 20 (November 1912): 456–57.

30. Buckman to Finegan, February 24, 1864, *ORA* XXXV, pt. 1, p. 342.

8. A Final Look

1. Shofner and Rogers, "Confederate Railroad Construction," 227.

2. W. W. Davis, *Civil War*, p. 191.

3. Milton to Seddon, January 11, 1864, *ORA* IV:III, p. 15.

4. Goff, *Confederate Supply*, pp. 247–48.

Bibliography

Primary Sources

Manuscripts

Appleton, John W. M. Papers. West Virginia University Library. Morgantown.

Boyd, Mary E. Papers, 1833–1916. P. K. Yonge Library of Florida History. University of Florida. Gainesville.

Comptroller's Letterbook, 1864–67. Florida State Library. Tallahassee.

Comptroller's Letterbook–Letters Received, 1860–65. Florida State Library. Tallahassee.

Duren, Charles M. Letters, February–April 1864. P. K. Yonge Library of Florida History. University of Florida. Gainesville.

Fessenden, W. P. Letter to his son James D. Fessenden, February 17, 1863. P. K. Yonge Library of Florida History. University of Florida. Gainesville.

Fleming, Francis P. Papers, 1852–1905. Florida Historical Society Library. University of South Florida. Tampa.

Fleming, Margaret. Documents concerning Hibernia Plantation on the St. John's River, 1864–76. P. K. Yonge Library of Florida History. University of Florida. Gainesville.

Gardner, J. "The Removal of Guns and Munitions from Fort Marion at St. Augustine, Florida, January 6th–12th, 1861." St. Augustine Historical Society. St. Augustine, Florida.

Jackson, Lawrence. "Memoirs of the Battle of Olustee, Fought in February 1864." In Edward C. Sanchez Papers, 1825–79. P. K. Yonge Library of Florida History. University of Florida. Gainesville.

Jenckes, H. B. Letters to Mrs. Mary Martha Reid, 1862–64. St. Augustine Historical Society. St. Augustine, Florida.

Jordan, James Matt. Papers. In "Letters from Confederate Soldiers, 1861–1865." 15 vols. Typescript collected by the Georgia Division, United Daughters of the Confederacy. Georgia Department of Archives and History. Atlanta.

Lee, Edmund C. "Civil War Letters." Copied by Historical Records Survey, State Archives Survey, 1937. Florida Room. Florida State Library. Tallahassee.

Linsley, Lt. James H. Diary, 1862–64. P. K. Yonge Library of Florida History. University of Florida. Gainesville.

Mason, Capt. Blaky. Letter from St. Augustine, Florida, April 24, 1863. St. Augustine Historical Society. St. Augustine, Florida.

Milton, John. Letterbook, 1861–63. Photocopy in Florida Historical Society Library. University of South Florida. Tampa.

———. Letterbook, November 27, 1863–March 21, 1865. Florida State Library. Tallahassee.

———. Papers, "Memoranda of Comptroller," October 10, 1862. Florida State Library, Tallahassee.

Mitchell, Dr. Joseph D. "Commencing with My Residence in Jacksonville, East Florida, November 1852–June 2, 1853." P. K. Yonge Library of Florida History. University of Florida. Gainesville.

Murphy, Cornelius. "The Battle of Olustee: A Draft Speech Prepared according to the Instructions of the Honorable Spessard L. Holland." P. K. Yonge Library of Florida History. University of Florida. Gainesville.

Noyes, Alonzo P. Papers. P. K. Yonge Library of Florida History. University of Florida. Gainesville.

Pelot, Dr. John Crews. "A Reconnaissance on Amelia Island, Florida, and an Attempted Capture of Yankee Pickets at the Harrison and Vaughn Places." St. Augustine Historical Society. St. Augustine, Florida.

Penniman, William. Papers. Southern Historical Collection. University of North Carolina. Chapel Hill.

Raysor, Michael Oliver. Family Correspondence, 1861–64. P. K. Yonge Library of Florida History. University of Florida. Gainesville.

Reed, A. M. Diary, 1848–99. P. K. Yonge Library of Florida History. University of Florida. Gainesville. Original in possession of Mrs. J. Reed Pierson, Jacksonville, Florida.

Roach, Jacob. Papers. Georgia Historical Society. Savannah.

Robinson, Calvin. "An Account of Some of My Experiences in Florida during the Rise and Progress of the Rebellion." P. K. Yonge Library of Florida History. University of Florida. Gainesville.

Sheldon, Capt. R. "The Civil War Fights at New Smyrna As Related by Capt. Sheldon." P. K. Yonge Library of Florida History. University of Florida. Gainesville.

Steedman, Charles. Letters, 1862–64. P. K. Yonge Library of Florida History. University of Florida. Gainesville.

Stephens, Winston. Papers. P. K. Yonge Library of Florida History. University of Florida. Gainesville.

Sumner, A. G. Letter, March 23, 1864. P. K. Yonge Library of Florida History. University of Florida. Gainesville.

Taylor, Maria Baker. Diary, January–July 1864. P. K. Yonge Library of Florida History. University of Florida. Gainesville.

Thomas, David Yancy. "A History of Banking in Florida." P. K. Yonge Library of Florida History. University of Florida. Gainesville.

Tuttle, Edwin. Papers. Robert W. Woodruff Library. Emory University. Atlanta.

White, Pleasant Woodson. Papers. Florida Historical Society Library. University of South Florida. Tampa.

Yonge, Chandler Cox. Papers, 1860–67. P. K. Yonge Library of Florida History. University of Florida. Gainesville.

Federal Documents

A Compendium of the Ninth Census (June 1, 1870), Compiled Pursuant to a Concurrent Resolution of Congress and under the Direction of the Secretary of the Interior. Washington, D.C.: Government Printing Office, 1872.

Atlas to Accompany the Official Records of the Union and Confederate Armies. Washington, D.C.: Government Printing Office, 1891–95.

Eighth Census of the United States: 1860. 4 vols. Washington, D.C.: Government Printing Office, 1866.

Eighth Census of the United States: Population Schedules (1860). Microfilm in P. K. Yonge Library of Florida History, University of Florida, Gainesville.

Ninth Census (1870): The Statistics of the Population of the United States. Washington, D.C.: Government Printing Office, 1872.

Official Records of the Union and Confederate Navies in the War of the Rebellion. 30 vols. Washington, D.C.: Government Printing Office, 1894–1927.

Population of the United States in 1860: Compiled from the Original Returns of the Eighth Census, under the Direction of the Secretary of the Interior. Washington, D.C.: Government Printing Office, 1864.

Seventh Census of the United States: 1850. Washington, D.C.: Government Printing Office, 1853–55.

Supplemental Report of the Joint Committee on the Conduct of the War. 2 vols. Washington, D.C.: Government Printing Office, 1866.

U.S. Congress. House. *Committee Reports,* 36th Cong. 2d sess., 1860–61. Washington, D.C.: Government Printing Office, 1861.

——— . *Committee Reports,* 37th Cong., 3d sess., Report No. 5. Washington, D.C.: Government Printing Office, 1863.

——— . *Executive Documents,* 36th Cong., 2d sess., 1860–61. Washington, D.C.: Government Printing Office, 1861.

——— . *Executive Documents,* 38th Cong., 2d sess., Document No. 18. Washington, D.C.: Government Printing Office, 1865.

U.S. Congress. Senate. *Senate Report,* 38th Cong., 1st sess., Report No. 47. Washington, D.C.: Government Printing Office, 1864.

U.S. War Department. *War of the Rebellion: A Compilation of the Official Records of the Union and Confederate Armies.* 128 vols. Washington, D.C.: Government Printing Office, 1880–1901.

State and Other Records

The Acts and Resolutions Adopted by the General Assembly of the State of Florida. Tallahassee: Office of the *Floridian and Journal.* 10th sess., 1860; 11th sess., 1861.

American Annual Cyclopedia and Register of Important Events for the Year 1864. New York: Appleton, 1872.

Florida Executive Records. Office of the Secretary of State, Tallahassee.

Journal of the Convention of the People of Florida at a Called Session Begun and Held at the Capitol in the City of Tallahassee on Tuesday, January 14, 1862. Tallahassee: Office of the *Floridian and Journal,* 1862.

Journal of the Proceedings of the Convention of Florida Begun and Held at the Capitol of the State at Tallahassee, October 25th, A.D. 1865. Tallahassee: Office of the *Floridian,* 1865.

Journal of the Proceedings of the Convention of the People of Florida Begun and Held at the Capitol in the City of Tallahassee on Thurs-

day, January 3, 1861. Tallahassee: Office of the *Floridian and Journal,* 1861. Facsimile ed. Jacksonville: H. & W. B. Drew, 1928.

Journal of the Proceedings of the House of Representatives of the General Assembly of the State of Florida. Tallahassee: Office of the *Floridian and Journal.* 10th sess., 1860; 11th sess., 1861; 12th sess., 1862; 13th sess., 1864; 14th sess., 1865.

Journal of the Proceedings of the Senate of the General Assembly of the State of Florida. Tallahassee: *Florida Sentinel* Office. 10th sess., 1860; 11th sess., 1861; 12th sess., 1862; 13th sess., 1864; 14th sess., 1865.

Newspapers and Periodicals

Atlanta Constitution, 1931.
Atlanta Intelligencer, 1864.
Fernandina Peninsula, 1863.
Florida Sentinel (Tallahassee), 1852, 1854, 1862–63.
Floridian and Journal (Tallahassee), 1860–62 (scattered issues).
Jacksonville Peninsula, 1864.
Lake City Columbian, 1864.
New South (Hilton Head, S.C.), 1864.
New York Herald, 1861–65.
New York Times, 1861–65.
New York Tribune, 1864.
St. Augustine Examiner, 1860–65 (scattered issues).
Savannah Daily Morning News, 1864.

Secondary Sources

General

Akerman, Joe A., Jr. *Florida Cowman: A History of Florida Cattle Raising.* Kissimmee: Florida Cattlemen's Association, 1976.

Amann, William F., ed. *Personnel of the Civil War.* 2 vols. New York: Yoseloff, 1961.

Ammen, Daniel. *The Navy in the Civil War: The Atlantic Coast.* New York: Scribner's Sons, 1905.

Anderson, Bern. *By Sea and by River: The Naval History of the Civil War.* New York: Knopf, 1962.

Andreano, Ralph, ed. *The Economic Impact of the American Civil War.* Rev. ed. Cambridge, Mass.: Schenkman, 1967.

Andrews, W. H. *Diary of W. H. Andrews, 1st Sergt. Co. M, 1st Georgia Regulars, from February 1861 to May 2, 1865.* East Atlanta, Ga., 1891(?).

Baltzell, George F., Colonel, U.S.A. "The Battle of Olustee." *Florida Historical Quarterly* 9 (April 1931): 199–223.

Bearss, Edwin C. "Military Operations on the St. Johns, September–October, 1862." *Florida Historical Quarterly* 42 (January 1964): 232–47; (April 1964): 331–50.

Beecher, Herbert W. *History of the First Light Battery Connecticut Volunteers, 1861–1865: Personal Records and Reminiscences.* New York: DeLaMare, n.d.

Bickel, Karl A. "Robert E. Lee in Florida." *Florida Historical Quarterly* 27 (July 1948): 59–66.

Biddle, Margaret Seton Fleming. *The Unrelenting Tide.* New York: Vantage Press, 1974.

Bittle, George C. "Florida Prepares for War, 1860–1861." *Florida Historical Quarterly* 51 (October 1972): 143–52.

Blakey, Arch Fredric. *Parade of Memories: A History of Clay County, Florida.* Jacksonville, Fla.: Drummond Press, 1976.

Boyd, Mark E. "The Federal Campaign of 1864 in East Florida." *Florida Historical Quarterly* 29 (July 1950): 3–37.

———. "The Joint Operations of the Federal Army and Navy near St. Marks, March 1865." *Florida Historical Quarterly* 29 (October 1950): 96–124.

Bradlee, Francis B. C. *Blockade Running during the Civil War and the Effect of Land and Water Transportation on the Confederacy.* Salem, Mass.: Essex Institute, 1925.

Breeze, Lawrence E. "The Battle of Olustee (1864): Its Meaning for the British." *Florida Historical Quarterly* 43 (January 1965): 207–16.

Briggs, Walter De Bois. *Civil War Surgeon in a Colored Regiment.* Berkeley, Calif.: n.p., 1960.

Brown, William Wells. *The Negro in the American Rebellion: His Heroism and His Fidelity.* Boston: Lee & Shepard, 1867.

Buchholz, F. W. *History of Alachua County, Florida.* St. Augustine: Record Company, 1929.

Burchard, Peter. *One Gallant Rush: Robert Gordon Shaw and His Brave Black Regiment.* Battleboro, Vt.: St. Martin's, 1965.

Burnham, W. Dean. *Presidential Ballots, 1836–1892.* Baltimore: Johns Hopkins University Press, 1955.

Cabell, Branch, and A. J. Hanna. *The St. Johns: A Parade of Diversities.* New York: Farr & Rinehart, 1943.

Cadwell, Charles K. *The Old Sixth Regiment* (Connecticut Volunteers), *Its War Record, 1861–5.* New Haven: Tuttle, Morehouse & Taylor, 1875.

Califf, Joseph Mark. *Record of the Services of the Seventh Regiment U.S. Colored Troops, by an Officer of the Regiment, from September 1863 to November 1866.* Providence: E. L. Freeman, 1878.

Call, Richard Keith. "An Address to the People of Florida, from Gen. R. K. Call, December 1, 1860." N.p., 1860.

Cash, William Thomas. "Taylor County History and Civil War Deserters." *Florida Historical Quarterly* 27 (July 1948): 28–58.

Chamberlain, Capt. V. "A Letter of Captain V. Chamberlain, Seventh Connecticut Volunteers." *Florida Historical Quarterly* 15 (October 1936): 85–95.

Chase, Salmon Portland. *Inside Lincoln's Cabinet: The Civil War Diaries of Salmon P. Chase.* Edited by David Herbert Donald. New York: Longmans, Green, 1954.

Chesnut, Mary Boykin. *A Diary from Dixie.* Edited by Ben Ames Williams. Boston: Houghton Mifflin, 1949.

Clark, James H. *The Iron Hearted Regiment: Being an Account of the Battles, Marches, and Gallant Deeds Performed by the 115th Regiment N.Y. Vols.* Albany, N.Y.: Munsell, 1865.

Clarke, Robert L. "The Florida Railroad Company in the Civil War." *Journal of Southern History* 19 (May 1953): 180–92.

———. "Northern Plans for the Economic Invasion of Florida, 1862–1865." *Florida Historical Quarterly* 28 (January 1950): 262–70.

Cochran, Hamilton. *Blockade Runners of the Confederacy.* Indianapolis: Bobbs-Merrill, 1958.

A Committee of the Regimental Association. *The Story of One Regiment, the Eleventh Maine Infantry Volunteers in the War of the Rebellion.* New York: Little, 1896.

Connelly, Thomas Lawrence, and Archer Jones. *The Politics of Command, Factions, and Ideas in Confederate Strategy.* Baton Rouge: Louisiana State University Press, 1973.

Cornish, Dudley T. *The Sable Arm: Negro Troops in the Union Army, 1861–1865.* 1956. Facsimile ed. New York: Norton, 1966.

Coulter, E. Merton. *The Confederate States of America.* Vol. 7 of *A History of the South,* ed. Wendell Holmes Stephenson and E. Merton Coulter. Baton Rouge: Louisiana State University Press, 1950.

Cox, Merlin G., and J. E. Dovell. *Florida from Secession to Space Age.* St. Petersburg: Great Outdoors Publishing, 1974.

Craven, Avery Odelle. *Growth of Southern Nationalism, 1848–1861.* Baton Rouge: Louisiana State University Press, 1953.

Croom, Wendell D. *The War-History of Company "C" (Beauregard Volunteers), Sixth Georgia Regiment (Infantry), with a Graphic Account of Each Member.* Fort Valley, Ga.: Printed at the *Advertiser* Office, 1879.

Crowninshield, Benjamin W. *A History of the First Regiment of Massachusetts Cavalry Volunteers.* New York: Houghton Mifflin, 1891.

Dacy, George Harold. *Four Centuries of Florida Ranching.* St. Louis: Britt, 1940.

Dancy, James M. "Reminiscences of the Civil War." *Florida Historical Quarterly* 37 (July 1958): 66–89.

Davis, Thomas Frederick. "Engagements at St. John's Bluff, St. Johns River, Florida, September–October, 1862." *Florida Historical Quarterly* 15 (October 1936): 77–84.

———. *History of Early Jacksonville, Florida, Being an Authentic Record of Events from the Earliest Times to and Including the Civil War.* Jacksonville, Florida: H. & W. B. Drew, 1911.

———. *A History of Jacksonville, Florida, and Vicinity, 1513 to 1924.* St. Augustine: Florida Historical Society, 1925.

Davis, William Watson. *The Civil War and Reconstruction in Florida.* New York: Columbia University Press, 1913.

Dennett, George M. *History of the Ninth U.S. Colored Troops from Its Organization till Muster Out, with Lists of Names of All Officers and Enlisted Men Who Have Ever Belonged to the Regiment . . . Lieut. Col. Geo. M. Dennett, Commanding.* Philadelphia: King & Baird, 1866.

Dennett, Tyler. *Lincoln and the Civil War in the Diaries and Letters of John Hay.* New York: Dodd, Mead, 1939.

Dennison, Rev. Frederic. *Shot and Shell: The Third Rhode Island Heavy Artillery in the Rebellion, 1861–1865.* Providence: J. A. & R. A. Reid, 1879.

Dickison, John J. *Military History of Florida.* Vol. II of *Confederate Military History,* 12 vols., ed. Clement Anselm Evans. Atlanta: Confederate Publishing, 1898.

Dickison, Mary Elizabeth. *Dickison and His Men: Reminiscences of the War in Florida.* Louisville: Courier-Journal Job Printing, 1890.

Dodd, Dorothy. "Edmund Ruffin's Account of the Florida Secession Convention, 1861: A Diary." *Florida Historical Quarterly* 12 (October 1933): 67–76.

———. "The Manufacture of Cotton in Florida before and during the Civil War." *Florida Historical Quarterly* 13 (July 1934): 3–18.

———. "The Secession Movement in Florida, 1850–1861." *Florida Historical Quarterly* 12 (July 1933): 3–24, 45–66.

————. "Some Florida Secession History. *Tallahassee Historical Society Annual* 3 (1937): 1–7.

————, ed. "Volunteers Report Destruction of Lighthouses." *Tequesta* 14 (1954); 67–71.

Doherty, Herbert J., Jr. "Florida in 1856." *Florida Historical Quarterly* 35 (July 1956): 60–70.

————. *Richard Keith Call: Southern Unionist.* Gainesville: University of Florida Press, 1961.

————. "Union Nationalism in Florida." *Florida Historical Quarterly* 29 (July 1950): 83–95.

Dowdey, Clifford, ed. *The Wartime Papers of R. E. Lee.* Boston: Little, Brown, 1961.

Dupuy, Trevor N., Colonel, U.S.A., and Arnold C. Dupuy. "Understanding War from Historical Perspective." *Marine Corps Gazette* 69 (June 1985): 53–58.

Dyer, Frederick, ed. *A Compendium of the War of the Rebellion.* 3 vols. 1908. Facsimile ed. New York: Yoseloff, 1959.

East, Omega G. "St. Augustine during the Civil War." *Florida Historical Quarterly* 31 (October 1952): 75–91.

Eaton, Clement. *A History of the Southern Confederacy.* New York: Macmillan, 1954.

Egan, Patrick. *The Florida Campaign with Light Battery C, Third Rhode Island Heavy Artillery.* Providence: n.p., 1905.

Eldridge, D. *The Third New Hampshire and All about It.* Boston: Stillings, 1893.

Emilio, Luis F. *History of the Fifty-fourth Regiment of Massachusetts Volunteer Infantry, 1863–1865.* Boston: Boston Book, 1891.

Eppes, Susan Bradford. *Through Some Eventful Years.* Macon, Ga.: Burke, 1926.

Escott, Paul D. *After Secession: Jefferson Davis and the Failure of Confederate Nationalism.* Baton Rouge: Louisiana State University Press, 1977.

Federal Writers Project, Works Progress Administration. *History of Marion County.*

————. *History of Putnam County.*

Fleming, Francis. *Memoir of Capt. C. Seaton Fleming, of the Second Florida Infantry, C.S.A., Illustrative of the History of the Florida Troops in Virginia during the War between the States, with Appendix of the Casualties.* Jacksonville, Fla.: Times-Union Publishing House, 1884.

Folsom, James Madison. *Heroes and Martyrs of Georgia: Georgia's Record in the Revolution of 1861.* Macon: Boykin, 1864.

Foote, Shelby. *The Civil War: A Narrative.* 3 vols. New York: Random House, 1958–74.

Fort, John Porter. *A Memorial and Personal Reminiscences.* New York: Knickerbocker Press, 1918.

Fox, Charles Barnard. *Record of the Service of the Fifty-fifth Regiment of Massachusetts Volunteer Infantry.* Cambridge, Mass.: Wilson & Son, 1868.

Fox, William Freeman. *Regimental Losses in the American Civil War, 1861–1865.* Albany, N.Y., Albany Publishing, 1889.

Freeman, Douglas Southall. *R. E. Lee: A Biography.* 4 vols. New York: Scribners, 1934.

Futch, Ovid L. "Salmon P. Chase and Civil War Politics in Florida." *Florida Historical Quarterly* 32 (January 1954): 163–88.

Garvin, Russell. "The Free Negro in Florida before the Civil War." *Florida Historical Quarterly* 46 (July 1967): 1–17.

Gates, Paul W. *Agriculture and the Civil War.* New York: Knopf, 1965.

Gilchrist, David T., and David W. Lewis, eds. *Economic Change in the Civil War Era.* Greenville, Del.: Eleutherian Mills-Hagley Foundation, 1965.

Goff, Richard D. *Confederate Supply.* Durham: Duke University Press, 1969.

Gold, Pleasant Daniel. *History of Duval County, Including History of East Florida.* St. Augustine: Record Company, 1929.

———. *History of Volusia County.* DeLand, Fla.: Painter Printing, 1927.

Graff, Mary B. *Mandarin on the St. Johns.* Gainesville: University of Florida Press, 1953.

Graham, Thomas. *The Awakening of St. Augustine: The Anderson Family and the Oldest City, 1821–1924.* St. Augustine: St. Augustine Historical Society, 1978.

———. "Letters from a Journey through the Federal Blockade." *Florida Historical Quarterly* 55 (April 1977): 439–56.

Grande, Ray. "Slave Unrest in Florida." *Florida Historical Quarterly* 55 (July 1976): 18–36.

Gray, John Chipman, and John Codman Ropes. *War Letters, 1862–1865.* Boston: Houghton Mifflin, 1927.

Hadd, Donald R. "The Irony of Secession." *Florida Historical Quarterly* 41 (July 1962): 22–28.

Harley, James A. "The Battle of Olustee." *Confederate Veteran* 20 (November 1912): 456–57.

Harper, Roland M. "Ante-Bellum Census Enumeration in Florida." *Florida Historical Quarterly* 6 (July 1927): 41–52.

Haulman, C. A. "Changes in the Economic Power Structure in Duval County, Florida, during the Civil War and Reconstruction." *Florida Historical Quarterly* 52 (October 1973): 175–82.

Havard, William C. "The Florida Executive Council, 1862." *Florida Historical Quarterly* 33 (July 1954): 77–96.

Hayes, John D., ed. *Samuel Francis DuPont: A Selection from His War Letters.* 3 vols. Ithaca: Cornell University Press, 1969.

Hebel, Ianthe Bond, ed. *Centennial History of Volusia County, Florida, 1854–1954.* Daytona Beach, Fla.: Volusia County Historical Commission, 1955.

Higginson, Thomas Wentworth. *Army Life in a Black Regiment.* 1870. Facsimile ed. Williamston, Mass.: Corner House Publishers, 1971.

——. "Up the St. Johns." *Atlantic Monthly* 16 (September 1870): 311–25.

——. "Up the St. Mary's." *Atlantic Monthly* 15 (April 1865): 422–36.

Hodges, Ellen E., and Stephen Kerber, eds. "Children of Honor: Letters of Winston and Octavia Stephens, 1861–1862." *Florida Historical Quarterly* 56 (July 1977): 45–74.

——. "Rogues and Black Hearted Scamps: Civil War Letters of Winston and Octavia Stephens, 1862–1863." *Florida Historical Quarterly* 57 (July 1978): 54–82.

Holbrook, William C. *A Narrative of the Services of the Officers and Enlisted Men of the Seventh Regiment of Vermont Volunteers (Veterans) from 1862 to 1866.* New York: American Bank Note, 1882.

Hopley, Catherine Cooper. *Life in the South; from the Commencement of the War. Being a Social History of Those Who Took Part in the Battle, from a Personal Acquaintance with Them in Their Homes. Spring 1860 to August 1862.* London: Chapman & Hall, 1863.

Howard, Michael, and Peter Paret, eds. *Carl von Clausewitz: On War.* Princeton: Princeton University Press, 1976.

Johannes, Jan H., Sr. *Yesterday's Reflections: Nassau County, Florida.* Callahan, Fla.: Richardson, 1976.

Johns, John Edwin. *Florida during the Civil War.* Gainesville: University of Florida Press, 1963.

Jones, Allen W. "Military Events in Florida during the Civil War, 1861–1865." *Florida Historical Quarterly* 39 (July 1960): 42–45.

Jones, Charles C. *The Evacuation of Battery Wagner, and the Battle of Ocean Pond. An Address Delivered before the Confederate Survivors Association in Augusta, Georgia, on the Occasion of Its Tenth Annual Reunion on Memorial Day, April 26, 1888.* Augusta: Chronicle Publishing, 1888.

————. *Historical Sketch of the Chatham Artillery during the Confederate Struggle for Independence.* Albany, N.Y.: Munsell, 1867.

Jones, Samuel. "The Battle of Olustee, or Ocean Pond, Florida." In *Battles and Leaders of the Civil War,* ed. Robert U. Johnson and Clarence C. Buell. Vol. 4. New York: Yoseloff, 1888.

Jones, Sarah L. "Governor Milton and His Family: A Contemporary Picture of Life in Florida during the War, by an English Tutor." *Florida Historical Quarterly* 2 (July 1909): 42–50.

Keely, Capt. John. "Handclasps between the Lines: Diary of Captain Keely." *Atlanta Constitution,* March 22, 1931.

Keuchel, Edward. *A History of Columbia County, Florida.* Tallahassee: Sentry Press, 1981.

Kinsman, Oliver D. *A Loyal Man in Florida, 1858–1861.* Washington: n.p., 1910.

Le Diable, Captain [pseud.]. *Historical Sketch of the Third Annual Conquest of Florida.* Port Royal, S.C.: n.p.: 1864.

L'Engle, Gertrude. *A Collection of Letters, Information, and Data on Our Family.* 2 vols. Jacksonville, Fla.: n.p., 1949–51.

Little, Henry F. W. *The Seventh Regiment, New Hampshire Volunteers in the War of the Rebellion.* Concord, N.H.: Evans, 1896.

Livermore, Thomas Leonard. *Numbers and Losses in the Civil War in America, 1861–65.* Rev. ed. Bloomington: Indiana University Press, 1957.

Long, Ellen Call. *Florida Breezes; or, Florida, New and Old.* 1882. Facsimile ed. Gainesville: University of Florida Press, 1962.

Lonn, Ella. *Desertion during the Civil War.* New York: Century, 1928.

————. "The Extent and Importance of Federal Naval Raids on Salt-Making in Florida, 1862–1865." *Florida Historical Quarterly* 10 (October 1932): 167–84.

————. *Salt as a Factor in the Confederacy.* New York: Neale, 1933.

McKee, James Harvey. *Back in War Times: History of the 144th Regiment New York Volunteer Infantry.* New York: Lt. Horace E. Bailey, 1903.

McMorries, Edward Young. *History of the First Alabama Volunteer Infantry of the Confederate States of America.* Montgomery: Brown Printing, 1904.

McMurry, Richard. "The Battle of Olustee." *Civil War Times* 16 (January 1978): 12–24.

McPherson, James M., ed. *The Negro's Civil War: How American Negroes Felt and Acted during the War for the Union.* New York: Pantheon Books, 1965.

————. *Ordeal by Fire: The Civil War and Reconstruction.* New York: Knopf, 1982.

McWhiney, Grady, and Perry D. Jamieson. *Attack and Die: Civil War Military Tactics and the Southern Heritage.* University: University of Alabama Press, 1982.

Marcus, Edward, ed. *A New Canaan Private in the Civil War: Letters of Justus M. Silliman, Seventeenth Connecticut Volunteers.* New Canaan, Conn.: New Canaan Historical Society, 1984.

Martin, Richard A. "Defeat in Victory: The Yankee Experience in Early Civil War Jacksonville." *Florida Historical Quarterly* 53 (July 1975): 1–31.

———. "The *New York Times* Views Civil War Jacksonville." *Florida Historical Quarterly* 53 (April 1974): 409–29.

Meador, John A. "Florida and the Compromise of 1850." *Florida Historical Quarterly* 39 (July 1960): 16–33.

Merrill, James M. *The Rebel Shore: The Story of Union Sea Power in the Civil War.* Boston: Little, Brown, 1957.

Moore, Albert Burton. *Conscription and Conflict in the Confederacy.* New York: Macmillan, 1924.

Moore, Frank E., ed. *The Rebellion Record: A Diary of American Events, with Documents, Narratives, Illustrative Incidents, Poetry, Etc.: With an Introductory Address by Edward Everett.* 11 vols. New York: Putnam's Sons, 1861–68.

Morgan, David R. *Confederate Veteran* 26 (July 1918): 302.

Morris, Gouverneur. *The History of a Volunteer Regiment: Being a Succinct Account of the Organization, Services, and Adventures of the Sixth Regiment of New York Volunteers Infantry, Known as Wilson's Zouaves.* New York: Veteran's Publishing, 1891.

Myers, Robert M., ed. *The Children of Pride: A True Story of Georgia and the Civil War.* New Haven: Yale University Press, 1972.

Nevins, Allan. *The War for Union.* 4 vols. New York: Scribner, 1959–71.

Nichols, James M. *Perry's Saints; or, The Fighting Parson's Regiment in the War of the Rebellion.* Boston: Lathrop, 1886.

Nicolay, John G., and John Hay. *Abraham Lincoln: A History.* 10 vols. New York: Century, 1890.

Niven, John. *Connecticut for the Union: The Role of the State in the Civil War.* New Haven: Yale University Press, 1965.

Norton, Oliver Wilcox. *Army Letters, 1861–1865, Being Extracts from Private Letters to Relatives and Friends from a Soldier in the Field during the Late Civil War, with an Appendix Containing Copies of Some Official Documents, Papers, and Addresses of Later Date.* Chicago: Deming, 1903.

Opdyke, John B. *Alachua Country: A Sesquicentennial Tribute.* Gainesville, Fla.: Alachua County Historical Commission, 1974.

Ott, Eloise. "Ocala prior to 1860." *Florida Historical Quarterly* 6 (July 1927): 85–110.

Ott, Eloise Robinson, and Louis Hickman Chazel. *Ocali Country: Kingdom of the Sun. A History of Marion County, Florida.* Orlando, Fla.: Marion Publishers, 1966.

Paisley, Clifton. "How to Escape the Yankees: Major Scott's Letter to His Wife at Tallahassee, March 1864." *Florida Historical Quarterly* 50 (July 1971): 53–61.

Palmer, Abraham J. *The History of the Forty-eighth Regiment New York Volunteers in the War for the Union, 1861–1865.* Brooklyn: Veterans Association of the Regiment, 1885.

Parker, Daisy. "Governor John Milton." *Tallahassee Historical Society Annual* 3 (1937): 14–21.

——. "John Milton, Governor of Florida: A Loyal Confederate." *Florida Historical Quarterly* 20 (April 1942): 346–61.

Patrick, Rembert Wallace. *Florida under Five Flags.* Gainesville: University of Florida Press, 1945.

Peters, Thelma. "Blockade-Running in the Bahamas during the Civil War." *Tequesta* 5 (1945): 16–29.

Potter, David M. *The Impending Crisis.* Completed and edited by Don E. Fehrenbacher. New York: Harper Torchbooks, 1976.

Price, Isaiah. *History of the Ninety-seventh Regiment Pennsylvania Volunteer Infantry during the War of the Rebellion, 1861–1865, with Biographic Sketches of Its Field and Staff Officers and a Complete Record of Each Officer and Enlisted Man.* Philadelphia: Price, 1875.

Price, Marcus W. "Ships That Tested the Blockade of the Georgia and East Florida Ports, 1861–1865." *American Neptune* 15 (April 1955): 97–132.

Proctor, Samuel. "Jacksonville during the Civil War." *Florida Historical Quarterly* 41 (April 1963): 343–55.

——, ed. "The Call to Arms: Secession from a Feminine Point of View." *Florida Historical Quarterly* 35 (January 1957): 266–77.

——, ed. *Florida One Hundred Years Ago.* Coral Gables: Florida Library and Historical Commission, Civil War Centennial Committee, 1960–65.

Quarles, Benjamin. *The Negro in the Civil War.* Boston: Little, Brown, 1953.

Ramsdell, Charles W. *Behind the Lines in the Southern Confederacy.* Baton Rouge: Louisiana State University Press, 1944.

——. "Confederate Government and the Railroads." *American Historical Review* 22 (July 1917): 794–810.

Randall, James Garfield, and David Herbert Donald. *The Civil War and Reconstruction*. 2d ed. Lexington, Mass.: Heath, 1969.

Reed, Rowena. *Combined Operations*. Annapolis: Naval Institute Press, 1978.

Reiger, John F. "Deprivation, Disaffection, and Desertion in Confederate Florida." *Florida Historical Quarterly* 48 (January 1970): 279–98.

———. "Florida after Secession: Abandonment by the Confederacy and Its Consequences." *Florida Historical Quarterly* 50 (October 1972): 128–42.

———. "Secession of Florida from the Union—a Minority Decision?" *Florida Historical Quarterly* 46 (April 1968): 358–68.

Rerick, Rowland H. *Memoirs of Florida, Embracing a General History of the Province, Territory, and State; and Special Chapters Devoted to Finances, Banking, the Bench, and the Bar.* 2 vols. Atlanta: Southern Historical Association, 1902.

Robertson, Fred L., comp. *Soldiers of Florida in the Seminole Indian, Civil, and Spanish-American Wars.* Live Oak, Fla.: Democrat Book & Job Print, 1903.

Roe, Alfred S. *The Twenty-fourth Regiment Massachusetts Volunteers, 1861–1866.* Worcester, Mass.: Twenty-fourth Veterans Association, 1907.

Rogers, William Warren, ed. "Florida on the Eve of the Civil War, As Seen by a Southern Reporter." *Florida Historical Quarterly* 39 (October 1960): 145–58.

Roman, Alfred. *The Military Operations of General Beauregard in the War between the States.* Baton Rouge: Louisiana State University Press, 1955.

Sandburg, Carl. *Abraham Lincoln: The War Years.* 4 vols. New York: Harcourt, Brace, 1939.

Schellings, William J., ed. "Blockade Duty on the Florida Coast, Excerpts from a Union Naval Officer's Diary." *Tequesta* 15 (1955): 55–72.

Schwartz, Gerald, ed. *A Woman Doctor's Civil War: Esther Hill Hawks' Diary.* Columbia: University of South Carolina Press, 1984.

Shannon, Fred A. *Organization and Administration of the Union Army, 1861–1865.* 2 vols. 1928. Facsimile ed. Gloucester, Mass.: Peter Smith, 1965.

Shofner, Jerrell H. *Nor Is It Over Yet: Florida in the Era of Reconstruction, 1863–1877.* Gainesville: University of Florida Press, 1974.

Shofner, Jerrell H., and William W. Rogers. "Confederate Railroad Construction: The Live Oak to Lawton Connector." *Florida Historical Quarterly* 43 (January 1965): 217–28.

Smith, George Winston. "Carpetbag Imperialism in Florida, 1862–1868." *Florida Historical Quarterly* 27 (October 1948): 99–130; (January 1949): 259–99.

Soley, James R. *The Navy in the Civil War: The Blockade and the Cruisers.* New York: Scribner, 1883.

Sproull, Katherine. "The Forts of Duval County." *Papers of the Jacksonville Historical Society* 1 (1947): 67–76.

Staudenraus, P. J., ed. "A [Union] War Correspondent's [Noah Brook's] View of St. Augustine and Fernandina, 1863." *Florida Historical Quarterly* 41 (July 1962): 60–65.

Strickland, Alice. "Blockade Runners." *Florida Historical Quarterly* 36 (October 1957): 85–93.

Sweet, Zeba Wilson, and J. C. Marsden. *New Smyrna, Florida, Its History and Antiquities.* DeLand, Fla.: Painter Printing, 1925.

Sweet, Zelia Wilson. *New Smyrna, Florida, in the Civil War. . . .* Daytona Beach, Fla.: Volusia County Historical Commission, 1963.

Swift, Lester L., ed. "Capt. Dana in Florida: A Narrative of the Seymour Expedition." *Civil War History* 11 (September 1965): 245–56.

Taylor, Susie King. *Reminiscences of My Life in Camp: With the Thirty-third United States Colored Troops Late First S.C. Volunteers.* Boston: Published by the Author, 1902.

Tebeau, Charlton W. *A History of Florida.* Coral Gables, Fla.: University of Miami Press, 1971.

Tenney, John Francis. *Slavery, Secession, and Success: The Memoirs of a Florida Pioneer.* San Antonio, Tex.: Southern Library Institute, 1934.

Thomas, David Y. "Florida Finance in the Civil War." *Yale Review* 16 (November 1907): 311.

Thomas, Emory M. *The Confederate Nation, 1861–1865.* New York: Harper & Row, 1979.

Thompson, Arthur W. "Confederate Finance: A Documentary Study of a Proposal of David L. Yulee." *Florida Historical Quarterly* 30 (October 1951): 193–207.

———. "Political Nativism in Florida, 1848–1860: A Phase of Anti-Secessionism." *Journal of Southern History* 15 (February 1949): 39–65.

Thompson, Benjamin W. "Flight from Florida." *Civil War Times* 12 (August 1973): 12–21.

Tolles, Zonira Hunter. *Shadows on the Sand: A History of the Land and the People in the Vicinity of Melrose, Florida.* Gainesville, Fla.: Shorter, 1976.

Tourtellotte, Jerome. *A History of Company K of the Seventh Connecticut Volunteers Infantry in the Civil War.* N.p., 1910.

Turner, George Edgar. *Victory Rode the Rails: The Strategic Place of Railroads in the Civil War.* Indianapolis: Bobbs-Merrill, 1953.

Uhler, Margaret Anderson. "The Civil War Letters of Major General James Patton Anderson." *Florida Historical Quarterly* 56 (October 1977): 150–75.

Vandiver, Frank Everson. *Rebel Brass: The Confederate Command System.* Baton Rouge: Louisiana State University Press, 1956.

Verrill, Ruth. *Romantic and Historic Levy County.* Gainesville, Fla.: Shorter, 1976.

Walkley, Stephen. *History of the Seventh Connecticut Volunteer Infantry, Hawley's Brigade, Terry's Division, Tenth Army Corps, 1861–1865.* Hartford: n.p., 1905.

Warner, Ezra J. *Generals in Blue: Lives of the Union Commanders.* Baton Rouge: Louisiana State University Press, 1959.

———. *Generals in Gray: Lives of the Confederate Commanders.* Baton Rouge: Louisiana State University Press, 1964.

Weigley, Russell F. *The American Way of War.* Bloomington: Indiana University Press, 1973.

Weinert, Richard P. "The Battle of Olustee." *Civil War Times* 1 (June 1962): 12–23.

———. "The Confederate Swamp Fox." *Civil War Times* 5 (December 1966): 4–11.

West, Richard S., Jr. *Mr. Lincoln's Navy.* New York: Longmans, Green, 1957.

Wiley, Bell I. *Southern Negroes, 1861–1865.* 1938. Facsimile ed. New Haven: Yale University Press, 1965.

Wiley, Bell I., and Hirst D. Milhollen. *Embattled Confederates: An Illustrated History of Southerners at War.* New York: Harper & Row, 1964.

Williams, Edwin L., Jr. "Negro Slavery in Florida." *Florida Historical Quarterly* 28 (October 1949): 93–110; (January 1950): 182–204.

Williams, Walter L. "Again in Chains: Black Soldiers Suffering in Captivity." *Civil War Times* 20 (May 1981): 36–45.

Williamson, Edward C., ed. "Francis P. Fleming in the War for Southern Independence: Soldiering with the Second Florida Regiment." *Florida Historical Quarterly* 28 (July 1949): 38–52, 143–55, 205–10.

Woodford, Milton M. "A Connecticut Yankee after Olustee." Edited by Vaughn D. Bornet. *Florida Historical Quarterly* 27 (April 1949): 358–403.

————. "A Connecticut Yankee Fights at Olustee: Letters from the Front." Edited by Vaughn D. Bornet. *Florida Historical Quarterly* 27 (January 1949): 237–59.

Wooster, Ralph A. "The Florida Secession Convention." *Florida Historical Quarterly* 36 (April 1958): 373–85.

————. *The Secession Conventions of the South.* Princeton: Princeton University Press, 1962.

"Yellow Fever on the Blockade of Indian River; A Tragedy of 1864. Letters of Acting Master's Mate John F. Van Nest." *Florida Historical Quarterly* 21 (January 1943): 352–57.

Yonge, Julien C., ed. "The Occupation of Jacksonville, February 1864, and the Battle of Olustee: Letters of Lt. C. M. Duren, Fifty-fourth Massachusetts Regiment, U.S.A." *Florida Historical Quarterly* 32 (April 1954): 262–87.

Yulee, David L. "Two Letters of David L. Yulee: His Opinion on Secession in 1860." *Florida Historical Quarterly* 29 (October 1950): 125–31.

Zornow, William F. "State Aid for Indigent Soldiers and Their Families in Florida, 1861–1865." *Florida Historical Quarterly* 34 (January 1956): 259–65.

Theses and Dissertations

Bright, Samuel R., Jr. "Confederate Coast Defenses." Ph.D. diss., Duke University, 1961.

Coles, David James. "A Fight, a Licking, and a Footrace: The 1864 Florida Campaign and the Battle of Olustee." Master's thesis, Florida State University, 1985.

Davis, Horace Gibbs. "Florida Journalism during the Civil War." Master's thesis, University of Florida, 1952.

Dillon, Rodney E., Jr. "The Civil War in South Florida." Master's thesis, University of Florida, 1980.

Doherty, Herbert J., Jr. "The Florida Whigs." Master's thesis, University of Florida, 1949.

Ferrel, Sidney Scaife. "Public Opinion in Confederate Florida." Master's thesis, University of Florida, 1950.

Futch, Ovid. "Salmon P. Chase and Radical Politics in Florida, 1862–1865." Master's thesis, University of Florida, 1952.

Guinn, Gilbert Sumter. "Coastal Defenses of the Confederate Atlantic Seaboard States, 1861–1862: A Study in Political and Military Mobilization." Ph.D. diss., University of South Carolina, 1972.

Hadd, Donald R. "Secession Movement in Florida, 1850–1861." Master's thesis, Florida State University, 1960.

Hendricks, George Linton. "Union Army Occupation of the Southern Seaboard, 1861–1865." Ph.D. diss., Columbia University, 1954.

Itkin, Stanley L. "Operations in the East Gulf Blockade of Florida, 1862–1865." Master's thesis, Florida State University, 1962.

Meador, John. "Florida Political Parties, 1865–1877." Ph.D. diss., University of Florida, 1964.

Meredith, Evelyn T. "The Secession Movement in Florida." Master's thesis, Duke University, 1940.

Mool, J. B. "Florida in Federal Politics, Statehood to Secession." Master's thesis, Duke University, 1940.

Patterson, Ellen Hodges. "The Stephens Family in East Florida: A Profile of Plantation Life along the St. Johns River, 1859–1864." Master's thesis, University of Florida, 1979.

Reiger, John Franklin. "Anti-War and Pro-Union Sentiment in Confederate Florida." Master's thesis, University of Florida, 1966.

Sanford, Robert Meriwether. "The Literary Elements of the Florida Newspapers of the Civil War Period." Master's thesis, University of Florida, 1936.

Thompson, Arthur William. "David Yulee: A Study of Nineteenth Century American Thought and Enterprise." Ph.D. diss., Columbia University, 1954.

Weinberg, Sydney Jay. "Slavery and Secession in Florida, 1845–1861." Master's thesis, University of Florida, 1940.

Williams, Edwin L., Jr. "Florida in the Union, 1845–1861." Ph.D. diss., University of North Carolina, 1951.

Index

Mrs. Simon Baruch University Award

The United Daughters of the Confederacy established the Mrs. Simon Baruch University Award for the purpose of encouraging research in Southern history. Recipients of the award are:

1927   Carpenter, Jesse Thomas, *The South as a Conscious Minority, 1789–1861*

1929   Whitfield, Theodore M., *Slavery Agitation in Virginia, 1829–1832*

1931   Flanders, Ralph Betts, *Plantation Slavery in Georgia*

1933   Thompson, Samuel, *Confederate Purchasing Agents Abroad*

1935   Wiley, Bell Irvin, *Southern Negroes, 1861–1865*

1937   Hill, Louise Biles, *Joseph E. Brown and the Confederacy*

1940   Haydon, F. Stansbury, *Aeronautics of the Union and Confederate Armies*

1942   Stormont, John, *The Economic Stake of the North in the Preservation of the Union in 1861*

1945   Schultz, Harold Sessel, *Nationalism and Sectionalism in South Carolina, 1852–1860*

1948   Tankersly, Allen P., *John Brown Gordon, Soldier and Statesman*

1951   Todd, Richard C., *Confederate Finance*

1954   Morrow, Ralph E., *Northern Methodism and Reconstruction*
Cunningham, Horace, *Doctors in Gray*

1957   Hall, Martin H., *The Army of New Mexico: Sibley's Campaign of 1862*

1960   Robertson, James I., Jr., *Jackson's Stonewall: A History of the Stonewall Brigade*

1969   Wells, Tom Henderson, *The Confederate Navy: A Study in Organization*

1970   Delaney, Conrad, *John McIntosh Kell of the Raider Alabama*

1972   Dougan, Michael B., *Confederate Arkansas: The People and Politics of a Frontier State*

1974   Wiggins, Sarah Woolfolk, *The Scalawag in Alabama Politics, 1865–1881*

1976   Nelson, Larry Earl, *Bullets, Ballots, and Rhetoric*

1978   Franks, Kenny A., *Stand Watie and the Agony of the Cherokee Nation*

1980   Buenger, Walter L., *Stilling the Voice of Reason: The Union and Secession in Texas, 1854–1861*

1982   McMurry, Richard M., *John Bell Hood and the War for Southern Independence*

1984   Daniel, Larry J., *Cannoneers in Gray: The Field Artillery of the Army of Tennessee, 1861–1865*

1988   DeCredico, Mary Ann, *Patriotism for Profit: Georgia's Urban Entrepreneurs and the Confederate War Effort*

1990   Nulty, William H., *Confederate Florida: The Road to Olustee*

1992   Willoughby, Lynn, *Fair to Middlin': The Antebellum Cotton Trade of the Apalachicola/Chattahoochee River Valley*